The Feeling of Kinship

DAVID L. ENG

The Feeling of Kinship

QUEER LIBERALISM

AND THE RACIALIZATION

OF INTIMACY

Duke University Press ⊗ Durham and London ⊗ 2010

© 2010 Duke University Press

Printed in the United States
of America on acid-free paper ⊗
Designed by Amy Ruth Buchanan
Typeset in Chaparral Pro by
Keystone Typesetting, Inc.
Library of Congress Cataloging-in-
Publication Data appear on the last
printed page of this book.

Frontispiece: Michele Carlson

"You say that two at Conway dwell,
And two are gone to sea,
Yet ye are seven!—I pray you tell,
Sweet Maid, how this may be."

Then did the little Maid reply,
"Seven boys and girls are we;
Two of us in the church-yard lie,
Beneath the church-yard tree."

"You run about, my little Maid,
Your limbs they are alive;
If two are in the church-yard laid,
Then ye are only five."

"Their graves are green, they may be seen,"
The little Maid replied,
"Twelve steps or more from my mother's door,
And they are side by side.

"My stockings there I often knit,
My kerchief there I hem;
And there upon the ground I sit,
And sing a song to them . . ."

—WILLIAM WORDSWORTH,
"We Are Seven" (1798)

I remember having this feeling growing up
that I was haunted by something, that I was
living within a family full of ghosts.

—REA TAJIRI,
History and Memory (1991)

Contents

⊗ ⊗ ⊗

Preface ix

Introduction 1
Queer Liberalism and the Racialization
of Intimacy

1 The Law of Kinship 23
Lawrence v. Texas and the Emergence of
Queer Liberalism

2 The Structure of Kinship 58
The Art of Waiting in *The Book of Salt* and
Happy Together

3 The Language of Kinship 93
Transnational Adoption and Two Mothers
in *First Person Plural*

4 The Prospect of Kinship 138
Transnational Adoption and Racial Reparation
(WITH SHINHEE HAN, PH.D.)

5 The Feeling of Kinship 166
Affect and Language in *History and Memory*

Notes 199
Bibliography 225
Index 239

Preface

⊛ ⊛ ⊛

The election of Barack Obama as the first African American president on November 4, 2008, was the same day that legalized marriage for gays and lesbians in the state of California, authorized by the State Supreme Court only six months earlier, was taken away through popular referendum. The combination of Obama's historic win with the passage of California's Proposition 8 by a narrow 2.3 percent margin initiated many rounds of recriminations—especially so, given the oft-cited statistic that 7 in 10 African Americans who came out to vote in the Presidential election also favored the ballot initiative. Yet, African Americans constituted only 10 percent of the California electorate who voted. Given the narrow margin of victory for Proposition 8, it would be a mistake to blame any one particular group for its passage: African Americans; other minorities; mainstream gay organizers who failed to provide effective outreach to communities of color; liberals who did not bother to vote; staunch moral-majority Republicans; or even the Mormon Church in Utah, which reputedly provided over 40 percent of the funding for the initiative.

The key issue is not that there is plenty of blame to spread around; there is. Rather, the important point is that the promise of progressive coalitional politics failed—a failure exacerbated by repeated contentions that African American communities (as well as other communities of color) are especially homophobic, coupled with the simultaneous insistence that "Gay is the New Black," as the December 16, 2008 cover of *The Advocate* proclaimed after the November elections. Equating gay and lesbian struggles for civil rights in the present to black civil rights movements in the past not only consigns racism to the dustbin of history—as a historical project "completed"—but also suggests that all gays are white while all blacks are heterosexual. Such an equation authorizes a political rhetoric of colorblindness that refuses to recognize the ways in which race, gender, sexuality, class, and nation continue to be articulated and constituted in relation to one another in the ongoing struggles for equality and social belonging. In short, by analogizing Proposition 8 to *Loving v. Virginia*, the 1967 Supreme Court decision overturning the state of Virginia's anti-miscegenation laws, mainstream gay and lesbian advocates deny the coevalness of sexual and racial discrimination, subjecting them to a type of historicist violence by casting them as radically discontinuous.

Today, under the shadows of neoliberalism, a politics of colorblindness helps to instrumentalize the hyper-extraction of surplus value from racialized bodies. It helps to legitimate a system of capitalist exploitation and accumulation largely favoring the industrialized North over the global South, a history tracing itself to the emergence of European colonialism in the fifteenth century and the establishment of the Enlightenment project in the eighteenth century that marks the rise and expansion of European modernity in the West and elsewhere. As the uncontested superpower on the world stage today, the United States is not just the custodian of empire but indeed the guardian of a European tradition of modern liberal humanism, one now mobilized to declare that the project of human freedom has been accomplished within the domestic borders of the nation-state. Our putatively colorblind moment is marked by the assertion that racial difference has given way to an abstract and universal U.S. community of individualism and merit. This is so even as it demands the inexorable growth of the prison industrial complex and ever-increasing militarization and unfreedom in global locales such as the Middle East, Afghanistan, and Guantánamo Bay, continued racialized violence and racialized labor exploitation and domination, and a vast redistribution of wealth to the already richest few as the just entitlements of multicultural, cosmopolitan world citizens— recent upheavals in the global economy notwithstanding.

In this ostensibly colorblind new world order of privilege and stigma, it is not surprising that the historic election of President Obama—who has not explicitly supported gay marriage rights (or single-payer health care, for that matter)—was accompanied by the passage of Proposition 8. To the contrary, it might have been expected insofar as the affirmation of freedom for African Americans, embodied in the extraordinary rise of this singular figure of racial unity, now leads to the final chapter of U.S. liberalism and progress. From this perspective, multiculturalism, as the key to a contemporary post-racial new world order of freedom, opportunity, and choice, might be seen not as the culmination but the continuing legacy of the long history of the world division of freedom and labor in New World modernity, with gay and lesbian marriage now constituting, as the subtitle of *The Advocate* cover also declares, "The Last Great Civil Rights Struggle."

In recent years, there has been a lot of debate in both queer and critical race studies about the value of intersectional and comparative approaches to the analysis of identity and difference. "Queer" was once understood as the name for a political movement and an extensive critique of a wide range of social normalizations and exclusions. However, in our putatively post-identity age, the term has become increasingly unmoored from its theoretical potentials and possibilities. Instead, it has come to demarcate more narrowly pragmatic gay and lesbian identity and identity politics, the economic interests of neoliberalism and whiteness, and liberal political norms of inclusion—including access to marriage, custody, inheritance, and service in the military. Today, "queer" and "rights" as well as "queer" and "marriage" no longer strike us as paradoxical terms or antithetical propositions.

I describe this remarkable consolidation as "queer liberalism," and it is the purpose of this book not only to explore the historical emergence of queer liberalism, but also to rethink the significant cleavings and dissociations of sexuality from race, and race from sexuality, that organize contemporary structures of family and kinship as well as the privatized space of the intimate in our colorblind age of global capitalism. Charting the multiple tensions between queer liberalism and what I describe as "queer diasporas," the unpredictable and unsettled migrations of queer Asian bodies in the global system, this book also seeks to retheorize conventional notions of family and kinship outside the geographical boundaries of the nation-state and beyond the ideological boundaries of U.S. exceptionalism, from a poststructuralist and psychoanalytic perspective.

❦ ❦ ❦

The Feeling of Kinship: Queer Liberalism and the Racialization of Intimacy
has been long in the making. Its completion finally allows me to thank
the many colleagues and friends to whom I owe much gratitude. First, I
would like to acknowledge the numerous students I have taught at
Columbia, Harvard, Rutgers, and the University of Pennsylvania who,
through their very serious engagement and concerns in my undergradu-
ate and graduate classes, continue to push me toward emergent forms of
social belonging and exclusion on the horizons of political thought. I
also want to thank the many individuals, as well as departments and
programs, who invited me to present various parts of this book and, in
the process, revise, rework, and refine my ideas. In particular, I would
like to acknowledge the intellectual generosity and hospitality of Henry
Abelove, Lisa Arellano, Brian Axel, Houston Baker, Ian Baucom, Kim
Benston, Mary Pat Brady, Laura Briggs, Cathy Caruth, Fu-jen Chen,
Kandice Chuh, Patricia Clough, Christina Crosby, Muriel Dimen, Brian
Edwards, Jillana Enteen, Martha Ertman, Melissa Fisher, Anne-Marie
Fortier, Carla Freccero, Michele Goodwin, Lori Gruen, Jan Gump, Gil-
lian Harkins, Neville Hoad, Alice Hom, Grace Hong, Hsinya Huang,
Sonia Katyal, Gail Lewis, Earl Liao, Marie Lo, Michael Lucey, Iona Man-
Cheong, Anita Mannur, Amy Martin, Dwight McBride, Lee Medovoi,
Jodi Melamed, Sean Metzger, Greg Moynahan, Fawzia Mustafa, Vivien
Ng, Don Pease, Lene Myong Petersen, Claire Potter, Rick Rambuss,
Russell Robinson, Mari Ruti, Jeff Santa Ana, Peter Schmidt, James
Schultz, Robert Schwartzwald, Laurie Shannon, Ta Trang, and Robyn
Wiegman.

I recently moved to the University of Pennsylvania, where I find
myself continually enchanted—up and down the hallways—by colleagues who combine intellectual rigor with great charm, collegiality,
and capaciousness. Special thanks to Charles Bernstein, Toni Bowers,
Virginia Chang, Stuart Curran, Thad Davis, Jim English, Grace Kao,
David Kazanjian, Amy Kaplan, Suvir Kaul, Ania Loomba, Heather Love,
Jo Park, Jean-Michel Rabaté, Melissa Sanchez, Deborah Thomas, Sala-
mishah Tillet, and Chi-ming Yang for being so warm and welcoming.

Some of the friends whose invaluable conversations, feedback, and
support allowed me to forge ahead through the ups and downs of writing
this book include Ritu Birla, Judy Butler, Ann Cvetkovich, Cathy Davidson, Gina Dent, Martha Fineman, Katherine Franke, Gayatri Gopinath,

Judith Halberstam, Sharon Holland, Janet Jakobsen, Heather Love, Lisa Lowe, Martin Manalansan, Fred Moten, Geeta Patel, Sonali Perera, Cathy Prendergast, Jasbir Puar, Camille Robcis, Shuang Shen, Shu-mei Shih, Ken Wissoker, and Sau-ling Wong. Their scholarship and institutional support—as well as their generosity of mind and spirit—continue to inspire and provide me with a model for scholarly brilliance and emulation.

There are, of course, those comrades and loved ones without whom anything much would not be possible. I completed the first draft of this book as my dear dad, Philip B. Eng, became increasingly ill. He passed away in May 2006, and for a while everything was rather hazy, as the reality of this divide sank in. I deeply thank Bernard Arias, Ed Cohen, Shinhee Han, Amy Kaplan, Farhad Karim, David Kazanjian, Homay King, Sanda Lwin, Susette Min, Rob Miotke, Mae Ngai, Ann Pellegrini, Josie Saldaña, Kaja Silverman, Lance Toma, Leti Volpp, Serena Volpp, Hiro Yoshikawa, Priscilla Wald, Dorothy Wang, Erik Webb, and Deborah White not just for reading again and again but, more importantly, for always staying in touch and for gifting me the sense of a collective project—a continuity and togetherness that can only be described as my very sense of the social. It is to Teemu Ruskola—my companion, editor, and chit-chatter in life—that I send my biggest love and thanks.

Portions of the preface, the introduction, and chapters one, two, three, and four were published previously in different forms. Chapter one appeared as "Freedom and the Racialization of Intimacy: *Lawrence v. Texas* and the Emergence of Queer Liberalism" in *A Companion to Lesbian, Gay, Bisexual, Transgender and Queer Studies,* edited by George E. Haggerty and Molly McGarry (Malden, Mass.: Blackwell, 2007), 38–59. Sections of the preface, introduction, and chapter two appeared as "The End(s) of Race" in *PMLA* 123, no. 5 (October 2008): 1479–93. Chapter three appeared as "Transnational Adoption and Queer Diasporas" in *Social Text* 21, no. 3 (Fall 2003): 1–37. Chapter four appeared as "Desegregating Love: Transnational Adoption, Racial Reparation, and Racial Transitional Objects" in *Studies in Gender and Sexuality* 7, no. 2 (2006): 141–72. I thank Blackwell, *PMLA*, Duke University Press, and the Analytic Press for allowing me to republish these materials.

Lastly, I would like to acknowledge Leigh Barnwell, Courtney Berger, Amy Ruth Buchanan, Katie Courtland, Tim Elfenbein, and Ken Wissoker at Duke University Press for shepherding through this second book project with the Press, and Derek Gottlieb for helping me to prepare the index. I would also like to thank Michele Carlson for allowing me to use her beautiful and startling image, "Roses," for the cover of this book. I met Michele as she was completing her MA and MFA at the California College for the Arts in San Francisco. Having read my *Social Text* article on transnational adoption, Michele asked me if I might help advise her thesis on this topic. "Roses" captures in the most visceral of ways the feelings of kinship and the problem of "girl love" that I explore in this book. At the same time, the power of this image—two graceful Asian women among a cascade of red roses and in a moment of unde-fined congress—is subtended by violence: a stack of gruesome China dolls that accumulates at the feet of one, like the debris of catastrophic wreckage that piles up before Walter Benjamin's Angel of History, while the other brandishes a handgun, prepared to shoot. Let me end this preface, then, and begin *The Feeling of Kinship* with the epigraph that accompanies Carlson's print:

> *Everything seemed to be piling up, or floating away*
> *But maybe those young gunners could hold it down.*

Introduction

ⓥ ⓥ ⓥ

QUEER LIBERALISM AND THE

RACIALIZATION OF INTIMACY

Such changes can be defined as changes in *structures of feeling*. The term is difficult, but "feeling" is chosen to emphasize a distinction from more formal concepts of "world-view" or "ideology." It is not only that we must go beyond formally held and systematic beliefs, though of course we have always to include them. It is that we are concerned with meanings and values as they are actively lived and felt.
—RAYMOND WILLIAMS, "Structures of Feeling"

In many ways this project began in the classroom. For over a decade now, I have been teaching on a regular basis an intro-duction to Asian American literature and culture. Although initially I could not have predicted that I would come to write a book about queer liberalism, the racialization of inti-macy, Asian diaspora and migration, and the politics of fam-ily and kinship, I became increasingly interested in these issues for a simple reason. Over the years, a growing number of students in my Asian American literature and culture classes have come out to me—not as gay or lesbian but as transnational adoptees.

In recounting their experiences, my students would often employ the language of the closet and the vocabulary of shame.[1] They stressed how they felt invisible as trans-national adoptees and how they felt compelled to come out of the closet time and again. They also admitted how such personal disclosures exacerbated their anxieties of being stigmatized and of feeling neither adequately Asian American nor suffi-ciently white. Finally, they emphasized how such ambivalent impulses provoked fears that they were being disloyal or ungrateful toward their adoptive parents. The complexity of these issues sparked a series of extended classroom discussions: Is the transnational adoptee an immi-grant? Is she Asian American? In turn, are her white adoptive parents Asian American?

Even more, such issues emerging at the intersection of queer studies and the contemporary politics of race made me start to think about transnational adoption as a new form of passing in our so-called "color-blind" age. Unlike prior histories of sexual or racial passing, however, the inscription of the closet in transnational adoption seemed to be less about the problem of detecting a hidden sexual or racial trait than about our collective refusal to see difference in the face of it. This refusal to see difference—to acknowledge race—marks the politics of colorblindness in our "post-identity" U.S. nation-state, which is characterized by the persistent disavowal of race in the name of freedom and progress.

Over time, the increasing presence of transnational adoptees in my Asian American literature and culture classes initiated a more sustained meditation on the unacknowledged ways in which race continues to structure and define both the public sphere and the private space of family and kinship relations. Moreover, it has demanded consideration of how contemporary evolutions in the meanings and values of social organization and community are, in Raymond Williams's terms, "ac-tively lived and felt" as structures of feeling.[2] In short, my students challenged me to examine emergent patterns of social belonging, both concrete and ephemeral, as they pushed me to reflect upon the feelings of kinship—the collective, communal, and consensual affiliations as well as the psychic, affective, and visceral bonds—that drew them to the intellec-tual and political projects of Asian American and critical race studies, as well as to theories of queerness and diaspora, as sites of critical response to the conundrums of race we face today. It is these cumulative reflec-tions that shape the arguments and analyses of The Feeling of Kinship.

Queer Liberalism

This book begins with an analysis of the historical emergence of what I describe as "queer liberalism" as well as its impact on conventional structures of family and kinship. Simply put, queer liberalism articulates a contemporary confluence of the political and economic spheres that forms the basis for the liberal inclusion of particular gay and lesbian U.S. citizen-subjects petitioning for rights and recognition before the law.[3] While gays and lesbians were once decidedly excluded from the normative structures of family and kinship, today they are re-inhabiting them in growing numbers and in increasingly public and visible ways. (Contemporary political debates on same-sex marriage and the inclusion of gay and lesbian couples on the "Wedding-Celebrations" pages of the venerable Sunday *New York Times* exemplify this remarkable historical shift.[4]) Our current moment is marked by the merging of an increasingly visible and mass-mediated queer consumer lifestyle with recent juridical protections for gay and lesbian rights to privacy and intimacy established by a number of interrelated court rulings on both the federal and the state levels. Most prominent among these is the landmark 2003 Supreme Court decision *Lawrence v. Texas*, overturning a Texas statute criminalizing homosexual sodomy as unconstitutional.[5] Moreover, recent legal decisions in Massachusetts and Connecticut legalizing same-sex marriage, as well as existing domestic partnership programs on the state level, in the municipal domain, and in the corporate arena, have remade the politics of kinship into "families we choose," to invoke anthropologist Kath Weston's important study of queer kinship, the lesbian baby boom, and the AIDS epidemic in 1980s San Francisco.[6]

Paradoxically, prior historical efforts to defy state oppression and provide a radical critique of family and kinship have given way to a desire for state legitimacy and for the recognition of same-sex marriage, adoption, custody, inheritance, and service in the military. In the following chapter, I explore the historical conditions of possibility for queer liberalism and its normative politics of family and kinship through an extended analysis of the *Lawrence* decision. Here, I emphasize how queer liberalism relies upon the logic of colorblindness in its assertion that racial difference has given way to an abstract U.S. community of individualism and merit.[7]

Today we inhabit a political moment when disparities of race—not to mention sex, gender, and class—apparently no longer matter; they neither signify deep structural inequities nor mark profound institutional emergencies. Our historical moment is overburdened by the language of colorblindness—especially with the recent election of our nation's first African American President, Barack Obama—one marked by the erosion of a public language for discussing race and racism. At the same time, it is distinguished by the cleaving of race from (homo)sexuality, and (homo)sexuality from race, the systematic dissociation of queer politics from critical race politics, the denial of their coalitional and intellectual possibilities. As I note in the Preface, the election of President Obama, accompanied by the passage of Proposition 8 in California, which invalidated the California Supreme Court's affirmation of same-sex marriages, marks one such significant cleaving.

Indeed, one of the main contentions of *The Feeling of Kinship* is that queer liberalism does not resist, but abets, the forgetting of race and the denial of racial difference. That is, the logic of queer liberalism in our colorblind moment works to oppose a politics of intersectionality, resisting any acknowledgment of the ways in which sexuality and race are constituted in relation to one another, each often serving to articulate, subsume, and frame the other's legibility in the social domain. In short, queer liberalism is predicated on the systematic dissociation of (homo)-sexuality from race as coeval and intersecting phenomena. The "completion" of the racial project that marks the advent of colorblindness in the U.S. nation-state thus becomes the condition of possibility for the historical emergence of queer freedom as the latest political incarnation of "the rights of man." In this regard, the election of President Obama and the passage of Proposition 8 are not oppositional or irreconcilable events. Rather, they function within an entirely predictable teleology of (racial) progress and (queer) freedom.

How did we get to such a historical juncture? In the legal domain of family and kinship, we are said to have formally entered a colorblind society with the 1967 Supreme Court decision *Loving v. Virginia*, in which the Court struck down as unconstitutional Virginia's anti-miscegenation statute prohibiting marriages between whites and blacks. While *Brown v. Board of Education* (1954) is typically regarded as the beginning of the end of legalized segregation in the *public* domain of education, *Loving* is commonly interpreted as the official end to legalized segregation in the *private* realm of family and kinship relations.[8] As such, *Loving* is seen as the legal culmination of a series of Constitutional challenges finally reversing the "separate but equal" doctrine of institutionalized segregation established by the 1896 *Plessy v. Ferguson* Supreme Court decision upholding state-sponsored separation of the races.

Today, after the formal end of state-sponsored segregation of the races—and under the official banner of colorblindness, multiculturalism, and neoliberalism—race is said to be irrelevant to the law, to political doctrines of the liberal individual, and to U.S. citizens as abstract and equal subjects. Legal scholar Rachel Moran remarks that, in a colorblind society, race is nothing but an "accident of birth," a "matter of physical appearance . . . no more germane to winning a government contract, getting a job, or gaining a seat at a public university than small ears or a freckled complexion."[9] Along similar lines, legal scholar Twila L. Perry observes that race today can no longer be debated as a collective injury but can only be discussed as individual harm. In response, Perry seeks to develop a language of "private" racial torts in lieu of a "public" language of discrimination and Constitutional redress for racial conflict and tension that continue to haunt and fracture U.S. society.[10]

Importantly, if race is defined in terms of its enduring social consequences, its ongoing legacies, and its continuing present of substantive inequalities, we can hardly say that we have entered a colorblind age. Indeed, our historical moment is defined precisely by new combinations of racial, sexual, and economic disparities—both nationally and globally— which are disavowed, denied, and exacerbated by official state policies that refuse to see inequality as anything but equality, and by a pervasive language of individualism, personal merit, responsibility, and choice. Contrary to liberal aspiration, the formal legal institution of colorblindness has not led to a U.S. society free of racial conflict, discrimination, and contradiction, as millions of people continue to be affected by race and afflicted by racism. Instead, a politics of colorblindness willfully refuses to acknowledge the increasing socio-economic disparities that mark our society, while also refusing to see these disparities as anything other than the just distribution of inequality to those who are unwilling to participate on the so-called level playing field of the neoliberal market.

Rather than accepting this teleological narrative of freedom and progress at face value, we ought to consider how colorblindness after *Brown* and *Loving* is only the latest historical incarnation of what legal scholar Cheryl I. Harris has described as a long and enduring history in U.S. law of "whiteness as property." Harris argues that U.S. jurisprudence has continually evolved in both explicit and implicit ways—from the period of slavery to emancipation, from the era of Reconstruction to Jim Crow segregation, and from the time of "separate but equal" to desegregation under civil rights movements—to connect property rights to race, and to legitimate a property interest in whiteness as the persistent and continuing right to exclude others across different historical periods. Although *Brown* and *Loving*, unlike *Plessy*, might be seen as taking "opposite interpretative stances regarding the constitutional legitimacy of legalized racial segregation," Harris observes, "the property interest in whiteness was transformed, but not discarded, in the Court's new equal protection jurisprudence."[11] In other words, through each shifting era of U.S. racial history, the law has not de-legitimated whiteness as property. Rather, it has adapted and re-adapted it for a changing historical landscape in which "whiteness as property evolved into a more modern form through the law's ratification of the settled expectations of relative white privilege as a legitimate and natural baseline."[12] In short, racial attitudes shift, but the right to exclude remains a historical constant, one ultimately rendering liberal notions of continuous social progress illusory.

Today, we might consider how the politics of colorblindness reconfigure whiteness as property to focus critical attention on the private structures of family and kinship as the displaced but privileged site for the management of ongoing problems of race, racism, and property in U.S. society. That is, in a colorblind age, the intimate sphere increasingly becomes a crucial site for a reconsideration and reevaluation of racial conflict organizing not just the private domain but the public sphere as well. The current evisceration of a political and public language to address social inequality across both realms reveals only one part of a historical process that Lauren Berlant identifies as the incredible "shrinking public sphere," a process solidified by the neoconservative Reagan-Thatcher revolution of the 1980s. Reacting against identity politics, the culture wars, and to the possibilities of a transformative multiculturalism, the Reagan-Thatcher revolution obviated the possibility for national political debates about race, sex, and class by displacing them into the "intimate public sphere" of privatized citizenship, normative family, and hetero-sexist morality.[13] Public discussions of race and racial discrimination have been systematically and precisely precluded through a rhetoric of colorblindness accompanying the incredible shrinking public sphere. As such, we must develop a critical vocabulary and analysis of the ways in which racial disparities and property relations embed and recode themselves within the private realm of family and kinship relations, only to seep back into circulation within the public domain.

Thus, for instance, while *Loving* may be said to have ended formal state-sponsored racial segregation in the private sphere of intimacy, this ruling (as all legal rulings regarding segregation) did not necessarily abolish *personal* prejudices, which are allowed to circulate, influence, and redefine family and kinship relations outside the formal reach of the law. As Moran observes, "having required government to behave hyperrationally in matters of race and marriage, *Loving* refrained from any discussion of how individuals should responsibly choose a spouse."[14] Building upon this argument, legal scholar Randall Kennedy points out that, while "statutes, judicial opinions, presidential directives, and voluminous commentary prepare us to assess racial discrimination in employment, housing, public accommodations, and the administration of criminal justice," there are in contrast "relatively few sources [to] give us guidance in evaluating racial discrimination in the choice of friends, dates, or spouses."[15] If the law no longer formally discriminates as a matter of public policy (and there is certainly robust debate over such a contention), it certainly does little to redress private racism or discrimination.

To take a critical page from Eve Kosofsky Sedgwick's monumental book on the persistence of homophobia in the age of sexual toleration, contrary to popular opinion "advice on how to help your kids turn out gay, not to mention your students, your parishioners, your therapy clients, or your military subordinates, is less ubiquitous than you might think. On the other hand, the scope of institutions whose programmatic undertaking is to prevent the development of gay people is unimaginably large."[16] In a similar vein, while the law no longer criminalizes interracial marriage, advice on how to promote interracial union and harmony is less ubiquitous than our colorblind pundits would have it. Likewise, while the law no longer enforces racial segregation in schools, it certainly does little to abet the disestablishment of racism in the educational hierarchy, to redress the education achievement gap between white and black students, or to prevent the ever-increasing segregation of the races in schools. The systematic dismantling of affirmative action after *Grutter v. Bollinger* and *Gratz v. Bollinger,* legal rulings handed down by the U.S. Supreme Court only a week after the *Lawrence* decision, as well as the more recent *Parents Involved in Community Schools v. Seattle School District No. 1,* underscores the law's simultaneous endorsement of formal equality through the language of colorblindness, coupled with its willful refusal to acknowledge continuing racial disparities, to enforce the material redistribution of resources, or to "de-legitimate," in Harris's words, an unwavering property interest in whiteness.[17]

In a colorblind society, firmly based on liberal distinctions between the public and private sphere, the state regulation of race and racial discrimination within the private realm of family and kinship relations would seem to be a preposterous idea, a fundamental affront to our sense of individual liberty and freedom. Indeed, it would seem to be an assault on privacy itself as a fundamental right to be protected. As the guardians of the liberal tradition, mainstream legal scholars thus find themselves at a conceptual loss to tackle enduring legacies of race and racial discrimination in the private domain of individual choice and economic self-determination, and in proffering adequate political as well as intellectual responses to the "afterlife" of post-identity politics.[18]

In this context, *The Feeling of Kinship* turns to the fields of critical race studies, queer studies, diaspora studies, transnational feminism, psychoanalysis, Marxism, cultural studies, and anthropology, which provide us with a thick critical vocabulary for examining the political, economic, and cultural processes by which race and racial difference continue to saturate our material and psychic lives, all the while denaturalizing liberal distinctions between the public and private domains by challenging its false divisions—"No More Separate Spheres!" in Cathy Davidson's memorable phrase.[19] In other words, we must contest romanticized notions of privacy and family as outside capitalist relations of exploitation and domination or—as generations of feminist scholarship has taught us—as free of gendered labor and value. At the same time we must remind ourselves of Karl Marx's insight in "On the Jewish Question," that the public sphere presupposes the hierarchies of the private sphere, guided and regulated by norms that are not neutral but conditioned by the particular interests of the dominant group.[20] Even more, we must resist the idealized notion of family and kinship relations as somehow removed from or eccentric to the racial tensions, cultural differences, and national conflicts that continue to define our domestic and global political economies and conditions of existence.

Here, it might be useful to keep in mind Amy Kaplan's insights on "manifest domesticity," on the ways in which "international struggles for domination abroad profoundly shape representations of American national identity at home, and how, in turn, cultural phenomena we think of as domestic or particularly national are forged in a crucible of foreign relations."[21] For instance, to return to an example from above, how is the practice of transnational adoption connected to modern histories of U.S. militarism and military intervention in Asia during Cold War conflicts and expansionism in the "American century"? More recently, how does the extension of liberal rights to privacy and family for gays and lesbians "over here," facilitated by the *Lawrence* ruling, relate to the demonizing of Arab and Muslim populations deemed intolerant, uncivilized, or inhuman "over there"? Both queries insist that we examine the ways in which liberal conceptions of the "domestic"—as public nation and private home—are "inextricable from the political, economic, and cultural movements of empire, movements that both erect and unsettle the ever-shifting boundaries between the domestic and the foreign, between 'at home' and 'abroad'."[22]

Today, under the shadows of a U.S-led globalization—capitalist development as freedom—the politics of colorblindness employs the depoliticized language of what Jodi Melamed describes as "neoliberal multiculturalism," the most recent historical phase of U.S. racial advancement on a global scale.[23] Neoliberal multiculturalism, Melamed argues, functions to support U.S. ascendancy on the global stage today, as racial liberalism did for U.S. global power following World War II. It seeks to manage racial contradictions in both the national and the international arena by masking the centrality of race for an ever-increasing global system of capitalist exploitation and domination. The biologization and capitalization of human life that defines neoliberal multiculturalism, under the shadow of global capitalism, is premised on the naturalization of a "system of capital accumulation that grossly favors the global North over the global South" and depends upon the "hyperextraction of surplus value from racialized bodies."[24] In the final analysis, neoliberal multiculturalism portrays racism as nonracialism and neoliberalism as the key to a multicultural, post-racist world order of freedom, opportunity, and choice. Under its mandates, "racism constantly appears as disappearing . . . even as it takes on new forms that can signify as nonracial or even antiracist."[25]

Economists and legal scholars tend to view choice as the very definition of (neo)liberal freedom. In rethinking neoliberal multiculturalism in the context of the private sphere, it is important to emphasize that nowhere is the language of choice more important than in the intimate space of family and kinship relations. However, anthropologists Susan Coutin, Bill Maurer, and Barbara Yngvesson argue that choice "is part of the morality tale that animates Western stories of self and of nation," justifying rampant practices of exploitation and domination.[26] Indeed, the neoliberal language of choice now helps to reconfigure not just the domestic but indeed the global marketplace as an expanded public field in which private interests and prejudices are free to circulate with little governmental regulation or restriction. As such, we need to ask how neoliberalism's rhetoric of choice works in tandem with a domestic politics of colorblindness precisely to subsume race within the private sphere of family and kinship relations. Such efforts to isolate and manage the private as a distinct and rarified zone outside of capitalist relations and racial exploitation, as well as dissociated from its domestic and global genealogies, express what I describe throughout this book as the "racialization of intimacy."

The Racialization of Intimacy

The racialization of intimacy marks the collective ways by which race becomes occluded within the private domain of private family and kinship today. Attention to the racialization of intimacy draws awareness to the ways in which racialized subjects and objects are reinscribed into a discourse of colorblindness. It brings critical focus on the processes by which race is exploited to consolidate idealized notions of family and kinship in the global North, for instance, through the practice of transnational adoption, the outsourcing of productive as well as reproductive labor, and the importation of careworkers from the global South. Furthermore, an examination of the racialization of intimacy reveals the political, economic, and cultural processes by which race has been forgotten across a long history of colonial relations and imperial practices, dissociated from or subsumed by other axes of social difference, such that it can only return as a structure of feeling, as a melancholic trace demanding historical explanation. Finally, the racialization of intimacy indexes other ways of knowing and being in the world, alternative accounts of race as an affective life-world within but ultimately beyond the dictates of a liberal humanist tradition, eluding conventional analytic description and explanation. At a time when race appears in official U.S. political discourse as only ever disappearing, it becomes increasingly urgent to contest such sanguine pronouncements with, among other things, this one simple fact: ever since the Enlightenment race has always appeared as disappearing.

In "The Intimacies of Four Continents," Lisa Lowe examines the sublation of African slave and Asian coolie labor that facilitated the rise of modern Europe, providing material support for the rise of republican states in Europe and North America, while helping to structure Enlightenment thought and the philosophical foundation for the universal "rights of man." Colonial labor relations on the plantations of the New World, Lowe writes, "were the conditions of possibility for European philosophy to think the universality of human freedom, however much freedom for colonized peoples was precisely foreclosed within that philosophy." Modern racial hierarchies "appear to have emerged in the contradiction between humanism's aspirations to universality and the needs of modern colonial regimes to manage work, reproduction, and the social organization of the colonized."[27] This dynamic stretches back to colonial labor relations organizing the plantations of the New World, and reaches forward to our contemporary moment of U.S.-led globalization, whose political culmination is the official disappearing act of race under the banner of liberal freedom and progress. We need to investigate this dialectic of disappearance—to reflect upon, as Lowe urges, the ways in which the "affirmation of the desire for freedom is so inhabited by the forgetting of its conditions of possibility, that every narrative articulation of freedom is haunted by its burial, by the violence of forgetting. What we know as 'race' or 'gender' are the *traces* of this modern humanist forgetting. They reside within, and are constitutive of, the modern narrative of freedom, but are neither fully determined by nor exhausted by its ends."[28]

In our colorblind age, it becomes increasingly important to draw attention to the ways in which intimacy has always been—and continues to be—racialized across what Fernand Braudel has described as the *longue durée*.[29] From this perspective, we come to apprehend the spectrality of race, which, like capital in Jacques Derrida's analysis, resists any straightforward narrative of affirmation and presence, any teleological progression from before to after.[30] As such, the advent of colorblindness in contemporary U.S. society might not be seen as the end of race. Instead, it might be approached as one significant event in a larger historical structure organized by colonialism's world division of racialized labor and freedom, a division materially and philosophically consolidated by the economic, political, and aesthetic tenets of the Enlightenment. Across this *longue durée*, race is constantly rendered ghostly. Colorblindness is merely the latest installment in this historical narrative of freedom and progress.

Seen from this perspective, intimacy might be thought of less as the sexual, romantic, and conjugal relations defining the liberal individual, serving to consolidate and separate the private domain of the bourgeois home from the public realm of work, society, and politics. To the contrary, Lowe's "Intimacies of Four Continents" underscores how a world division of racialized labor on the plantations of the New World provided the very conditions of possibility for the emergence of bourgeois notions of intimacy and concepts of privacy marking the rise of Euro-American modernity and the production of the liberal individual. That is, the racialized political economy of colonialism "founded the formative wealth of the European bourgeoisie," while the "labor of enslaved and indentured domestic workers furnished the material comforts of the bourgeois home."[31] In turn, the material consolidation of the bourgeoisie as a distinct class provided the ideological support for the separation of private and public spheres, all the while fueling the demand for the universal "rights of man" defining eighteenth-century revolution and the Enlightenment tradition.

Today, we continue to struggle with the political, economic, and cultural legacies of colonialism and its constructions of race as one significant project of Euro-American modernity. *The Feeling of Kinship* enters this critical conversation by examining the historical rise of queer liberalism as one recent incarnation of liberal freedom and progress, constituted by the racialization of intimacy and the forgetting of race. At the same time, the book explores how we might read through and against this history of racial forgetting—acknowledging its ghost and identifying its contradictions and denials—by turning to the concept of "queer diasporas."

Queer Diasporas

Much of *The Feeling of Kinship* focuses on the impact of queer diasporas —in particular, queer Asian diasporas—on conventional structures of family and kinship. Turning to queer Asian diasporas opens up forgotten histories of racialized intimacy within the received genealogies of liberal humanism, one largely defined by the dialectic of white-black race relations in the black Atlantic. A turn to queer diasporas allows us not only to queer the black Atlantic by expanding the oceanic limits of its social cartographies into other geographical spaces and times but also to consider the dynamic relationship between Asian migrant and African slave labor in a comparative context.

From this perspective, *The Feeling of Kinship* seeks to constitute one piece of a larger intellectual endeavor for the study of race and racialization in our colorblind age: the collective rethinking of the Enlightenment project and New World modernity from the perspective of Asia and Africa. In doing so, it attempts to move beyond the geographic boundaries of the nation-state and, more urgently, beyond the ideological boundaries of U.S. exceptionalism, which insists on the disappearance of race in the name of freedom and progress. It is precisely Asian American and Latino studies that brought the question of area studies —of other Asias and other Americas—into the field of American studies, provincializing the U.S. and its dominant critical discourses.

In this book, queer diasporas is not only an object of knowledge—a collection of novels, films, documentaries, legal decisions, and case histories—highlighting intersections of queerness with the global impact of Asian diasporas and migrations. Equally important, it is also a critical methodology, a reading practice that responds to queer liberalism and its racialization of intimacy by imagining otherwise, and by providing alternative knowledges and possibilities.[32] Diaspora, meaning "to disperse" or "to sow," is conventionally understood as the scattering of a people from a single place of origin. Khachig Tölölyan notes that today "[we] use 'diaspora' provisionally to indicate our belief that the term that once described Jewish, Greek, and Armenian dispersion now shares meanings with a larger semantic domain that includes words like immigrant, expatriate, refugee, guest-worker, exile community, overseas community, ethnic community."[33]

The political implications of diasporas, both old and new, are unstable in regard to the entity of the modern nation-state. While diasporas can be sites of resistance to the nation-state, they can also function, Tölölyan argues, as "its ally, lobby, or even, as in the case of Israel, its precursor."[34] From either perspective, diaspora is firmly attached to genealogical notions of racial descent, filiation, and biological traceability. Configuring diaspora as displacement from a lost homeland or exile from an exalted origin can thus underwrite regnant ideologies of nationalism, while upholding virulent notions of racial purity and its structuring heteronormative logics of gender and sexuality.

By invoking queer diasporas as a methodological approach, I seek to explore contemporary Asian movements and migrations in the global system not through a conventional focus on racial descent, filiation, and biological traceability, but through the lens of queerness, affiliation, and social contingency. The methodology of queer diasporas draws attention both to the nostalgic demands of diaspora and to a history of modernity built on the forgetting of race. It declines the normative impulse to recuperate lost origins, to recapture the mother or motherland, and to valorize dominant notions of social belonging and racial exclusion that the nation-state would seek to naturalize and legitimate through the inherited logics of kinship, blood, and identity. Instead, the methodology of queer diasporas denaturalizes race precisely by contesting and rethinking the pervading rhetoric that "situates the terms 'queer' and 'diaspora' as dependent on the originality of 'heterosexuality' and 'nation'."[35]

Gayatri Gopinath observes, "If 'diaspora' needs 'queerness' in order to rescue it from its genealogical implications, 'queerness' also needs 'diaspora' in order to make it more supple in relation to questions of race, colonialism, migration, and globalization."[36] Refusing to subsume sexuality within overarching narratives of national identity and racial belonging, or to incorporate these latter categories within a Western developmental narrative of capitalism and gay identity, the methodology of queer diasporas becomes a theoretical approach for telling a different story about the contemporary politics of nation-building and race under globalization, along with its accompanying material and psychic processes of social belonging and exclusion.

If the methodology of queer diasporas provides critical resources to denaturalize heteronormative discourses of racial purity underwriting dominant nationalist as well as diasporic imaginaries, it simultaneously complicates the homogenizing narratives of globalization that take for granted the totalizing logic of commodification, the inexorable march of economic development as the guiding beacon of (neo)liberal rights and freedoms. Rather, if capitalism, contrary to its classical formulation by Marx, has proceeded not through the homogenization of the globe but through the racialized differentiation of labor markets, production, and consumption, the turn to queer diasporas methodology serves to mark the uneven effects of capitalist exploitation and social domination "over there" as well as "over here."[37] In the process, it provides a particular perspective on globalization and reveals "alternative modernities," other cultural forms and practices that operate as potential sites of contradiction and refusal.[38]

The resistance to the universal translatability of (homo)sexuality as a stable category of knowledge traveling across different times and spaces is one such important site. As a methodological tool, queer diasporas draws attention to other forms of family and kinship, to other accounts of subjects and subjectivities, and to other relations of affect and desire dissonant to traditional conceptions of diaspora, theories of the nation-state, and the practices and policies of neoliberal capitalism. In short, it highlights the breaks, discontinuities, and differences, rather than the origins, continuities, and commonalities, of diaspora. By indexing what Dipesh Chakrabarty calls the "diversity of human life-worlds," outside of capitalism's logics of empty, homogeneous time and space, the methodology of queer diasporas offers a critique of modernity and its forgetting of race that calls attention to unauthorized subjects and to unacknowledged structures of feeling beyond an empirical tradition of liberal rights and representation.[39]

From this perspective, the concept of queer diasporas focuses attention on the epistemological and ontological limits of the liberal humanist tradition, bringing into relief disparate ways of knowing and being in the world that evade the purview of capitalist modernity. Even more, by providing a site for the interrogation of what Williams terms the "affective elements of consciousness and relationships," queer diasporas mark not only the tangible but also intangible areas of social existence and belonging, the feelings of kinship that threaten, in Walter Benjamin's words, "to disappear irretrievably" if we do not recognize and seize hold of them.[40] Throughout, *The Feeling of Kinship* thus explores not only the political economy of globalization, which gives rise to new forms of family and kinship, but also the psychic economy of globalization and the psychic dimensions of queer diasporas. It pays particular attention to structures of feeling, not just to formal concepts, structural analyses, and systematic beliefs, but also to the more ephemeral, intangible, and evanescent feelings of kinship as they are "actively lived and felt," in Williams's words, "thought as felt and feeling as thought."[41]

From a slightly different perspective, this book focuses on the following theoretical question: Why do we have numerous poststructuralist accounts of language but few poststructuralist accounts of kinship? In the 1970s, feminist anthropologists such as Gayle Rubin turned to structuralist accounts of kinship, most notably those of Claude Lévi-Strauss, to compare the exchange of women to the exchange of words.[42] Judith Butler observes that, when the study of kinship was combined with the study of structural linguistics, the exchange of women was likened to the trafficking of a sign, the linguistic currency facilitating a symbolic bond among men. To recast particular structures of kinship as "symbolic," Butler warns, "is precisely to posit them as preconditions of linguistic communicability and to suggest that these 'positions' bear an intractability that does not apply to contingent social norms."[43] In this manner, structuralist accounts of language have burdened us with structuralist accounts of kinship underwritten by the dominance of the Oedipus complex. Here, the Oedipus complex is not a developmental moment but a constitutive prohibition that emerges with the very inception of language, a structuralist legacy privileging certain forms of kinship as the only intelligible, communicable, reproducible, and livable ones.

We have moved beyond structuralist accounts of language, but have we moved beyond structuralist accounts of kinship? In our colorblind age of globalized capitalism, is the Oedipus complex still the guiding principle by which we can describe and measure structures of family and kinship? If not, how might we delineate a new terrain of material and psychic relations not bounded by the foundational structures of the incest taboo and the Oedipal myth, one attentive to questions of race and (homo)sexuality not withstanding the amnesias of modernity? The incest taboo inscribes a psychic pathway for displacement into the social world, while the Oedipus complex mandates the psychic affiliations—the normative identifications and desires—that we must make within this social world in order to live as intelligible beings and recognizable subjects. Queer diasporas fall out of normative Oedipal arrangements precisely by carving out other psychic pathways of displacement and affiliation, by demarcating alternative material structures and psychic formations that demand a new language for family and kinship. If poststructuralist theories of language reveal the ways in which our identities are discursively inscribed and thus open to the possibilities of re-signification, the concept of queer diasporas helps us rethink a poststructuralist account of language precisely in order to develop a poststructuralist account of kinship attentive to questions of state formation, racial taxonomies, sexual politics, and globalization—indeed, a retheorization of family and kinship relations after poststructuralism still largely absent in current debates in queer theory and anthropological accounts of kinship.

The Feeling of Kinship

The remainder of this book is organized into five chapters. Chapter one, "The Law of Kinship" begins with the law and an analysis of the landmark 2003 U.S. Supreme Court ruling, *Lawrence v. Texas,* in relation to the contemporary emergence of queer liberalism. As I note above, *Lawrence* overturned the Court's infamous 1986 *Bowers v. Hardwick* decision, and declared a Texas statute banning same-sex sodomy unconstitutional. By offering legal protections to gay and lesbian intimacy, *Lawrence* marks a significant historical moment in which a long Enlightenment liberal tradition of privacy, as a political right to be protected, is for the first time being extended to certain gay and lesbian U.S. citizen-subjects willing (and able) to accept a heteronormative version of bourgeois family, domesticity, and marriage.

Chapter one considers how the *Lawrence* decision inaugurates queer liberalism by marking a particular confluence between the political and economic spheres, but it also questions whether the ruling can be considered an unmitigated victory for queer liberalism. Mainstream gay and lesbian activists frequently invoke *Lawrence* in relation to a legalized past of racial discrimination—that is, invoke *Lawrence* as "our" *Brown v. Board of Education* or "our" *Loving v. Virginia.* By analogizing *Lawrence* to *Brown* and *Loving,* gay and lesbian activists configure queer liberalism as a political project in the present while consigning racism as a political project to the past. This analogy denies the coevalness of sexual and racial discrimination, subjecting them to a type of historicist violence by casting them as radically discontinuous. In other words, queer liberalism functions not in opposition to but with the logic of colorblindness that deems the racial project historically "complete."

In contrast, chapter one argues that the ghost of miscegenation haunts this landmark legal decision—that the emergence of queer liberalism depends upon the active management, repression, and subsuming of race. It asks what it might mean to begin with the material facts of the case: that the plaintiffs were a mixed-race black-white "couple" (according to legal scholar Dale Carpenter, they were, in fact, a one-night stand involved in a messy love triangle); that the Houston police entered Lawrence's apartment on the report of a weapons disturbance; that the caller who phoned in this racial trespass used the following language: "[There's] a nigger going crazy with a gun."[44] How is it, then, that what begins as a story of racial trespass ends as a narrative of queer freedom?

Ultimately, by bringing together a longer history of privacy rights in liberal legal theory with more recent scholarship from critical race theory, I describe the emergence of privacy in the *Lawrence* decision as a racialized property right, one extending the long juridical history of "whiteness as property"—a long legal legacy of property and racial privilege in U.S. law—into our colorblind moment. Through this extension, a long and troubling history of African American race and intimacy as spoiled kinship is transformed into idealized notions of queer family and kinship precisely by folding domesticated gays and lesbians into the liberal project of the U.S. nation-state.

Chapter one concludes with a coda that turns our attention to the psychic structures of queer liberalism. The coda focuses on Sigmund Freud's infamous case history of Dr. Daniel Paul Schreber (1842–1911). In his 1911 "Psychoanalytic Notes Upon an Autobiographical Account of a Case of Paranoia (Dementia Paranoides)," Freud analyzes the mental gymnastics of the paranoid Schreber, a distinguished German judge and once chief justice of the Saxony Supreme Court, in order to explore how Oedipal norms conscript the voice of the law to enforce and maintain its normative boundaries of family and kinship. This reading of Schreber illuminates the psychic structure of queer liberalism by illustrating how homosexuality can be reconciled with the demand of the super-ego, good citizenship, and the moral majority. At the same time, this reading of Schreber establishes a tension between the material and the psychic registers—the political and psychic economies of queer diasporas—that the remainder of the book examines in its exploration of poststructuralist accounts of family and kinship.

In sum, *Lawrence v. Texas* traces the advent of queer liberalism in a U.S. domestic landscape ordered by the politics of colorblindness and post-identity. In subsequent chapters of the book, I turn from the domestic to the diasporic in order to investigate queer diasporas as concerted political, economic, and cultural response to the predicaments of our colorblind age. Chapter two, "The Structure of Kinship," begins with a consideration of the incest taboo as that primary psychic structure regulating the emergence of the social, and with a meditation on subjects of modernity who, in Joseph Roach's memorable phrase, are "forgotten but not gone."[45] Monique Truong's novel, *The Book of Salt* (2003), set in 1930s Paris, and Wong Kar-wai's film, *Happy Together* (1997), set in late-1990s Buenos Aires, bookend the early- and late-twentieth century through their focus on queer Asian migrants laboring in the diaspora. Collectively, Truong's and Wong's bachelors draw attention away from authorized East-West movements of immigration and assimilation to focus instead on unauthorized South-South axes of migration and disenfranchisement. In the process, Truong's novel and Wong's film transport us from the realm of fiction to the domain of history by considering how queer diasporas and desires become central to the narration of modernity, to the problems of historicism, and to the dialectic of affirmation (of freedom) and forgetting (of race) that defines the liberal humanist tradition.

Bình, Truong's fictionalized distillation of a series of Indo-Chinese cooks appearing on the pages of the eponymous *Alice B. Toklas Cookbook,* is employed as household chef and servant to Gertrude Stein and Toklas during the couple's famous expatriate residency in Paris. By installing her protagonist in the intimate quarters of the Stein Salon, and by centering him in the historical margins of Old World Europe, Truong draws insistent attention to who and what must be forgotten so that the high modernism exemplified by Stein and Toklas might be affirmed. Truong asks, what remains unassimilable, unrecognizable, and untold in the making of the political and aesthetic realm of Euro-American modernity? How is it that Stein and Toklas can appear in history as the iconic lesbian couple of both literary modernism and historical modernity while Bình, the queer Vietnamese colonial, can never appear in history? In this regard, what is the relationship between the aesthetic inscription of Stein as the doyenne of literary modernism in her time and the current political inscription of Stein and Toklas as the exemplars of queer liberalism in our time?

Bình inhabits the interwar years, which mark the political and aesthetic upheaval of European modernity and enlightenment in the face of total war. In turn, Wong Kar-wai's protagonists Lai and Ho are part of a queer diasporic underclass whose unacknowledged labor secures the boundaries of a globalizing new world order under the shadows of late capitalism and decolonization. Wong's couple departs (post)colonial Hong Kong on the brink of its 1997 turnover from British to Chinese authority. They travel halfway around the world in order to jump-start their failing relationship—in the words of Ho, "to start over." In the final analysis, the impossibility of the couple's relationship—their consummate psychic deadlock—forces us to imagine an alternative sphere of family and kinship relations lived outside the sanctioned boundaries of the Oedipus complex and incest taboo. If the incest taboo demands displacement from kin or, more accurately put, establishes kinship relations precisely on the basis of displacement, Lai and Ho challenge particular mobilizations of the incest taboo and its principles of displacement that sanction and establish the Oedipal as the only livable, knowable, or inevitable form of family and kinship.

Chapter three, "The Language of Kinship," extends this exploration of displacement and the incest taboo by focusing on an ostensibly "privileged" figure of neoliberalism—the transnational adoptee—along with the problems of affiliation coerced and configured by the dominant language of kinship, the Oedipus complex. In this chapter, I explore the psychic and material histories of postwar transnational adoption from Asia through an analysis of Deann Borshay Liem's documentary *First Person Plural* (2000), a film that examines both Borshay Liem's 1966 adoption from a Korean orphanage by a white American couple in Fremont, California, and her discovery, some twenty years later, of her Korean birth mother. *First Person Plural* situates the practice of transnational adoption firmly within gendered histories of military violence. At the same time, by focusing on Borshay Liem's dilemmas, both on not having enough space in her mind for two mothers and on her wayward feelings of kinship, the film highlights the psychic consequences of the transfer of infants in the global system from South to North.

In the age of global capitalism, domestic and reproductive labor are increasingly outsourced to women from and in the global south. *First Person Plural* suggests how transnational adoptees today, in turn, provide a new type of affective labor, one helping to consolidate the social and psychic boundaries of white middle-class nuclear families in the global north by shoring up Oedipal ideals of family and kinship not only for heterosexual but also, and increasingly, for homosexual couples and singles. Borshay Liem's "documentary of affect" also illustrates how the transnational adoptee's assimilation into her new American family depends on the strict management of her affect, in which racial difference and the racial past—losses associated with a Korean birth mother and motherland—remain unaffirmed by those closest to her. Ultimately, I argue in chapter three, transnational adoption is not just another unacknowledged instance of the racialization of intimacy; even more, the practice opens upon and complicates the terrain of racial melancholia and loss, which is particularly complicated due to its profoundly unconscious and intrasubjective nature. As such, chapter three concludes with an analysis of Freud's concept of the negative Oedipus complex as rejoinder to the traditional Oedipal romance of one father and one mother. Only here can the psychic possibility of two mothers outside of normative structures of the positive Oedipus complex become thinkable and the possibility of a poststructuralist language for family and kinship become viable.

Chapter four, "The Prospect of Kinship," expands upon this reading of racial melancholia through a psychoanalytic case history about a U.S. transnational adoptee from Korea, Mina. Co-written with Shinhee Han, a New York-based psychotherapist, the chapter analyzes Mina's racial melancholia by turning to theories of affect in object relations that bring us to another psychic alternative and possibility: the prospect of racial reparation. Mina's loss of mother and motherland triggers a series of primitive and violent psychical responses such that we are forced to rethink Melanie Klein's theories of infantile development—of good and bad objects, and good and bad mothers—in terms of good and bad *racialized* objects, good and bad *racialized* mothers. Mina's case history demands a consideration of racial difference as constitutive of, rather than peripheral to, Klein's fundamental notions of splitting and idealization, of depression and guilt, and of reinstatement and reparation. In short, we come to recognize that Klein's psychic positions are also and at once *racialized* positions. For Mina, negotiating the depressive position and addressing her racial melancholia ultimately entails the racial reparation of the lost and devalued Korean birth mother.

Chapter four concludes by focusing on the ways in which Mina's case history draws attention to the materiality of the psychotherapist as a racialized subject. In particular, we consider how the dynamic of transference between the patient and her Korean American analyst is framed by the public fact of their shared racial difference as well as by the public nature of the analyst's pregnancy, which ensued during the course of the Mina's treatment. Here, we examine how Han's pregnancy constitutes her, to reformulate D.W. Winnicott, as a "racial transitional object" for Mina, which allows her to negotiate a reparative position for race by resignifying her vexed identifications with not only a disparaged Koreanness but also an idealized whiteness. Ultimately for the transnational adoptee, racial reparation involves creating psychic space for two "good-enough" mothers—the Korean birth mother as well as the white adoptive mother.

In the final chapter of the book, "The Feeling of Kinship," I turn from racial reparation as an individual psychic problem to racial reparation as a collective political predicament of our colorblind age by examining the relationship between psychic and political genealogies of reparation. Chapter five analyzes a growing body of U.S. cultural productions—novels, documentaries, and films about Japanese internment by *sansei* (third-generation) artists born after World War II. It focuses on vexed feelings of kinship and on affect as a political project. Unlike their parents and grandparents, these writers and directors did not live through internment. For the most part, their works have been published and produced after House Resolution 422, the Civil Liberties Act of 1988. Signed into law by Ronald Reagan, H.R. 422 not only offered a national apology for the evacuation, internment, and relocation of 112,000 Japanese Americans during World War II; it also provided monetary restitution of $20,000 to each surviving internee. The Civil Liberties Act of 1988 is commonly heralded as the conclusion to a regrettable but anomalous chapter of U.S. history. But, as these cultural works collectively insist, political reparation and psychic reparation are hardly coterminous.

Thus, we are left with an urgent question: What does it mean to take responsibility for a historical event one never actually experienced? Ultimately, I argue, to take responsibility is as much an affective as a political affair—all the more so in the face of internment's putative historical resolution, and in a U.S. political climate that declares the project of human freedom accomplished within the domestic borders of the nation-state. Chapter five analyzes Rea Tajiri's documentary on Japanese internment, *History and Memory: for Akiko and Takashige* (1991), as a documentary of affect, like *First Person Plural*. I argue that, unlike mainstream gay and lesbian activists who enact a certain form of historical violence by reifying an analogy between (homo)sexual and racial progress, Tajiri presents us with an unexpected set of *affective* correspondences. These emotional analogies and feelings of kinship world forgotten creatures and things by bringing them into the time and space of history in a fundamentally different manner from that of historicism. In the process, Tajiri helps us to rethink the parameters, not just of family and kinship, but of identity and history, by insisting on a new relationship between affect and language after poststructuralism.

By configuring affect and language not as oppositional but as supplemental, *History and Memory* illustrates how the linguistic binds of identity might be loosened while the dominant narratives of historicism are simultaneously redefined. In this respect, Tajiri's film returns us to a set of issues raised here, and expanded upon throughout the pages of this book, concerning the affirmation of freedom and the forgetting of race that mark the establishment of the Enlightenment project, the rise of Euro-American modernity, and the tenets of liberal humanism under which we continue to labor in our colorblind age. Like the other cultural productions in this book of queer diasporas, Tajiri's feelings of kinship demand a new model of historical understanding animated under the sign of the affective, one keeping us open to the world, and one for which we all must learn to take responsibility.

The Law of Kinship

       ⊗ ⊗ ⊗

LAWRENCE V. TEXAS AND THE

EMERGENCE OF QUEER LIBERALISM

Since then I have wholeheartedly inscribed the cultivation of femininity on my banner, and I will continue to do so as far as consideration of my environment allows, whatever other people who are
ignorant of the supernatural reasons may think of me. I would like
to meet the man who, faced with the choice of either becoming a
demented human being in male habitus or a spirited woman, would
not prefer the latter.
—DANIEL PAUL SCHREBER, *Memoirs of My Nervous Illness*

Trans-Atlantic slave and trans-Pacific coolie migrations to
the New World constituted not only the material but also the
philosophical foundation for liberal humanism to think the
universality of human freedom and progress. This historical
legacy continues to haunt the disavowed racial ground of our
contemporary U.S. political moment. Our putatively colorblind age is replete with assumptions that freedom is made
universal through liberal political enfranchisement and the
rights of citizenship, and through the globalization of capitalism and the proliferation of "free" markets. Indeed, under
the neoliberal mandates of the "ownership" society, political
and economic rights—citizenship and property—are increasingly conflated. As Aihwa Ong observes, neoliberal rational-
ity is marked by the "infiltration of market-driven truths and
calculations into the domain of politics," with political and

social problems insistently recast as non-ideological issues in need of technical, economic response.[1]

Such a narrow discourse of human emancipation underwrites what Gayatri Chakravorty Spivak has described as "a history of the vanishing present," making it exceedingly difficult to imagine alternative knowledges, political possibilities, and social communities—especially in a post-9/11 world order.[2] Today, ideals of a unified and ascendant U.S. national culture on the global stage are mobilized to distinguish a freedom-loving and civilized U.S. nation-state against its freedom-hating and uncivilized Muslim other. This genealogy of freedom simultaneously underwrites the contemporary emergence of what I describe as "queer liberalism." Queer liberalism marks a particular confluence of political and economic conditions that form the basis of liberal inclusion, rights, and recognitions for particular gay and lesbian U.S. citizen-subjects willing and able to comply with its normative mandates.

In this chapter, I explore queer liberalism's law of kinship by examining the landmark June 2003 Supreme Court decision *Lawrence v. Texas,* which struck down as unconstitutional a Texas statute banning same-sex sodomy while reversing the infamous 1986 Supreme Court ruling *Bowers v. Hardwick.*[3] Here, the Court had earlier affirmed the constitutionality of a Georgia statute under which Michael Hardwick had been convicted for engaging in sodomy with a consenting adult male in the privacy of his Atlanta home.[4] In *Bowers,* the majority opinion, written by Justice Byron White, formulated its judicial task in the following, and as many have noted disingenuous, terms: whether the U.S. Constitution "confers a fundamental right upon homosexuals to engage in sodomy."[5] In reversing *Bowers,* the majority opinion in *Lawrence,* written by Justice Anthony Kennedy, reformulated the legal problem not merely as a question of same-sex sodomy, but as a question of the fundamental right to privacy and intimacy.[6] Stating that the Court failed "to appreciate the extent of the liberty at stake" in *Bowers, Lawrence* reinterpreted the problem to consider whether one could be criminalized for loving someone of the same sex: "The question before the Court is the validity of a Texas statute making it a crime for *two persons* of the same sex to engage in certain *intimate sexual conduct.*"[7]

In conferring on gays and lesbians the Constitutional right to "intimate sexual conduct" as couples ("two persons"), and by describing this right to privacy "as an integral part of human freedom," the majority opinion in *Lawrence* constituted gay and lesbian political recognition, enfranchisement, and inclusion among "We the People" as a privileged relationship between freedom and intimacy, domesticity and couple-dom. Under the banner of freedom and progress, queer liberalism thus becomes linked to a politics of good citizenship, the conjugal marital couple, and the heteronormative family. In this context, we need to ask how a constitutive violence of forgetting resides at the heart of queer liberalism's legal victory, its (re)inhabiting of conventional structures of family and kinship. Doctrinally *Lawrence* appears in the pages of Consti-tutional Law textbooks as a watershed decision concerning rights to liberty and privacy for gays and lesbians. I would suggest, however, that repressed legacies of race and property constitute the core narrative of queer freedom and progress underwriting this legal decision. While race is not the doctrinal issue in *Lawrence*, I contend that it should be central to our thinking about the case politically and socially, and subsequently to our thinking about the historical emergence of queer liberalism. In-deed, as I argue in this chapter and this book, a long history of *racialized* intimacy subtends liberal narratives of freedom and progress, which require a more comprehensive analysis of the intersections of race and sexuality in U.S. law and society.

Chapter one offers an intersectional analysis of the *Lawrence* decision. *Lawrence*'s legal victory might be something, in Spivak's words, that we "cannot not want."[8] Indeed, in our conservative times, it is something we cannot afford not to want. Needless to say, the decriminalization of same-sex sodomy in U.S. law is an event of tremendous political signifi-cance. Nevertheless, it is crucial to explore the historical conditions of possibility as well as the social costs and limits of this latest episode in the story of human freedom and progress.

This chapter is divided into several sections. I begin with a historical elaboration of the emergence of queer liberalism onto the U.S. political stage. Departing from John D'Emilio's well-known analysis of "Capital-ism and Gay Identity," I examine the logic of *late* capitalism and gay identity as a function of a contemporary U.S.-led political economy of neo-liberal globalization and governmentality. Next, I follow with a detailed analysis of the *Lawrence* ruling in order to delineate how queer liberalism's freedom and progress is predicated on the systematic dissociation of race from (homo)sexuality as coeval phenomena. This dissociation marks the emergence of gays and lesbians from what Dipesh Chakrabarty has de-scribed as the "imaginary waiting room of history."[9] However, this "com-ing out" into history and into the liberal polity, as it were, requires not only the domestication of gay and lesbian intimacy but also, and equally important, its differential distribution as a racialized property right—what I am describing here as the "racialization of intimacy." I conclude the chapter with a meditation on the psychic structure of queer liberalism. Analyzing Freud's 1911 "Psychoanalytic Notes Upon an Autobiographical Account of a Case of Paranoia (Dementia Paranoides)," I explore the mental gymnastics of Daniel Paul Schreber (1842–1911), the distinguished albeit psychotic German judge who served as chief justice of the Saxony Supreme Court of Appeals before a series of mental breakdowns left him permanently incapacitated and confined to a mental asylum. Understanding the "supernatural reasons," as Schreber puts it in his *Memoirs of My Nervous Illness*, compelling his transformation from "a demented human being in male habitus" to a "spirited woman," promises to provide insight on the psychic demands and limits of queer liberalism. Even more, it promises to shed light on queer liberalism's current renaturalization of Oedipal norms, long under duress through evolving forms of family and kinship.

Queer Liberalism, or Late Capitalism and Gay Identity

The contemporary emergence of queer liberalism marks an unsettling, though perhaps not entirely unexpected, attempt to reconcile the radical political aspirations of queer theory's subjectless critique with the liberal demands of gay and lesbian U.S. citizen-subjects petitioning for rights and recognition before the law.[10] Our current moment is marked by a particular coming together of economic and political spheres that form the basis for liberal inclusion: the merging of an increasingly visible and mass-mediated queer consumer lifestyle (emerging post-Stonewall and ascendant during the 1980s and 90s) with recent juridical protections for gay and lesbian rights to privacy and intimacy established by the *Lawrence* ruling; the legalization of same-sex marriage in the state of Massachusetts during the same year; and the California and Connecticut State Supreme Courts' recent decision to do the same.[11]

In his well-known 1983 essay "Capitalism and Gay Identity," John D'Emilio argues that gay identity first emerged at the turn of the nineteenth century through the ascent of wage labor in industrializing cities and the independent sexual lifestyle this wage labor afforded.[12] The creation of urban zones of gay life was facilitated by the movement of individuals away from agrarian-based family units and actualized through the severing of family and kinship bonds—a severing later mirrored, even embraced, in the politics of gay liberation and "coming out." As the material bases for the family as an independent unit of production eroded in the face of an ever-expanding, wage labor-based capitalist "free" market system, the ideological and emotional weight of family and family values, as well as the divisions between the public sphere of work and the private sphere of family, intensified. D'Emilio observes that, through this historical expansion of the emotional bases for kinship relations, family took on increasing significance as an "affective unit," a social institution meant to produce "emotional satisfaction and happiness."[13] Sanctified as the source of love, affection, and emotional security, family became defined against the heartlessness of a capitalist system that was, in fact, the material source for its ideological evolution.

It is clear that while capitalism may have been instrumental in creating the conditions for the emergence of gay identity, it did not at the same time establish a *laissez-faire* attitude toward same-sex relations. If the 1980s and 90s witnessed the emergence of gay and lesbian identity and visibility as a function of the market, as well as the development of a political movement for rights and recognition, especially in response to the AIDS pandemic, it also marked the simultaneous consolidation of right-wing ideologies under the sign of family and family values.[14] From this perspective, (homo)sexual regulation cannot be thought as the antithesis of queer liberalism, freedom, and progress, but must be thought as constituting their very historical conditions of possibility. "Sexual regulation," as Janet Jakobsen suggests, "is such a passion in U.S. politics because sexual regulation is constitutive of (secular) American freedom."[15]

Today, we find ourselves at a remarkable historical juncture regarding queer liberalism and the politics of family and kinship. To come out of the closet still places family and kinship bonds at risk. At the same time, however, gays and lesbians are reinhabiting structures of family and kinship not only in growing numbers but also in increasingly public and visible ways. While in prior decades gays and lesbians sustained a radical critique of family and marriage, today many members of these groups have largely abandoned such critical positions, demanding access to the heteronormative nuclear family and the rights, recognition, and privileges associated with it. Paradoxically, prior historical efforts to defy state oppression and to oppose state regulation of family and marriage have, to a striking extent, given way to the desire for state legitimacy, sanction, and authorization of same-sex marriage. Once considered anathema to family and kinship, homosexuality in our current political moment is being legally and ideologically reconciled to its normative mandates, paving over alternative public worlds and social formations that previous generations of gays and lesbians have made. In this political calculus, the state emerges as the central locus and guarantor through which non-normative sexual identities it once criminalized are now protected, liberated, and reconfigured—in the words of conservative gay pundit Andrew Sullivan—as "virtually normal."[16]

Seen from this perspective, queer liberalism's appeals to the state mark a significant moment in which the politics of "Queer Nation" and "U.S. citizen" are no longer antithetical, a fact evident in the astonishing August 2004 coming-out statement, scripted with the assistance of the Human Rights Campaign, of the former New Jersey Governor James McGreevy: "My truth is that I am a gay American." As Hannah Arendt defines it in *The Origins of Totalitarianism*, citizenship is nothing less than "the right to have rights."[17] And from this perspective, queer liberalism's current claims to state-sanctioned rights, recognitions, and privileges implicitly reinforce a normative politics, not just of family and kinship, but of U.S. citizenship. In the process, the state's role as the legitimate arbiter of rights and guarantor of freedom and liberty—even as Constitutional protections are eroded under the U.S. Administration's infinite War on Terror—remains uncontested and is indeed strengthened. If, as Judith Butler observed in 1993, the "I do" of the wedding ceremony is a performative invocation sealing the heterosexual social contract through the disavowal of "You queer," today we witness the historical reordering of this antithetical bind: "I do" and "You queer" no longer need be at odds under the watchful eyes of the law.[18]

Teemu Ruskola points out that it might prove difficult to resist our present interpellation as law-abiding U.S. citizen-subjects, capable of intimacy, no longer Constitutionally criminalizable, worthy of national recognition, and deserving of judicial respect.[19] He cautions, however, that it is equally crucial at this historical juncture to remind ourselves of Giorgio Agamben's insight that "the spaces, the liberties, and the rights won by individuals in their conflicts with central powers always simultaneously prepared a tacit but increasing inscription of individuals' lives within the state order."[20] To be a subject of the law, Butler observes, requires a "passionate attachment" to our subjection.[21] And, as Saidiya Hartman reminds us in the context of slavery and emancipation, "the failures of Reconstruction cannot be recounted solely as a series of legal reversals or troop withdrawals; they also need to be located in the very language of persons, rights, and liberties."[22] The vocabulary of persons, rights, and liberties fully inhabits the politics of queer liberalism today, and it is a language that we need to interrogate with care.

In other words, we need to explore the critical assumptions and limitations of queer liberalism's narratives of freedom and progress. We need to remind ourselves that decriminalization and social belonging are not coterminous, as contentious same-sex marriage debates, with state amendments and initiatives defining marriage as "between one man and one woman," immediately underscore.[23] We need to reflect on the political and economic costs that underwrite the current inscription of queer U.S. citizen-subjects into a national order, the instability of a rights-based discourse that enables political legitimacy while exacerbating evolving relations of capitalist exploitation, racial domination, and gender subordination in a domestic as well as global context.[24] In short, we must reexamine our assumptions concerning queer freedom and progress.

Departing from D'Emilio, we might ask: What is the contemporary mode of production that allows for queer liberalism's reinhabiting of conventional family and kinship relations? From a slightly different angle, how might we describe the relationship between *late* capitalism and gay identity? We cannot underestimate the ways in which neoliberalism and its proliferating modes of consumer capitalism underpin the historical evolution and transformation of capitalism and of gay identity into queer family and kinship. Emerging in the late 1970s, alongside the ascension of various multicultural and identity politics movements, neoliberal practices and policies were predicated on the expansion of markets and the dismantling of barriers to free trade in a globally-integrated economy. Linked to structural adjustment programs meant to overhaul the economies of the global South, neoliberalism facilitated the financialization of currency regimes, demanded the privatization of the public sector, and enjoined the commodification and capitalization of biological life.[25] Neoliberal practices and policies organized the unequal distribution of social goods and human labor—indeed, human life and freedom—into a biopolitics of global capitalism, one in which an ascendant queer liberalism can be a (potentially) respectable rather than stigmatized social formation.

Shifting from a politics of protest and redistribution to one of rights and recognitions, queerness is increasingly rendered an aestheticized lifestyle predicated on choice. Queerness has come out of the closet, as it were, becoming in the process a mass-mediated commodity, a culture of beautiful objects (bodies, fashions, food, and furniture) to be consumed, a *Queer Eye for the Straight Guy,* to invoke the title of Bravo's popular television program in which five gay men work tirelessly to make over the flagging masculinity of one heterosexual man.[26] Organized around the principle that the heteronormative family needs all of our material and emotional support, *Queer Eye* defines good citizenship as never-ending consumption in the free market, serving as an uncanny reminder of President George W. Bush's infamous directive to Americans after September 11th to fight terrorism by shopping (rather than, say, voting).

A product of late capitalist rationalization, queer liberalism functions as a supplement to capital, but in a desexualized, repackaged, and contained form. In other words, we might say that neoliberalism enunciates (homo)sexual difference in the register of culture—a culture that is freely exchanged (purchased) and celebrated (consumed). Thus, from the legal perspective of *Lawrence,* we might say that as sodomy is transformed into intimacy—coming together with the logic of queer domesticity as an aestheticized ideal—homosexual particularity and difference are absorbed into a universalized heteronormative model of the liberal human, an abstract national culture and community. In the process, a political movement of resistance and redistribution has been reconfigured and transformed into an interest group and niche market—a commercial scene of entertainment venues, restaurants, and shopping—in which gays and lesbians are liberated precisely by proving that they can be proper U.S. citizen-subjects of the capitalist nation-state.[27] In this regard, family is not just whom you choose but on whom you choose to spend your money.

That the emergence of queer liberalism comes at a historical moment of conservative U.S. politics and policies on the domestic and global stage should give us immediate pause. It would be premature to embrace wholeheartedly what Lisa Duggan has aptly labeled "homonormativity," the gay and lesbian liberal platform advocating for so-called progressive causes such as same-sex marriage, while rhetorically recoding freedom and liberation in terms of privacy, intimacy, domesticity, marriage, and the unfettered ability to "shop until you drop."[28] Configuring queer politics in such narrow terms obviates the political possibility of democratizing the (supposedly) private sphere of family and kinship relations, of recognizing and responding to the diverse ways in which we now structure and live out our intimate lives. In its place, we are presented with a domesticated vision of family and kinship, one predicated on the conjugal family and its Oedipal arrangements as the only legally recognized and tenable household structure. The proposition that marriage should be the privileged way of legitimating sexuality is not just conservative; it does not reflect our present realities and social formations.

From this perspective, homonormativity collaborates with a neoliberalism willfully blind to unequal structures of globalization and its increasingly international gendered division of labor. It is a politics that, in Duggan's words, "does not contest dominant heteronormative assumptions and institutions but upholds and sustains them while promising the possibility of a demobilized gay constituency and a privatized, depoliticized gay culture anchored in domesticity and consumption."[29] This political economy remains unchallenged by U.S. conservative and liberal agendas alike; indeed it is the place in which the two converge (Reagan and Bush meet the Clintons and Obamas). The privatization of family underwrites the withdrawal of state funding and resources, as the promotion of "traditional" marriage is meant to replace state dependency and employer support. A larger world-historical context demands that we ask how queer liberalism's current turn to rights furthers rather than thwarts these logics of neoliberalism, with its political economy of capitalist development characterized as human freedom, its multicultural mandates as "anti-racist" progress.

Before turning to a reading of *Lawrence v. Texas,* I would like to gesture to the ways in which queer liberalism's turn to normative forms of family and kinship—its folding into a neoliberal U.S. state project—is constituted against the figure of the racialized immigrant "over there" as well as "over here." Chandan Reddy, for instance, notes how discourses of family and family values increasingly serve to mediate contradictions between the U.S. nation-state and a neoliberal global economy. He argues that, since the 1980s, family reunification laws have helped to produce a racialized and gendered noncitizen immigrant workforce for domestic and low-end labor markets in the U.S. The turn toward family values was initiated by the reformation of the 1965 Immigration and Nationality Act, which shifted U.S. immigration policies away from a quota system based on national origins to one predicated on principles of family reunification. In the process, it served to bring into the U.S. not only an expanded transnational capital class (the post-1965 middle-class professional brain drain) but also a transnational laboring class largely from the Southern hemisphere—Asia, Latin America, and the Caribbean.

From the perspective of this new transnational laboring class, we might note that while the Immigration Act of 1990 capped the number of immigrant visas for so-called unskilled workers at a mere 10,000, it also increased family-based immigration visas to an annual limit of 480,000 starting in 1995. Facially neutral, these immigration policies in fact created an enormous pool of racialized and gendered low-wage noncitizen labor for a metropolitan service economy. Yet by coding immigration as essentially produced by the petitioning activities of resident immigrants in the U.S. themselves, family reunification laws work to appease "capital's need for immigrant workers while projecting the state as either a benevolent actor reuniting broken families or an overburdened and effete agent unable to prevent immigrants' manipulations of its (mandatory) democratic and fair laws."[30] At the same time, they also shifted state responsibility for welfare and social services— such as workplace injury insurance, childcare, and healthcare—back onto the shoulders of the petitioning immigrant families themselves. In this way, Reddy concludes, "the state is absolved politically from having created and expanded the conditions of noncitizen life within the territorial parameters of the United States and, at the same time, distinguishes itself as the apotheosis of Western Democracy by achieving the status of depoliticized neutrality."[31]

On the one hand, the state manages to increase the numbers of immigrants arriving into the U.S. for a domestic economy demanding low-wage non-citizen labor for the industrial and service sectors. On the other hand, the state simultaneously mobilizes a xenophobic rhetoric of immigrant invasion in order to dismantle its welfare responsibilities and to enact immigration "reform" by criminalizing immigrants and those who dare to provide basic services to them. As social welfare programs for the racialized immigrant and the racialized poor disappear in the face of corporate welfare malfeasance, family must increasingly become that privatized institution that takes up the state's abnegation of its public and institutional obligations. In this regard, home and family are not "private," but serve as crucial sites within the global restructuring of capital and labor.

Importantly, as the state reconstitutes its power through family reunification laws and its accompanying discourse of family values, it also reinforces heteropatriarchal relations in immigrant communities. Immigrant workers brought under family reunification programs have increasingly been forced to depend on family ties for access to room and board, employment, and other services. Reddy observes: "Family reunification extend[s] and institute[s] heteronormative community structures as a requirement for accessing welfare provisions for new immigrants by attaching those provisions to the family unit."[32] In the process, the state can simultaneously blame immigrant communities for monocultural deficiencies and pathological cultural values brought with them from abroad, for being particularly homophobic, and queer immigrants of color (as well as queers of color, in general) for being particularly willing to accept homophobic silencing.[33] Here we might note the work of Étienne Balibar who observes that, while racism based on the nineteenth-century categories of biology and blood has receded, discrimination based on forms of perceived cultural differences and values have proliferated in our contemporary moment.[34]

These culturalist arguments serve to demonize immigrant communities as illiberal, while masking the complicity of the neoliberal U.S. state in helping to engender the very homophobia that both the state and the larger public insist is imported part and parcel from these immigrants' home countries. In the same political breath, such culturalist arguments also justify the exclusion of so-called intolerant, uncivilized, and illiberal racialized immigrant communities from the U.S. nation-state and civil society, through a liberal language of citizenship as the guarantor of freedom and liberty for all, including now normative gay and lesbian U.S. citizen-subjects claiming their rightful place at the citizenship table. In short, the production of queer liberalism and the discourse of racialized immigrant homophobia are two sides of the same liberal coin. For queer immigrants of color who compose this new transnational laboring class, late capitalism and gay identity, in contrast to D'Emilio's earlier claims, do not decrease but rather increase dependency on family and kinship as well as its heteronormative mandates.

Taken together, Reddy's and Duggan's observations underscore a significant cleaving between queer and critical race projects, progressive social movements once thought in the same political breath. This cleaving insists that we rethink how race and sexuality are systematically dissociated in a putatively colorblind age, demanding a more robust politics of intersectionality in the face of neoliberal practices and policies.

The turning away from a sustained examination of the vast political and economic inequalities in the state, civil society, and commercial life, marks the paradoxes of queer liberalism. A renewed queer studies must insist that problems of neoliberal political economy cannot be abstracted away from the racial, gendered, and sexual hierarchies of the nation-state, but must be understood as operating in and through them. In this regard the recent turn toward antirelationality in queer studies might also be thought as a turn toward anti-intersectionality in the field—a coming together of colorblind and queer politics. As José Muñoz observes, "denouncing relationality first and foremost distances queerness from what some theorists seem to think of as contamination by race, gender, or other particularities that taint the purity of sexuality as a singular trope of difference . . . Antirelational approaches to queer theory were . . . investments in deferring various dreams of difference."[35]

In a post-9/11 world order, a renewed queer critique must be vigilant to the fact that sexuality is intersectional and that queer is a political metaphor without a fixed referent. It would insist that we ask to what extent a progressive queer politics might be (in)compatible with the mandates of U.S. citizenship as well as state rights and recognitions. The turn to an unapologetic and militant U.S. heteropatriarchy on the world stage demands a renewed queer politics attentive not only to questions of neoliberalism and globalization but also to issues of empire, sovereignty, and terrorism. It demands a renewed queer politics focused on problems of immigration, citizenship, welfare, the prison industrial complex, and human rights, including the collective ways in which these various issues underwrite the contemporary emergence of queer liberalism's claims on family and marriage, and on intimacy and domesticity.

The Imaginary Waiting Room of History

To place *Lawrence v. Texas* in context, it is necessary to recall two other significant historical events of 2003: the U.S. invasion and occupation of Iraq three months prior to the *Lawrence* ruling, as well as the Supreme Court's *Grutter v. Bollinger* and *Gratz v. Bollinger* affirmative action decisions handed down only a week after *Lawrence*. How are these three significant historical events—of queer liberalism, U.S. imperialism, and racial (in)equality—connected to one another? How it is that the Supreme Court that effectively elected George W. Bush president is the same Supreme Court that resoundingly overturned *Bowers v. Hardwick* only seventeen years after the case was decided, while also upholding ever tenuously affirmative action by instituting a temporal limit to its application?

Justice Kennedy's majority opinion in *Lawrence* begins with "liberty" and ends with "freedom": "Liberty protects *the person* from unwarranted government intrusions into a dwelling or other private places . . . As the Constitution endures, *persons in every generation* can invoke its principles in their own search for greater freedom."[36] This slippage, from the abstract individual, "the person," deserving of liberty from unwarranted government intrusion into his/her private home, to the organization of these abstract individuals into an implied social group, "persons in every generation," in search of ever "greater freedom" and social belonging, is noteworthy. In the context of *Lawrence*, "liberty" is neither a positive nor a substantive liberty. The right to be left alone from state interference, surveillance, and criminalization is a negative liberty that does not, unlike affirmative action, require the material redistribution of resources. In this sense, liberty for the individual is not about substantive equality for all. Even more, liberty might be said to imply, indeed constitute, an intended social group to whom rights, recognition, and privileges are granted. From this perspective, the liberty of some can certainly be in conflict with the freedom of others. Hence, we need to ask, liberty and freedom for whom, where, and under what conditions?

Lawrence v. Texas is lauded by legal scholars and the mainstream press alike as an unmitigated victory for gay and lesbian politics, as an unquestionable advancement for queer freedom and progress. Indeed, numerous gay and lesbian advocates call *Lawrence* our *"Brown,"* in reference to *Brown v. Board of Education*, aligning homosexual with racial progress, while at the same time necessarily ignoring through this analogy the fact that the plaintiffs in the case, John Geddes Lawrence and Tyron Garner, were a mixed-race couple.[37] In fact, Lawrence and Garner were not a couple at all, but part of a vexed one-night love triangle, according to legal scholar Dale Carpenter.[38] This material fact, largely ignored by *Lawrence* commentators, renders queer liberalism's idealization of conjugal domesticity especially ironic. Even more, it insists that we analyze this landmark legal decision not only for its queer but also for its subsumed racial politics. In other words, what if we were to approach this ruling not as an unmitigated victory for queer liberalism, but as a symptom of the U.S. nation-state's enduring inability to deal with problems of racial segregation, and thus come to terms with its ghosts of miscegenation? To put it in terms of the focus of this book, how does the contemporary emergence of queer liberalism depend upon a constitutive forgetting of race—on the racialization of intimacy?

One of Justice Kennedy's central premises for overturning *Bowers v. Harwick* was the "outdated" nature of sodomy statutes. Noting that, of the twenty-five states prohibiting such conduct at the time of the *Bowers*, only thirteen remain. Kennedy observes that in "those States, including Texas, that still proscribe sodomy (whether for same-sex or heterosexual conduct), there is a pattern of nonenforcement with respect to consenting adults acting in private."[39] In his scathing dissent from the majority opinion, Justice Antonin Scalia argues that the lack of enforcement of sodomy laws does not prove that they are outdated. To the contrary, Scalia protests, lack of enforcement is understandable given the fact that "consensual sodomy, like heterosexual intercourse, is rarely performed on stage. If all the Court means by 'acting in private' is 'on private premises, with the doors closed and the windows covered,' it is entirely unsurprising that evidence of enforcement would be hard to come by." Scalia then immediately goes on to offer these telling parenthetical remarks: "(Imagine the circumstances that would enable a search warrant to be obtained for a residence on the ground that there was probable cause to believe that consensual sodomy was then and there occurring)."[40]

Scalia's sarcastic aside is a reminder that it was not the report of "consensual sodomy" that provided the legal basis for the intrusion of the Harris County Sheriff's Department into the privacy of Lawrence's Houston apartment. It was, in fact, the report of a weapons disturbance. Carpenter reports that Robert Eubanks, the jilted third in the Lawrence-Garner love triangle, called the Harris County police dispatcher using the following words: "[There's] a nigger going crazy with a gun."[41] Scalia is right. People do not call the police when their neighbors are in *flagrante delicto*. They do, however, call them when they see an unidentified black man on their property, and under such circumstances, the police always respond. It is this enduring and unresolved history of whiteness, private property, and black racial trespass that provides the material and ideological background through which the queer liberalism of *Lawrence* emerges. How is it, then, that what begins as a story of racial trespass can end as a narrative of queer freedom?

It is useful to address this question by focusing on the legal genealogy of the *Lawrence* ruling traced out by both the majority and dissenting opinions. Both Kennedy and Scalia place *Lawrence* in a genealogy of privacy cases related to a woman's control over her reproductive rights and access to abortion: *Griswold v. Connecticut* (1965); *Eisenstadt v. Baird* (1972); *Roe v. Wade* (1973); *Carey v. Population Services International* (1977); and *Planned Parenthood of Southeastern Pennsylvania v. Casey* (1992).[42] The legal genealogy of *Lawrence* traced here concerns issues of privacy, not race.[43] But what if we were to pursue a reading of *Lawrence* through an alternate legal genealogy, through the specter of race, through the ghost of miscegenation?

One central argument raised by the plaintiffs' attorneys—accepted in Justice O'Connor's concurrence though ultimately dismissed by the majority opinion—was framed in terms of equal protection. Orienting their argument around the question of equality, Lawrence's and Garner's lawyers insisted that Texas law regarding same-sex sodomy was a form of sex discrimination. That is, a sexual act committed by a man with a woman was permitted while the same act committed by a man with a man was criminalized. This equal protection argument emerged from the Reconstruction Era amendments to the U.S. Constitution—specifically, the equal protection clause of the 14th Amendment—and thus connects queer liberalism to histories of race, slavery, and segregation.

Justice Kennedy gestures to this history of race and slavery when he cites Justice Stevens's dissenting opinion in *Bowers,* that "neither history nor tradition could save a law prohibiting miscegenation from constitutional attack," in arguing that the Texas statute too was obsolete.[44] Here, Justice Kennedy links *Lawrence* with the 1967 *Loving v. Virginia* ruling, in which the Court struck down a Virginia statute banning mix-raced marriages.[45] In *Loving,* the Court held it unconstitutional for Virginia to allow a white person to marry a white person but not for a black person to marry a white person. I am fascinated by Kennedy's analogizing of homosexuality to race. Both Kennedy and same-sex marriage advocates continually invoke civil rights cases as the legal and political precedents for *Lawrence*; they insistently compare current public resistance to same-sex marriage to "outdated" anti-miscegenation laws. As the stigma against mixed-raced couples proved legally untenable in 1967, so too will social and legal resistance wane against same-sex marriage in our present moment.

Ironically, by turning to *Loving* as a source of queer liberation and freedom, these advocates ignore the historical fact that the overturning of anti-miscegenation law in *Loving* was accompanied by a simultaneous hardening of legal defenses against homosexuality in *Boutilier v. Immigra-*

tion Services (1967).[46] This Supreme Court ruling, handed down just prior to the *Loving* decision, affirmed the constitutionality of a federal law that excluded homosexuals from eligibility for immigration and naturalization as an issue of national security.[47] In 1963, Clive Michael Boutilier, a native of Canada, applied to become a naturalized U.S. citizen. Boutilier had earlier immigrated to the U.S. with his family in 1955, when he was twenty. Asked about his sexual history during his naturalization proceedings, Boutilier answered that, since the age of fourteen, he had engaged in sexual activity with both men and women. The U.S. government immediately began deportation proceedings against Boutilier, which he challenged all the way to the Supreme Court. In a 6–3 vote, the Court upheld the constitutionality of the INS deportation order.

Siobhan Somerville observes, "In the eye of the law, the interracial couple was imagined as having a legitimate claim on the state at the same time that the nation was defensively constituted as heterosexual, incapable of incorporating the sexually suspect body. That the Supreme Court had reaffirmed the exclusion of homosexuals from citizenship only three weeks earlier makes it particularly ironic that *Loving* is currently read as the precursor to gay and lesbian rights."[48] To represent *Loving* only as an expansion of marriage rights is misleading, Somerville argues, for *Loving* also simultaneously consolidated heterosexuality as a prerequisite for state recognition and the rights of citizenship.[49] By analogizing *Lawrence* to *Loving*, we not only ignore this constitutive history of racial and sexual regulation but also overlook at our own peril the ways in which the U.S. state continues to consolidate and enforce heteronormativity precisely through the language of colorblindness.

Furthermore, by analogizing same-sex marriage to this "settled" history of interracial union, queer liberalism is embedded in a narrative of *temporal* development. That is, homosexuals are now allowed to exit what Chakrabarty describes as the "imaginary waiting room of history." Emerging as queer liberals, they tacitly underwrite the unending march of human freedom and progress. In such a historical narrative, racial liberation is configured as a politics of the past, while queer liberalism is configured as a politics of the present. Racial liberation is thus deemed a completed project and consigned to a prior historical moment. From this perspective, the emergence of queer liberalism underwrites the simultaneous demise of affirmative action. In short, queer liberalism becomes thinkable precisely because racial equality has been settled and achieved. Hence, the possibility of reading homosexuality and race as constitutive, as intersectional, as politically and temporally coeval is foreclosed.

Let me elaborate upon this foreclosure by turning, once again, to Scalia's response to Kennedy's invocation of *Loving*. Scalia dismisses the heightened scrutiny claims associated with race as inapplicable to Lawrence's claim of sex discrimination, refusing to find any plausible connections between *Loving* and *Lawrence*. He notes that the Texas statute applies equally to all persons: men and women, homosexuals and heterosexuals alike. Scalia concedes that, although the statute distinguishes between the sexes insofar as the partner with whom the sexual acts are performed is concerned, "this cannot itself be a denial of equal protection, since it is precisely the same distinction regarding partner that is drawn in state laws prohibiting marriage with someone of the same sex while permitting marriage with someone of the opposite sex." He continues:

> The objection is made, however, that the antimiscegenation laws invalidating *Loving v. Virginia,* similarly were applicable to whites and blacks alike, and only distinguished between the races insofar as the *partner* was concerned. In *Loving,* however, we correctly applied heightened scrutiny, rather than the usual rational-basis review, because the Virginia statute was "designed to maintain White Supremacy." A racially discriminatory purpose is always sufficient to subject a law to strict scrutiny, even a facially neutral law that makes no mention of race. No purpose to discriminate against men or women as a class can be gleaned from the Texas law, so rational-basis review applies.[50]

Here, it is important to note that Scalia's legal reasoning, like Kennedy's, also functions within an analogical frame, only reversing its conclusions. The facially neutral Virginia statute was in practice "designed to maintain White Supremacy," so heightened scrutiny, Scalia contends, had to apply. But no such argument can be made in *Lawrence:* "No purpose to discriminate against men or women as a class can be gleaned from the Texas law." Hence, rational-basis review, not heightened scrutiny, must obtain.

Despite their very significant divergence of opinion, the perspectives of Scalia and Kennedy ultimately converge insofar as both Justices implicitly endorse a liberal narrative of temporal development in regard to racial progress. Kennedy seeks to extend this liberal narrative of racial inclusion and progress to gays and lesbians; Scalia will not. Nevertheless, in juxtaposing queer and racial liberation through a logic of temporal analogy, both Kennedy and Scalia implicitly consign racial libera-tion to the past, to the dustbin of history, a political project in our colorblind age both settled and achieved. In the process, the fact of Garner's blackness—the "nigger going crazy with a gun"—must neces-sarily be forgotten, its troubling presence banished in the face of queer liberalism's narrative of liberty, freedom, and progress.[51]

Such analogical reasoning, which resides at the heart of legal anal-ysis, must be deconstructed. For in configuring homosexuality and race as historical analogies, parallel issues that never cross, Kennedy, Scalia, same-sex marriage advocates, and indeed the law itself deny the ways in which sexuality and race function intersectionally—as supplements to one another. Through the inability to recognize the points of intersec-tion between race and (homo)sexuality, as well as the convergence of both then (*Loving*) and now (*Lawrence*), racial history is rewritten. Al-though numerous scholars in critical race, feminist, and queer studies have argued that identity categories are not analogous but intersec-tional, legal knowledge nevertheless remains insistently organized by such reasoning, by the notion that "sexual identity is in most ways, or at least in the most salient ways, like race."[52]

Legal scholar Janet E. Halley points out that "like race" arguments "are so intrinsically woven into American discourses of equal justice that they can never be entirely forgone."[53] It is important to recognize the "like race" comparisons are appealing precisely because of the his-torical role of race in Constitutional jurisprudence and the distinct his-tory of the 14th Amendment's due process and equal protection clauses. Nevertheless, Halley emphasizes, an effort to move beyond the per-sistence and intractability of "like race" arguments in the law offers the possibility of moving beyond liberal identity-based frameworks in order to emphasize not "who we are but how we are thought," thus drawing attention to the politics and problems of racial knowledge.[54]

From the perspective of shifting political economies, Miranda Joseph identifies analogy as the dominant trope of post-Fordist globalization processes.[55] Building upon Spivak's insights on questions of value in Marx, Joseph observes that analogy in late capitalism functions to ren-der an inchoate, emergent alterity into a known, recognizable, and in-ternally continuous other by focusing on similarity at the expense of difference. In the process, analogy levels what is heterogeneous and discontinuous in its objects of comparison, between what is known and what is unknown, and what is burdened and unburdened. Such a deployment of analogy disables a politics of intersectionality. It determinedly "amputates the incommensurable," in Horkheimer and Adorno's memorable words, which would focus on the interdependence of difference and alterity across various legal categories and social movements.[56]

Taken together, Halley's and Joseph's critiques of analogy draw attention to who and what must be forgotten in order to consolidate modernity's narrative of freedom and progress, its ceaseless march from before to after. In our putatively colorblind age, this shift from identity (who we are) to epistemology (how we are thought) helps to address the politics of racial knowledge and loss, allowing us to "imagine otherwise."[57] It focuses our attention less on the will to authenticity, the drive to recuperation, and the evidence of experience—tenets central to liberalism and its politics of recognition. Rather, it draws our critical focus to the ways in which heterogeneity is reduced to homogeneity, asking how the mobilization of "like race" arguments in our so-called colorblind age—one insistently configuring race in terms other than itself—poses significant challenges to a judicial system of precedent, which is premised on the heightened scrutiny of race only in its overt manifestations. As race disappears, how will the law ever come to see it?

In this regard, when queer liberals insist that *Lawrence* is "our *Loving*" or "our *Brown*," they foreclose the possibility of reading the *Lawrence* decision as part of a long legal tradition maintaining interlocking, indeed constitutive, systems of white supremacy and heterosexism foundational to liberal modernity's unending march of freedom and progress.[58] We cannot regard the *Lawrence* decision as an unmitigated victory for queer recognition and rights. For insofar as Lawrence and Garner are a mixed-raced—and not just a same-sex—"couple," the ruling insistently points to the unfulfilled promise of *Loving*, insofar as *Loving* is persistently read as ending the stigmatization of cross-racial intimacies dissociated from a politics of (hetero)sexual regulation and consolidation. From another perspective, this repressed history of race in *Lawrence* might be said to indict the unfulfilled dream of racial desegregation itself proffered by *Brown*. Why, in other words, must we think about the *Lawrence* case only in terms of queer liberalism's victory, rather than in terms of race, miscegenation, and segregation, unresolved in the past and persisting in the present? This forgetting, this conflation of *Lawrence* and *Loving* as a temporal analogy, underwrites the narrative of queer freedom and progress in our colorblind age. It demands a renewed intersectional approach.

The Racialization of Intimacy

My intersectional reading of homosexuality and race in *Lawrence v. Texas* must also be examined with a consideration of the insistent slide of homosexuality into discourses of intimacy and family, as well as marriage and coupledom, as they are expressed throughout the majority opinion and dissent, and in the social and political commentary that the ruling has generated.

Kennedy's majority opinion underscores the right to privacy as the *sine qua non* of gay and lesbian self-determination. He writes, "The petitioners are entitled to respect for their private lives. The State cannot demean their existence or control their destiny by making their private sexual conduct a crime. The right to liberty under the Due Process Clause gives them the full right to engage in their conduct without intervention of the government . . . The Texas statute furthers no legitimate state interest which can justify its intrusion into the personal and private life of the individual."[59] The right to privacy in the privileged form of what the Court variously describes as "consensual sexual intimacy" or "intimate sexual conduct" is not just the foundation from which contemporary notions of queer liberty and freedom emerge for gays and lesbians. The rhetoric of Kennedy's majority opinion, as Teemu Ruskola and Katherine Franke argue, ultimately speaks only to couples in the private domain of the monogamous bedroom. In the process, the ruling necessarily effaces the material facts of the Lawrence-Garner-Eubanks love triangle.[60]

Throughout the majority opinion, Kennedy constructs a second analogy, likening homosexual relationships to heterosexual marriage, thus inscribing queer liberalism into a normative discourse of family and family values. Kennedy writes: "To say that the issue in *Bowers* was simply the right to engage in certain sexual conduct demeans the claim the individual put forward, just as it would demean a married couple were it to be said that marriage is simply about the right to have sexual intercourse."[61] And again: "When sexuality finds overt expression in intimate conduct with another person, the conduct can be but one element in a personal bond that is more enduring. The liberty protected by the Constitution allows homosexual persons the right to make this choice."[62] The legal question emerging in *Lawrence* does not focus on a fundamental right to engage in sodomy, but in intimacy, the latter becoming the requirement for having a Constitutionally protected sex life.

In this shift, from sodomy to intimacy, *Lawrence* parallels the consumer logic of global capitalism by desexualizing homosexuality not in the economic but in the political-legal domain. The case, that is, deemphasizes acts (one night of sodomy) while inscribing a normative vision of acceptable queer identity and lifestyle (twenty years of intimacy, domesticity, coupledom, and consumption). It should not be a crime *just* to engage in homosexual sodomy. However, the legal rhetoric of *Lawrence*, Ruskola observes, "leaves little or no justification for protecting less-than-transcendental sex that is not part of an ongoing relationship." The implicit bargain the Court proposes is clear: "The Court, and the Constitution, will respect our sex lives, but on condition that our sex lives be respectable." In the process, "our sex lives begin to turn into entitlements recoded as part of universal human intimacy," a kind of " 'compulsory heterosexuality' in its new, second-generation form."[63] In our colorblind age, this might be described as one central aspect of queer liberalism's law of kinship.

By domesticating our sex lives, *Lawrence* removes queer liberalism from the public domain as an issue of homosexual equality and difference. Instead, it relocates it in the private sphere of intimacy, family, and bourgeois respectability as *sameness*. From another perspective we might say that *Lawrence* not only inducts gays and lesbians into the *time* of liberal progress but also places them into the *space* of the liberal nation-state. In other words, *Lawrence* reinscribes the traditional divide between the public and private, upholding conventional liberal distinctions between the state and the family, civil society and the home. Nevertheless, it is clear that, while intimacy confers the rights and privileges of queer citizenship on those willing to conform to its temporal and spatial mandates, privacy is not conferred on all involved. It emerges precisely as a function of the sublation of race, as the racialization of intimacy.

Indeed, as I discussed in the introduction, intimacy has had a philosophically central role in the evolution of the liberal human subject, the universal European man. In this genealogy, intimacy is indexed to a notion of privacy, insistently figured as relations of family and kinship in the space of the bourgeois home, as opposed to the public realm of work, civil society, and the state. Importantly, the evolution of the public and private spheres that characterized the rise of metropolitan European and North American societies depended on strict management of race. One only needs to think about the social organization of the slave plantation to appreciate the ways in which bourgeois privacy and intimacy was secured precisely through the subordination of African slaves, indentured Asians, and colonized natives. Under the political economy of colonialism, the exploitation of racialized labor underwrote the formative material wealth of the European and North American middle class, while contributing to the rise of the political values of the republican state.[64] As Ann Laura Stoler points out, this political economy was a form of racialized governmentality through which colonialism administered the enslaved and colonized, while insistently denying its racialized genealogy.[65]

G.W.F. Hegel defines the emergence of modern liberal personhood in *The Philosophy of Right* as the development of individual self-consciousness through ever-evolving forms of property.[66] Through property, the universal European man established his right to self-possession: of body, interiority, mind, and spirit. The evolution of property in its more complex political forms—in marriage, family, civil society, and the state—mark the dialectic sublation of social particularity and difference into an ever-expanding and more inclusive whole. *The Philosophy of Right*, Lisa Lowe observes, depends on the dialectical overcoming of slavery by modern human freedom, a contradiction resolved through the unity of human particularity within the universality of the state and the production of the abstract individual. But this "'overcoming' depends on a concept of slavery that located its practice in the 'Old World' of ancient Greece and Rome rather than in the 'New World' of the Americas."[67]

Hegel's definition of freedom emerges through a developmental process in which the individual first possesses himself, his own interiority, then embeds his will in an object through labor, and subsequently makes a contract to exchange that thing. "Marriage and the family," Lowe observes, "were primary and necessary sites of this investment of will in civil institutions; the 'intimacy' within the family was the property of the individual becoming 'free.'"[68] For European subjects in the nineteenth century, this notion of intimacy in the private sphere became the defining property of the modern individual. Ideals of privacy in bourgeois domesticity were thus configured as the individual's possession, to be politically protected, as in "the right to privacy." It is this longer colonial history of intimacy as property and possession of the liberal individual—a history built on the repressed legacies of slave, indentured, and colonized labor—that serves as the backdrop for my comments on the racialization of intimacy securing the queer liberalism of *Lawrence*.

Intimacy's unfolding on the terrain of political freedom and progress through the rights of property, marriage, family, and children is an entitlement now being extended to domesticated gay and lesbian U.S. citizen-subjects, an entitlement that continues to displace its racialized conditions of possibility. In other words, gay and lesbian political enfranchisement colludes with conventional liberal distinctions between family and the state. Legacies of racial domination and segregation become subsumed under the sign of (gay) intimacy, privacy, family, and kinship. Ultimately, it is this highly regulated and dichotomized public-private social formation that *Lawrence* invites queer liberals to join. It is no surprise, then, that what begins as queer liberation has ended up at the political doorstep of same-sex marriage.[69] Today, neoliberal governmentality as a world-historical phenomenon universalizes freedom in the language of choice. More specifically, in the intimate realm of family and kinship relations, we are free to choose whom to marry. Jakobsen observes, the "Reformation ties the idea of individual freedom to the institution of marriage . . . Marriage, then, like the market, is part of the freedom from the church that marks the beginning of modernity . . . It is through marriage—by being able to say who we freely choose to marry— that gay people fully become individuals."[70]

In tracing this longer genealogy of intimacy in liberal political thought to *Lawrence* and to the contemporary emergence of queer liberalism, I would like to suggest that intimacy might be regarded as a type of racialized property right that remains unequally and unevenly distributed among gay and lesbian populations today. In other words, queer liberalism extends the right of privacy to gay and lesbian U.S. citizen-subjects willing to comply with its normative dictates of bourgeois intimacy, and able to afford the comforts of bourgeois domesticity in their reconfigured globalized incarnations. In this sense, queer liberalism is not necessarily about excluding bourgeois racial subjects from its aegis. To the contrary, it is about failing to recognize the racial genealogy of exploitation and domination that underwrites the very inclusion of queers and queers of color in this abstract liberal polity.

Legal formalists will most certainly take issue with this formulation of intimacy as a (racialized) property right, insisting that privacy is inalienable, and that it can neither be bought nor sold as property. The important work of legal feminists, however, illustrates how certain forms of property thought to be inalienable—including licenses, degrees, and welfare benefits—might be regarded as property in, for example, divorce proceedings. Equally crucial, critical race scholars have also rethought legal conceptions of property in the context of a long U.S. history of slavery, racial segregation, and racial subordination. Highlighting the more metaphysical aspects of property as the right to things that are intangible—not just tangible, physical entities that can be bought and sold—critical race scholars trace how the law established a property interest in whiteness itself. Historically, whiteness came to assume the critical characteristics and status of property across several legal registers and social domains. These range from first possessor rules during colonial settlement, to the creation of value in the cultivation of barren land, to Lockean labor theory under industrialization, to utilitarian theory under modern forms of capitalism.

In her groundbreaking 1993 article "Whiteness as Property," Cheryl I. Harris offers us one genealogy of this enduring connection.[71] She notes how whiteness, initially constructed as racial identity, evolved into other forms of property protected in both explicit and implicit ways by U.S. law and society. Whiteness and property share a common premise in the right to exclude. Prior to emancipation, black slaves were literally considered to be objects of property, while whites were constituted as subjects of freedom. Whiteness, Harris observes, was the "characteristic, the attribute, the property of free human beings." After Emancipation, across the Jim Crow era, and even after the overturning of legalized segregation and the advent of affirmative action, whiteness as property continued to evolve into more complex and modern forms "through the law's ratification of the settled expectations of relative white privilege as a legitimate and natural baseline."[72]

The law's construction of whiteness "defined and affirmed critical aspects of identity (who is white); of privilege (what benefits accrue to that status); and, of property (what *legal* entitlements arise from that status). Whiteness at various times signifies and is deployed as identity, status, and property, sometimes singularly, sometimes in tandem."[73] Whiteness was, and continues to be, a valuable and exclusive property essential to the self-possession of the liberal individual, to the value of his or her reputation, and to the normative definitions of the enfranchised U.S. citizen-subject. Whiteness and property, liberty and freedom, are and continue to be inextricably intertwined.

I would like to connect Harris's conception of white privilege as a natural baseline for freedom—the property of free human beings, guarded by U.S. law and society—to my longer discussion of bourgeois intimacy, in European liberal political thought, as a racialized property right now being brought together and reconfigured by queer liberalism. Linking these two arguments from Enlightment philosophy and critical race theory, I would suggest that intimacy as a racialized property right—one predicated on a long U.S. history of racial subordination and the legal protection of white privilege—now serves to constitute normative gay and lesbian U.S. citizen-subjects as possessive individuals. It inducts them into an enlightened realm of being proper U.S. citizen-subjects, into an abstract and universalizing liberal narrative of political enfranchisement and inclusion, and into the proper time and space of the modern U.S. nation-state. In the era of late capitalism and gay identity, whiteness as property has now evolved to create new queer subjects for representation, demanding a more thorough investigation of the degree to which (homo)sexuality and race constitute and consolidate conventional distinctions between the time and space of civilization and barbarism.

When queer liberalism is declaring victory in the name of freedom and liberty, we are at a moment of critical urgency for sustained intersectional analyses. To rethink *Lawrence v. Texas* from this perspective is to return the ghost of miscegenation to queer liberalism's putative legal victory. To deny the analogy of *Lawrence* to *Brown* and *Loving* would be to rethink queer liberalism's unending storm of progress, to reconsider a historical genealogy of freedom through its unremitting deployments and disavowals of race and the racialization of intimacy. To resist the analogy of homosexual to racial progress is to understand what is politically at stake in a colorblind U.S. society in which, to borrow from Wahneema Lubiano, "race no longer talks about race," but is sublated into normative discourses of privacy, intimacy, bourgeois domesticity, marriage, family, and kinship.[74]

"Our Western Civilization"

Before concluding this chapter with some speculations on Dr. Schreber, I would like briefly to situate queer liberalism and its racialization of intimacy in a more global frame. In a post-9/11 world order, as legal scholar Leti Volpp observes, the opposite of the U.S. citizen is no longer the illegal alien but the terrorist.[75] From this perspective, the discourse of queer liberalism and family values during an unending U.S. "War on Terror" serves to decriminalize queer identity, placing it under the aegis of constitutional rights, recognitions, and privileges at the very moment that racialized immigrants are presumptively criminalized, subject to indefinite detention and illegal surveillance in the name of U.S. security, security for U.S. civil society, and protection for U.S. citizen-subjects.

Lawrence comes at a moment when the enfranchisement of the normative gay and lesbian U.S. citizen-subjects "over here" as liberated and free is accompanied by the simultaneous annihilation of Muslim populations deemed unfree and uncivilized "over there." This dialectic of inclusion and exclusion represents two sides of the same liberal coin. That is, U.S. led neoliberalism legitimates its global mission by coding the political power and economic wealth of its beneficiaries as the just rewards of a multicultural, cosmopolitan world citizenry. At the same time, as Jodi Melamed notes, it justifies the plight of the dispossessed through the rhetoric of mono-culturalism and other pathological cultural deficiencies demanding military force to save lives, rescue women, provide basic needs, and promote democracy.

Let us remember that the majority opinion in the *Lawrence* decision is remarkable not just for its insistence that "Freedom extends beyond spatial bounds." Such a universalizing gesture is ironic given the fact that the liberty interest at stake is rhetorically figured as a bourgeois intimacy insistently tethered to the domestic space of the private home. The decision is equally notable for its gestures toward the European Court of Human Rights and the Canadian legislature, international and national legal bodies that have upheld the right of homosexual adults to engage in intimate consensual conduct and same-sex marriage, rulings not only at odds with the stated premise of the *Bowers* decision but also with the stated mission of the former Bush Administration and its numerous fundamentalist religious supporters. From this perspective, the assertion of queer liberalism on the global stage may be less about gay and lesbian rights, recognitions, and privileges than about codifying across the planet a Euro-American liberal humanist tradition of freedom and democracy.

In *Lawrence's* time of intense U.S. exceptionalism and unilateralism, what does this turning toward a global community suggest? How does such a turning underwrite the collective and superior liberal humanist achievements of, in the words of Kennedy's majority decision, "our Western civilization"?[76] What kind of truth claims do statements about freedom and liberty have in the face of our former Administration's abrogation of international laws and treaties and its secret policies on torture, spying, and indefinite detention, as well as current political disasters in Iraq, Pakistan, and Afghanistan, along with the continuing evisceration of welfare, healthcare reform, and other social services with the upward redistribution of wealth to the already richest few? What kinds of unstated logics of civilization and barbarism, of the human itself, are being animated by the decriminalization of same-sex intimacy at the precise moment when racialized immigrants and the racialized poor—both "over there" and "over here"—are presumptively criminalized or killed? What type of political response would be adequate to a morality tale that passes itself off as foreign diplomacy and human rights? What does it mean when right-wing pundits such as Charles Krauthammer employ the language of gay liberation and freedom to describe in dulcet tones contemporary incarnations of U.S. imperialism, militarism, and the politics of force? "People are now coming out of the closet on the word empire."[77]

It means that those of us committed to a renewed politics of identity in our colorblind age must concern ourselves with the problems and predicaments of intersectionality and insist on new approaches to intersectionality in queer studies. It means that we must reconsider how the emergence of queer freedom is produced in relation to a long racialized history of whiteness as property. It means that we must examine how the promulgation of abstract equality displaces the language of race into the register of privacy and intimacy, family and kinship. In other words, we must recognize how queer liberalism secures its legal, social, and moral claims through the simultaneous dismantling of affirmative action and the configuration of normative gay and lesbian U.S. citizen-subjects as a new model minority on the global stage. Such an account tracks the folding in of those individuals once sexually stigmatized into the mandates of U.S. empire, whether in the form of territorial occupation and abrogation of sovereignty, the exportation of democracy and the rule of law, or the rights of free trade and unfettered consumption in a neoliberal politics of globalization. The dissociation of queer liberalism from its racialized genealogy constitutes the new neoliberal multiculturalism of our current times. Freedom and the racialization of intimacy mark queer liberalism's normative politics of family and kinship as only the most recent incarnation of the "rights of man." It is this particular configuration of U.S. self-fashioning—not the maligned triumvirate of race, sex, and class—that constitutes the most virulent form of identity politics on the global stage today.

I have investigated some of the political limits of queer liberalism and its desire for the right to have rights. How, in turn, might we describe the psychic structure of such desire? What are the psychic lineaments of late capitalism and gay identity, the psychic structures of normalization underwriting queer liberalism's fidelity to privacy and intimacy, its laws of family and kinship? Arguably, *Lawrence* marks a significant legal shift in terms of same-sex sodomy laws in the U.S., but has there been a concomitant psychic shift?

In order to explore these queries, I would like to conclude this chapter with some speculations concerning Freud's reading of the memoirs of the infamous German lawyer and judge Daniel Paul Schreber. The son of Moritz Schreber, a famous nineteenth-century medical authority know for his stringent theories on child-rearing, the younger Schreber was the one-time *Senatspräsident* of the Saxony Court of Appeals. In Eric Santner's estimation, Schreber's psychotic episodes were triggered by a dis-ease with power, one initiated by his "crises of investiture" in symbolic authority and legitimation. For Schreber, his failure to be elected to the Reichstag, followed by his subsequent installation as presiding judge of the Saxony Court, became symbolic processes of nomination and inscription that he simultaneously accepted and rejected with ambivalence.[78] After suffering a number of debilitating breakdowns, in 1903 Schreber published *Memoirs of my Nervous Illness* (*Denkwürdig-keiten eines Nervenkranken*), which he had written during the course of his second hospitalization.[79] Incapacitated by the demand to speak through or for the law, Schreber nonetheless managed to find a voice linking his symbolic nomination (*Ernennung*) and his paranoid unmanning (*Entmannung*).

Although Freud never treated Schreber as a patient, he immortalized the psychotic judge—known as the most famous mental patient of his time—through his analysis of Schreber's *Memoirs of My Nervous Illness*, elevating it into one of the most important psychiatric textbooks on paranoia. In his 1911 "Psychoanalytic Notes Upon an Autobiographical Account of a Case of Paranoia (Dementia Paranoides)," Freud reads Schreber's autobiographical account of his mental illness—his elaborate delusional system—to propose a theory about the ways in which repressed homosexual wish-fantasies reside at the core of the formation of paranoid psychoses. The quavering voice of the law through which

Schreber's paranoid fantasies are mobilized and take hold provides one way of analyzing the psychic structure and limits of queer liberalism.

In "'Civilized' Sexual Morality and Modern Nervous Illness" (1908), Freud asserts that it "is one of the obvious social injustices that the standard of civilization should demand from everyone the same conduct of sexual life—conduct which can be followed without any difficulty by some people, thanks to their organization, but which imposes the heaviest psychical sacrifices on others."[80] Nonetheless, throughout his meta-psychological writings, Freud repeatedly asserts that the emergence of the social is dependent on the sublimation of homosexuality, its foreclosure from psychic as well as social life. "On Narcissism" (1914), for instance, concludes with the following observations:

> The ego ideal opens up an important avenue for the understanding of group psychology. In addition to its individual side, this ideal has a social side; it is also the common ideal of a family, a class or a nation. It binds not only a person's narcissistic libido, but also a considerable amount of his homosexual libido, which is in this way turned back into the ego. The want of satisfaction which arises from the non-fulfillment of this ideal liberates homosexual libido, and this is transformed into a sense of guilt (social anxiety). Originally this sense of guilt was a fear of punishment by the parents, or, more correctly, the fear of losing their love; later the parents are replaced by an indefinite number of fellow-men. The frequent causation of paranoia by an injury to the ego, by the frustration of satisfaction within the sphere of the ego ideal, is thus made more intelligible, as is the convergence of ideal-formation and sublimation in the ego ideal, as well as the involution of sublimations and the possible transformation of ideals in paraphrenic disorders.[81]

"On Narcissism," as well as numerous other meta-psychological texts, underwrite a conventional understanding of the emergence of the social as contingent upon the transformation of homosexual desire for the father into heterosexual identification with him. In this passage, the emergence of a "common ideal of a family, a class or a nation" is brought about through the sublimation of homosexual libido into a collective social conscience and through the affective charge of guilt. The disavowal and management of homosexual desire emerges precisely as a feeling of custodial dread in relation to a judgmental ego-ideal, what Freud later will describe as the super-ego.

Here, paranoia and the ego-ideal seem to derive their coherence from their mutual exclusion of one another, by drawing a strict boundary between pathologized homosexuality and homosocial *esprit de corps*. Yet these divisions are not so distinct, but in constant danger of collapsing. If the ego-ideal is meant to consolidate and shore up errant libido, transforming homosexual desire into a displaced homosocial identification, paranoia marks the dissolution of this consolidation. In his "Psychoanalytic Notes," Freud points out that as hysteria condenses, paranoia decomposes.[82] Through the disavowal and projection of forbidden desires, what was first abolished internally (i.e. homosexual libido) appears to return from without, from elsewhere in multiple and manifest forms.[83] Paranoia's emergence on the psychic scene demolishes the sublimations that have worked to direct homosexuality into homosociality, threatening in the process to expose and transform the social ideals that found them. As the residue and sign of the psychic displacement of homosexual libido, paranoia's presence not only threatens to sexualize the social instincts through the return of the repressed but also marks the ego's continued "frustration of satisfaction within the sphere of the ego ideal."[84]

In spite of Freud's attempts to separate and segregate paranoia and the space of the ego-ideal, they often become mixed up and confused. Indeed, this mixing is paradoxically symptomized both by Freud's over-identification with Schreber and by his inability to maintain any analytical distance from the paranoid insights of the judge. Their voices, too, overlap and are confused: "It remains for the future to decide," Freud writes, "whether there is more delusion in my theory than I should like to admit, or whether there is more truth in Schreber's delusion than other people are as yet prepared to believe."[85] Agreeing with Schreber's self-assessment as "a man of superior mental gifts and endowed with an unusual keenness alike of intellect and of observation,"[86] Freud tells us that psychiatrists might take a lesson from this patient, that "the wonderful Schreber . . . ought to have been made a professor of psychiatry and director of a mental hospital."[87] What is it that Freud thinks we must come to learn from him?

In Schreber's memoirs, Freud encounters a voice and manner that is, at times, all too reasonable and rational. Schreber's paranoid wish-fantasies reveal a fundamental fault-line between the pathological and normative. Precisely at the point where paranoid narcissism seems to present itself as unambiguously separate from the space of the ego-ideal, a confusion of voices arises: the voice of censorship associated with paranoia and the unrelenting voice of guilty conscience associated with the ego-ideal cannot be distinguished from one another. In "On Narcissism," Freud notes that the voices brought into the foreground by paranoia mark the evolution of conscience "in a regressive form as a hostile influence from without. The complaints made by paranoiacs also show that at bottom the self-criticism of conscience coincides with the self-observation on which it is based."[88] Here, Freud suggests that the voice of conscience and its paranoid facsimile are indistinguishable because they are fundamentally identical. In short, social conscience and paranoid self-censorship are rendered coterminous insofar as both emanate from the judgments of a lacerating ego-ideal that, as Freud puts it, is brought into the foreground again by the disease, such that we are not able to distinguish our own voice from that of others. *"The delusion-formation,"* Freud concludes, *"which we take to be the pathological product, is in reality an attempt at recovery, a process of reconstruction"* of this psychic and social management of homosexual desire.[89]

From this perspective, while it is a common assertion by right-wing pundits that homosexuality—and now same-sex marriage—will be the end of western civilization as we know it, I would like to propose that Schreber's case history illustrates how homosexuality, rather than being antipathetic to the mandates of the ego-ideal, might indeed be confused with them, and even reconcilable to their demands. If so, Schreber thus functions as a prescient role model for our current times. Insofar as queer liberalism marks the folding of a domesticated homosexuality into the conjugal ideals of a heternormative social order, Schreber illustrates the elaborate mental gymnastics required by such a project on the level of the psyche. Indeed, Schreber's *Memoirs* reveal how a (re)mixing and (re)coding of the normative mandates of the ego-ideal through a confusion of voices can come to be folded into the social text of Schreber's delusional system.

For Freud, the most "salient feature" of Schreber's delusional system concerns the judge's repressed homosexual wish-fantasies, his emasculation and belief that he was "being transformed into a woman" through the persecutory whims of God.[90] Schreber's psychotic fantasy is triggered one morning "between sleeping and waking," by the idea "that after all it really must be very nice to be a woman submitting to the act of copulation."[91] Freud tells us that such an idea "would have [been] rejected with the greatest indignation if he [Schreber] had been fully conscious."[92] Indeed, Schreber recounts in his *Memoirs* that he initially construed his transformative "unmanning" as a conspiracy in which "God Himself had played the part of accomplice, if not of instigator," in the plot against him.[93]

It is only later, Schreber slowly comes to realize, that he is part of a grander religious schema. That is, God's use of his transformed female body like that of a "strumpet" is intended for a much higher purpose, one entirely consonant with the "Order of Things."[94] Schreber plays a pivotal role in this "divine miracle" as God's personal concubine: his sexual relations with his master and impregnation by his "divine rays" are ultimately meant to create a new race of men to populate the earth. Here, Schreber's delusional fantasies take on a prescient eugenic shine, triggering many commentators to note the similarities between Schreber's paranoia and the paranoia of fascism that underwrites the emergence of National Socialism and the totalitarian German state some three decades later.[95] Only from this perspective can Schreber reconcile himself to his fate and embrace this higher Spiritual calling, this "mission to redeem the world and to restore it to its lost state of bliss."[96] In Freud's estimation, what initially begins as a (homo)sexual delusion of persecution is converted through Schreber's psychotic musings into a religious delusion of grandeur meant to ensure the reproduction of nation and national culture across generations. This is an intersection of race and homosexuality, miscegenation and kinship, that we would do well to note. In the context of such a divine mandate, the judge wonders rhetorically, what man "faced with the choice of either becoming a demented human being in male habitus or a spirited woman, would not prefer the latter"?[97]

Kendall Thomas notes that Freud's reading of the *Memoirs of My Nervous Illness* has "suffered a curious fate. Although it should have been plain enough that the project of the 'Psychoanalytic Notes' was to demonstrate the psychopathological effects that the repression of homosexual desire produced in a socially *heterosexual* man, Freud's study was quickly put to a very different use. As Eve Kosofsky Sedgwick has observed, later interpretations of the 'Psychoanalytic Notes' deployed Freud's psychoanalysis of the Schreber *Memoirs* 'not against *homophobia* and its schizogenic force, but against *homosexuality*' and homosexuals."[98] Needless to say, these misreadings have tended to blur the eugenic aspects of Schreber's delusional fantasies as well as the focus of Freud's insights concerning "the violent psychic pressures compulsory heterosexuality exerts on homosexual desire in those who consider themselves to be heterosexual."[99] In the process, it is the homosexual rather than the homophobe who becomes the subject of mental illness.

It is entirely appropriate, as Thomas and Sedgwick indicate, to evaluate Schreber's memoirs and case history in terms of a pervasive homophobia, rather than homosexuality, that defines the social order. Nevertheless, I would like to perform a slightly different reading here. I would like to focus on Schreber's ambivalence toward his symbolic inscription into the social order, one marking the difficulty of ever finally drawing a definite line separating homosexual libido from heterosexual *esprit de corps,* of dissociating the judge's delusional system from that of a wider social and discursive community into which it both blends and bleeds. Schreber's delusional fantasies reveal a particular form of homosexuality that delineates the psychic compromises one might make in order to reconcile homosexuality to the moral demands of the ego-ideal—to blend into its confusion of voices through a particular form of family and kinship. Today, we might say that such a reconciliation defines the psychic structure and limits of queer liberalism.

Let us remember that Schreber's homosexual wish-fantasy takes the curious corporeal form of what might be described not so much as an interdicted homosexual tableau, but perhaps more accurately as a transgendered heterosexuality. Schreber straightens his relationship to God by becoming a voluptuous woman, only after which he is used by God like a "strumpet." In this regard, if Freud chooses to describe Schreber's transformation into a voluptuous woman as a "homosexual" wish-fantasy, it may be equally accurate to describe this psychic scenario as a homosexual wish-fantasy surprisingly compliant with the heteronormative mandates of the ego-ideal—indeed, Oedipal norms of family and kinship. In slightly different terms, if Schreber allows his desire for (God) the father to be manifested and revealed, he dares only to do so not in his own appointed and interdicted corporeal form, but in the authorized guise of an acceptable heterosexuality and social propriety.

Indeed, Freud tells us that throughout his life and career, Schreber is a man of "high ethical standing."[100] In this regard, it is important to note that, even and especially, in his psychotic state, Schreber continues to maintain a strict and slavish devotion to his ego-ideal. Put otherwise, we might say that Schreber's homosexual wish-fantasy is ultimately meant to install a form of the heteronormative bourgeois domesticity and coupledom that is not reflected in his actual life. Freud reminds us that Schreber's marriage, "which he describes as being in other respects a happy one, brought him no children."[101] As Freud concludes, "Dr. Schreber may have formed a phantasy that if he were a woman he would manage the business of having children more successfully . . . If that were so, then his delusion that as a result of his emasculation the world was to be peopled with 'a new race of men, born from the spirit of Schreber' . . . would also be designed to offer him an escape from his childlessness."[102] (Note how Schreber's paranoid fantasies disavow homosexuality in the name of race, thus "a new race of men, born from the spirit of Schreber." In this way, Schreber's homosexual delusions pave the way for our current moment in which the racial project is rendered "complete" in the name of queer liberalism and neoliberal multiculturalism.) Even more, we might describe Schreber's particular vision of immaculate conception as homosexuality without homosexuals.

Here, are we not strikingly close to contemporary political debates regarding the moral respectability of same-sex marriage, the conjugal couple, and joys of parenting—that is, the mental vicissitudes of being virtually normal? What the Schreber case so emphatically underscores is the reconciliation of a certain version of fantasized homosexuality to the moral demands of the super-ego and its authorized Oedipal ideals. Schreber's repressed homosexual wish-fantasies reveal not a poststructuralist disavowal of Oedipal arrangements, but a kind of postmodern mental gymnastics meant to reconcile the judge's paranoid delusions with his high ethical standing and his ventriloquizing of "the common ideal of a family, a class or a nation." In strict compliance with the social demands of conjugal domesticity, privacy, and intimacy, Schreber's decision to publish his memoirs for a general *fin-de-siècle* Victorian public opens onto the terrain not of social humiliation and gay shame, but of family values and gay pride.

Schreber, the psychotic judge but upright citizen-subject, clearly believes in the didactic and moral lesson to be learned from his story of homosexuality lost and heterosexuality found. In this light, we might think of Schreber as the precursor and poster child to the gay pundits of our contemporary times who instruct us to "grow up" and to "get married," who share their triumphs of personal adversity among the ruling classes at elite prep schools and universities, and who come to the conclusion that heteronormative values of family and kinship are indeed a preferable and desirable cover for other material and psychic arrangements less socially acceptable or palatable.[103] Furthermore, similar to "like-race" arguments that deny the enduring legacy of racism in our liberal order, these like-marriage mandates enshrine the domesticated conjugal family as the only legally and socially recognized household structure.[104] In the process, they deny the coevalness of other social and psychic formations of family and kinship, the heterogeneity of domestic arrangements that we live today and that do not resolve themselves into comfortable zones of privacy and intimacy.[105] How, we must consider, does this turn to marriage make it more difficult to imagine and live alternative kinship structures? How does it make it more difficult to advocate for the well-being of children in any number of social forms and formations? As Duggan and Richard Kim point out, the current attack on domestic partnership and other civil contracts "rolls back decades of success in winning recognition and benefits for couples of all gender combinations who could not or would not marry."[106] From this perspective, refocusing progressive efforts on household diversity, rather than organizing solely for same-sex marriage, could generate a broad vision of social justice that resonates on many fronts. "If we connect this democratization of household recognition, with advocacy of material support for caretaking, as well as for good jobs and adequate benefits (like universal health care), then what we have in common will come into sharper relief."[107]

Schreber's paranoid delusions were ahead of his time, transported to the *Lawrence* court of 2003. His homosexual like-marriage wish-fantasies assert a kind of distorted ownership over his queer desires through the creation of a delusional system meant to rationalize and reconcile homosexual difference in the guise of heterosexual similitude. In this particular psychic tableau, homosexuality would not be the end of Western civilization as we know it, the antithesis of the super-ego, the source of social reason's erosion and dissolution. Rather, Schreber shows us how a particular homosexual life and lifestyle might indeed be the foundation for the ego-ideal's continued support and renewal. In Schreber we discover one way in which queer liberalism might be reconciled to the moral majority, one particular route through which it may indeed have a psychic life.

TWO *The Structure of Kinship*

ⓖ ⓖ ⓖ

THE ART OF WAITING IN *THE BOOK
OF SALT* AND *HAPPY TOGETHER*

The photographer could rehearse the efforts to picture these men in
the usual ways, but there was always a remainder. The men resisted
all attempts to order them, no matter the orthodoxy of conventions
brought to bear in arranging and deciphering them. They had their
own desires.
—ANTHONY W. LEE, *Picturing Chinatown*

Two American ladies wish—
—ALICE B. TOKLAS, *The Alice B. Toklas Cookbook*

How might we imagine otherwise? How might we visualize
loss and the forgetting of race? How might we imagine a
psychic landscape beyond Schreber's mental gymnastics, a
social terrain beyond the limits of queer liberalism?

This—and each subsequent—chapter of *The Feeling on
Kinship* turns to the concept of queer diasporas as a rejoinder to the political and psychic dilemmas of queer liberalism. As a methodological tool, queer diasporas directs
our attention to other communities—to other humanities
within modernity and its received traditions of liberal humanism. In doing so, it moves us beyond identity-based
frameworks in order to emphasize the epistemological coordinates of how we are thought—in order to focus on the
politics and problems of racial knowledge. As a structure of
feeling, queer diasporas also indexes lost and forgotten de-

sires, those stubborn remainders of affect that individuate through their ardent refusal of the orthodoxy of conventions, the great expectations of social agreement. Lastly, in the binding force of the what-can-be-known, queer diasporas suggests how we might think the unknowable, and indeed mourn, as William Faulkner writes, "a might-have-been which is more true than truth."[1] Queer diasporas thus opens upon a landscape of other histories and knowledges, preserving in the process a space for social and political reinvestment.

Monique Truong's novel, *The Book of Salt* (2003), and Wong Kar-wai's film, *Happy Together* (1997), tell such stories of lost and forgotten desires.[2] Truong and Wong focus on that stubborn remainder—a reservoir of insistent, queer desire—that individuates their protagonists through the singularity of their longings. Truong and Wong rethink the what-can-be-known by drawing insistent attention to the epistemological as well as the ontological limits of a liberal humanist tradition that affirms particular subjects while excluding others from historical consideration. They imagine those who have yet to be visualized or articulated within these restricted paradigms of knowing and being—others who constitute and haunt, but are nevertheless foreclosed, from the domain of the properly historical. Truong and Wong thus saturate the what-can-be-known with the persistent, melancholic trace of the what-might-have-been, the what-could-have-been. This chapter focuses on queer Asian migrants in the diaspora. Unlike queer liberals today, who appear before the law demanding rights and legal protection for their intimacies, these queer Asian migrants remain subjects in waiting. Waiting structures the temporal and spatial logics of the dis-appearance of their communities of intimacies in the global system. In this manner, queer diasporas functions as a critical tool that interrupts the contemporary emergence of queer liberalism.

The Book of Salt, set in early 1930's Paris, and *Happy Together*, set in late 1990's Buenos Aires, bookend the twentieth century through their sustained attention to the figure of the Asian coolie, toiling anonymously in global streams of migrant labor. Bình, the narrator of *The Book of Salt*, is a Vietnamese colonial, an exiled queer and a queer exile, who is forced to leave Vietnam after an illicit love affair with the young French chef who oversees the kitchen of the governor-general of Saigon. Eventually, after various travails at sea as a galley cook, Bình ends up employed as household chef to Gertrude Stein and Alice B. Toklas during the couple's famous residence in Paris as American expatriates and icons of the Lost Generation. Bình is a fictionalized composite inspired by two historical figures—two Vietnamese cooks who appear briefly in the pages of the eponymous *Alice B. Toklas Cookbook* (1954). Though richly imagined, Bình is ultimately an unverifiable presence, conjured forth more by American desire, by the call for hired help that Toklas places in the local newspaper: "Two American ladies wish—"[3]

Bình's dim presence in the archive compels Truong's fictional narrative as a historical supplement. It invokes Gayatri Chakravorty Spivak's caveat that "the subaltern is necessarily the absolute limit of the place where history is narrativized into logic."[4] Yet *The Book of Salt* is less an instance of the subaltern writing back than an exploration of the limits of such writing for the politics of history. Through the course of Truong's novel, the eloquence of Bình's queer desires comes to entangle and reconfigure the domains of both history and fiction by drawing insistent attention to who and to what must be forgotten so that the high modernism exemplified by Stein and Toklas might come to be affirmed.

Set in early-twentieth century Old World Paris, *The Book of Salt* rewrites the narrative of the inscrutable Asian bachelor-laborer, insisting that we consider how the colonial subtends the emergence of the modern. Set in late-twentieth century New World Argentina, *Happy Together* follows an underclass of queer Asian migrant workers who struggle under the shadows of globalization, demanding in turn a reflection on how the postcolonial subtends the development of the global. Two lovers, Lai Yiu-fai (Tony Leung Chiu-wai) and Ho Po-wing (Leslie Cheung Kwok-wing), depart Hong Kong a few years before the colony's 1997 retrocession from British to Chinese sovereignty. They travel halfway around the world, to Buenos Aires, in order to jump start their failing relationship—in the words of Ho, to "start over."

The affective intensity of the couple's queer diaspora—their impossible psychic attachments to one another—negates any generic story of the anonymous Chinese bachelor-laborer quietly toiling away in effeminized celibacy. Indeed, so compelling is the force of Lai's and Ho's inexorable desires that, ultimately, we come to witness a social and psychic reconfiguration: we witness the emergence of an alternative structure of family and kinship, a social organization and belonging not running under but alongside the normative mandates of the Oedipal. If historicism's charge is to legislate a privileged way of knowing and being in the world, *The Book of Salt* and *Happy Together* present, to borrow from

Martin Heidegger, a "worlding" of the colonial and postcolonial subject in terms other than modernity's social contract.[5] Truong's novel and Wong's film thus represent two exceptional archives for a critical investigation of the dialectic of affirmation (of freedom) and forgetting (of race) that both constitutes and confounds the emergence of queer liberalism.

Naming

In chapter nine of *The Book of Salt*, Bình recollects a curious meeting with a fellow Vietnamese colonial he encounters one evening on a bridge over the Seine. It is 1927, over two years before Bình will find his Madame and Madame and join the Stein-Toklas household in their renowned 27 rue de Fleurus home, the illustrious literary salon of 1930s Paris. The "man on the bridge," as Bình refers to him, is an enigmatic figure. Wearing a "black suit, coarse in fabric, too large for his frame, and many years out of fashion," the stranger, whose name we never learn, tells Bình that he has also been a cook, as well as a "[k]itchen boy, sailor, dishwasher, snow shoveler, furnace stoker, gardener, pie maker, photograph retoucher, fake Chinese souvenir painter, your basic whatever-needs-to-be-done-that-day laborer, and . . . letter writer."[6]

Over the course of a shared evening and meal, Bình learns that this handsome fellow is thirty-seven years old, that he left Vietnam at age twenty-two, and that he has not been back since. Now just a visitor to *la ville lumière*, the unnamed man had once resided in Paris for almost four years. Their supper ends with a steaming plate of watercress, wilted by a flash of heat and seasoned perfectly with a generous sprinkling of *fleur de sel*, "salt flowers." Bình observes a "gradual revelation of its true self, as I was beginning to learn, is the quality that sets *fleur de sel* apart from the common sea salt that waits for me in most French kitchens. There is a development, a rise and fall, upon which its salinity becomes apparent, deepens, and then disappears. Think of it as a kiss in the mouth."[7] Thus inspired, Bình shifts his attention once again to his attractive dinner companion, wondering if this anonymous stranger might, indeed, be the long-lost scholar-prince for whom he has been tirelessly searching.

Bình's encounter and Truong's chapter concludes with a slow after-dinner stroll in the Jardin du Luxembourg, and the hint of a mutual desire fulfilled:

A kiss in the mouth can become a kiss on the mouth. A hand on a shoulder can become a hand on the hips. A laugh on his lips can become a moan on mine. The moments in between these are often difficult to gauge, difficult to partition and subdivide. Time that refuses to be translated into a tangible thing, time without a number or an ordinal assigned to it, is often said to be "lost." In a city that always looks better in a memory, time lost can make the night seem eternal and full of stars.[8]

Bình's encounter with this stranger is "lost" to time, their desire and brief affair untranslatable "in between" moments of laughter and moaning, movements of shoulders, hips, and lips. Unmatched to any cardinal or ordinal assignment that would render it a "tangible thing"—unmatched, that is, to the abstract time of capitalism or to its calculated wages—their fleeting liaison confounds the domain of historical understanding if we come to recognize the biographical details Truong sparsely scatters across this ephemeral meeting: that the unnamed scholar-prince is one Nguyen That Thanh, also known as Nguyen Ai Quoc.[9] Readers familiar with the public life of Nguyen will know that nearly fourteen years later he will finally return to his homeland, Vietnam, and under the name Ho Chi Minh ("He Who Enlightens") will become the political leader of a successful anticolonial revolution that will humble the Western empires of France and the United States.

I begin with this episode of the man on the bridge not only to raise the specter of a scandalous, perhaps unthinkable, desire that binds Bình and Ho Chi Minh in their shared queer diasporas but also to emphasize how queer desire is not peripheral, but indeed central, to the narration of race, modernity, and the politics of history in *The Book of Salt*. More specifically, how does queer diasporas as a conceptual category—outside the boundaries of territorial sovereignty and in excess of sanctioned social arrangements—bring together dissonant desires with the political, thereby forcing in the process a crisis in historicism, in the idea of history as "the way it really was?"[10] Queer desire in Truong's novel enables a productive reading practice that, in Walter Benjamin's words, would "brush history against the grain."[11] Such action, mobilized through the politics of naming and misnaming in Truong's novel, is what I call historical catachresis.

The Oxford English Dictionary (2nd ed. 1989) defines "catachresis" as the "improper use of words; [the] application of a term to a thing which it does not properly denote; [or the] abuse or perversion of a trope or metaphor." In refusing to name the handsome stranger on the bridge, Truong insists on a consideration of how the politics of *naming* and *misnaming* works to stabilize—indeed, to justify—the historical order of things. Through the problematics of naming, historical catachresis works to dislodge a particular version of history as "the way it really was" by denying the possibility of a singular historical context in which the past has transpired and reemerges in the present as a reified object of investigation. Truong's refusal to name the man on the bridge presents us with a dialectic of affirmation and forgetting: How is it that Stein and Toklas can appear in history as the iconic lesbian couple of literary modernism and historical modernity while Bình can never appear and Ho Chi Minh must wait to appear? How is it that Stein and Toklas are placed in history while Bình and Ho Chi Minh are displaced from it?

In her analysis of historical catachresis in the context of modern Chinese women, the historian Tani Barlow stresses the temporality of its grammar: the future perfect tense. By focusing on what Chinese women "will have been" in the "what was" of sanctioned Chinese history, Barlow seeks to destabilize the force of historicism's documentary evidence.[12] Drawing attention to the what-will-have-been challenges the what-can-be-known by asking who must be forgotten and what must be passed over, homogenized, and discarded, in order for history to appear in the present as a stable object of contemplation. In this manner, the what-will-have-been reopens the question of the future in a settled past. It simultaneously transports that past into what Benjamin describes as a "history of the present," which is the recognition that history is always and insistently re-presented to us, mobilized for present political purposes. In the same breath, it recognizes the fact that there are, as Michel Foucault argues, "multiple time spans, and each one of these spans is the bearer of a certain type of events. The types of events must be multiplied just as the types of time span are multiplied."[13]

Reflection on historical catachresis in this scene from *The Book of Salt* highlights the imperial ambitions of modernity's deployments of empty homogeneous time and space—the endless flow of past, present, and future—in the name of historicism. Truong's refusal to attribute a proper name to the man on the bridge who will have been Nguyen That Thanh—and Ho Chi Minh only after returning to Vietnam—underscores the logic of waiting that structures European modernity in relation to its colonial others: the what-will-have-been of the Vietnamese nationalist independence movement in relation to the what-was, and is, of European modernity, liberal progress, and capitalist development.

Even more, Truong's refusal of the moniker Ho Chi Minh declines a process of nomination, dislodging the proper name from its referent; indeed, it allows the problem of historical referentiality to interrupt and reinhabit the accumulated weight of documentary evidence accrued around this famous revolutionary name. (Significantly, we also learn that Bình is a pseudonym the narrator chooses for himself when he first ships out from Saigon; the proper name is one that no one can own.) Through the irruption—indeed, the interruption—of queer desire, Truong stages the emergence of an alternative historical time and space discontinuous with the sanctioned historical development, conventional historical narratives, and authorized historical representations of this hallowed revolutionary hero.

We might also observe that historical catachresis more broadly understood implies that every naming is also a misnaming. Truong's stranger without a name responds to the what-will-have-been of Ho Chi Minh by keeping open a permanent space of differentiation between the proper name and its intended referent. Here, the query, "Did Ho Chi Minh *really* sleep with men?" is lost; the impossibility of the question and a response opens up a tear in historical time, a space of disappearance and forgetting in which time never quite coincides with itself. Through this slippage in time, Truong not only draws attention to the limits of historicism's idealization of presence and progress, but also creates a queer time and space outside teleological histories of state and family, infused with heterogeneity and intractability and lacking proper historical destination or documentary intent. In short, Truong opens up an epistemological space for a consideration of the unknowable and unthinkable—other possibilities and other possible times and spaces—that inhabit and saturate the emergence of modernity's now.

In this regard, we might consider how Truong's crossing of fiction into history and history into fiction is the condition of possibility for the epistemological exploration of subalternity as the absolute limit of the place where history is narrativized into logic. Since the establishment of ethnic studies in the late 1960s as a political movement as well as scholarly endeavor, the ethnic literary text in the U.S. has often been said to function as a proxy for history. This has placed particular pressure and urgency on the literary to perform what is "missing" in history and to represent otherwise unrepresentable communities. Here, the burden of authenticity and the evidence of experience inveigh against the bind and sting of injurious racial stereotypes as well as the lack of minority presence and power in the academy.

With the unnamed stranger on the bridge, however, we encounter a critical project focused less on recovery of what is a lost and irrecoverable past or on the correction of historical error through the positing of unvarnished truth—history the way it really was. We encounter less the real story of Ho Chi Minh than one in which the unknowable and unthinkable mobilized under the sign of the literary, under the sign of queer diasporas, become the conditions of possibility by which the "properly" historical, the what-can-be-known, is consolidated and affirmed. In short, by refusing to name, Truong asks us to reflect on what it means to answer forgetting and disappearance with new and ever more narratives of affirmation and presence. She encourages us to reconsider the binds of authenticity central to liberalism's affirmation of identity and its politics of recognition. Through historical catachresis, she shifts our attention from the problem of the real to the politics of our lack of knowledge—to the dialectic of affirmation and forgetting through which historical knowledge and reality are constituted, named, and established.

Indeed, Truong's emphasis on a scandalous queer desire binding this stranger without a proper name to Bình, the servant-cook, shifts our temporal grammar altogether. It raises the specter of the what-could-have-been in relation to the what-was of European modernity, liberal progress, and capitalist development, as well as the subsequent Vietnamese independence movement, its revolutionary discourses of postcolonial subversion and resistance, and its gendered discourses of aggrieved masculinity.[14] The past conditional inflection of what-could-have-been indexes a space of melancholic loss and forfeiture, a privileged time of the possible, albeit unverifiable, and a privileged space of the forgotten, albeit persistent.

By enveloping the lost stranger in his desirous embrace, Bình opens up a permanent space for the ghostly in the real.[15] He preserves room for thinking the what-could-have-been in the what-can-be-known of historicism. We might say that Bình's queer desires, his melancholic attachments to this stranger without a name, highlight another realm of historical possibility altogether. Disturbing rather than stabilizing identity, Bình's queer desires stage another time and space of historical *becoming*. They supplement the dialectic of affirmation and forgetting that subtends historicism's now, its empty homogeneous time and space. "Although we strap time to our wrists, stuff it into our pockets, hang it on our walls, a perpetually moving picture for every room of the house," Bình reminds us in the closing lines of chapter nine, "it can still run away, elude and evade, and show itself again only when there are minutes remaining, and there is nothing left to do except wait till there are none."[16] The moments in between, though desirous, are evanescent. Lost and forgotten, they saturate the what-can-be-known.

Waiting

Considering such moments in between draws attention to the temporal and spatial heterogeneity that both conditions and cuts the what-can-be-known of historicism, bringing us firmly into the folds of haunted history, one in which ghosts and spirits, as Dipesh Chakrabarty emphasizes, "are not dependent on human beliefs for their own existence."[17] Such a critical insight demands reflection on the ways in which historicism serves, to borrow from Heidegger, as a type of violent "worlding" process through which certain creatures and things are brought into the time and space of European modernity ("worlded") while others are consigned to wait, excluded and concealed ("earthed").[18]

Chakrabarty observes that historicism enabled European domination of the world in the nineteenth century through a particular logic of time and space, embedded in the philosophical mandates of political modernity, in everyday habits of conscious as well as unconscious thought. "Historicism," he writes, "is what made modernity or capitalism look not simply global but rather as something that became global *over time*, by originating in one place (Europe) and then spreading outside it. This 'first in Europe, then elsewhere' structure of global historical time was historicist; different non-Western nationalisms would later produce local versions of the same narrative, replacing 'Europe' by some locally constructed center. It was historicism that allowed Marx to say that the 'country that is more developed industrially only shows, to the less developed, the image of its own future.' "[19] The development of European modernity and liberal capitalism over time, as well as their globalization across space, beginning in Europe and then spreading to the New World and beyond, make the possibility of imagining alternative modernities— different knowledges, alternative political possibilities, and other social communities—exceedingly difficult. They universalize the centrality of European political, economic, and aesthetic thought in relation to its colonial others, while presuming that progress and development in the non-West must invariably take place through mimetic fidelity to European images and ideals. Rendered an obsolete remainder of a superseded past, the perpetually anachronistic non-West is forced to play catch-up with an exalted European present and presence invariably constituted as the here and now.

Chakrabarty explores how historicism employs an analytic tradition (exemplified for him by Marx) that abstracts heterogeneity and particularity by sublating them into a universalizing narrative of European historical consciousness. But he also stresses the necessity to contest and supplement the analytic tradition through consideration of a hermeneutic tradition (exemplified for him by Heidegger).[20] The hermeneutic tradition, relentlessly dominated by the inexorable temporal march of modernity and the globalization of capitalism, operates both within and beyond historicism's epistemological reach. It generates "a loving grasp of detail in search of an understanding of the diversity of human lifeworlds. It produces what may be called 'affective histories' . . . [and] finds thought intimately tied to places and to particular forms of life."[21]

These structures of feeling, to return to a concept from Raymond Williams, are those emergent social forms, ephemeral and difficult to grasp or to name, that appear precisely at a moment of emergency, when dominant cultural norms go into crisis.[22] They evoke one important way by which hauntings are transmitted and received as an affective mood, communicating a sense of the ghostly as well as its political and aesthetic effects. The evolution of modernism in the interwar years might be characterized as such a moment of political and aesthetic upheaval in the face of total war. Nevertheless, it remains crucial to examine how this emergency not only signals a crisis internal to European thought and its history of consciousness but also marks the irruptions of race into a privileged narrative of European modernity and progress, the interruptions of a sublated and spectralized colonial world into the European universal. Here it is important to emphasize how race functions beyond the realm of the visible and the protocols of the empirical. Race, that is, is more than just an epiphenomenon of Euro-American capitalism's differentiation, division, and management of Asian and African bodies in New World modernity. As Vilashini Cooppan points out, race "mirrors one logic of capital (the body as commodity) while inter-rupting another (the stages of capitalist development)."[23]

In *The Book of Salt*, queer diasporas emerges as a conceptual wedge in the homogenizing march of the analytic tradition, while affective his-tory marks the ghostly and the evanescent of a spectralized in-between. Bình, whose queer desires and narrative voice illuminate an alternative human life-world, reveals the return of the subject. This position is precarious, however, and hardly inured to the annihilating intents of anachronism: its discourse of citizenship and rights, its mantra of cap-italism and consumption, its protocols of "Repetition and routine. Ser-vitude and subservience. Beck and call," in Bình's words.[24] The disciplin-ing intent of historicism, its abstracting and atomizing of heterogeneity into empty, homogenous time and space, is revealed in a fascinating scene of travel in the middle of Truong's novel. Here, Bình tells us about Stein and Toklas's yearly sojourn in their country home in Bilignin, a trip he is enjoined to facilitate. "When summer comes to Paris," Bình relates,

> my Madame and Madame pack their clothes and their dogs into their automobile, and they drive themselves and their cargo down to the Rhône Valley to the tiny farming village of Bilignin. I am left behind to lock up the apartment and to hand the keys over to the concierge, whom I have always suspected of being overly glad to see these two American ladies go . . . With my Mesdames already on the road for over a day, I pack up whatever warm-weather garments I have that year, and I go and splurge on a hat for the hot summer sun. If I find a bargain, then I also treat myself to lunch at an establishment with cloth on the table and an attentive waiter who is obliged to call me "Monsieur." I then take what is left of the money that my Mesdames gave me for a second-class train ticket, and I buy a third-class one instead. I sleep all the way down to Bilignin, where I open the house and *wait* several more days—as my Mesdames drive at a speed that varies somewhere between leisurely and meandering—before I hear the honking of their automobile and the barking of the two weary dogs. I *wait* for them on the terrace.[25]

Bình packs away whatever warm-weather garments he has for that year, locks up the Stein-Toklas residence, and hands the keys over to the custodianship of the French concierge. Bình's human life-world outside the beck and call of domestic servitude—his new hat, his lunch at an upscale bistro where the waiter is obliged to call him "Monsieur"— emerges only in between the time of his Mesdames' departure and arrival, their disappearance and re-appearance. Here the in-between is configured as a privileged and paradoxical key to a hermeneutic tradition, a structure of feeling that defies the temporal and spatial logic of modernity's ceaseless progress, its homogenous march from before to after. Affective history—a structure of feeling—appears both before *and* after: in between the time before Stein and Toklas's arrival in the rural French countryside and after their departure from the city, in between the space before Bilignin and after Paris. In the process, an alternative human life-world is given shape and form, a worlding of the colonial subaltern that Johannes Fabian might describe as the emergence of "coevalness."[26]

Focusing on modernity's persistent denial of such coevalness, its disciplining of time and space into the political logic of liberal humanism and the economic logic of liberal capitalism, Chakrabarty observes that John Stuart Mill's historicist arguments "consigned Indians, Africans, and other 'rude' nations to an imaginary waiting room of history. In doing so, it converted history itself into a version of this waiting room. We were all headed for the same destination, Mill averred, but some people were to arrive earlier than others. That was what historicist consciousness was: a recommendation to the colonized to wait. Acquiring historical consciousness, acquiring the public spirit that Mill thought absolutely necessary for the art of self-government, was also to learn this art of waiting. This waiting was the realization of the 'not yet' of historicism."[27] The "not yet" of European historicism governs Bình's narrative of simultaneous migration, a process in which the servant-cook is relegated to the imaginary waiting room of history. Through the disappearance of other possible pasts as well as the forgetting of other possible futures, the colonized can only await the colonizer. Bình must learn this art of waiting. And while both must necessarily be "headed for the same destination," Chakrabarty emphasizes, it is the colonizer who must invariably arrive first, the colonized trailing behind, an anachronistic relic of the not yet of modernity's now.

In this passage from *The Book of Salt*, however, we are presented with a further twist of colonial logic: even when the colonized arrives early, he *still* must wait. That is, even though Bình is ahead of his Mesdames, he still must work and he still must wait. The first to reach Bilignin, the servant-cook is compelled to resume his domestic duties of beck and call. He opens up and prepares the house for the arrival of Stein and Toklas, waiting "several more days" for his Mesdames to arrive at their appointed (historical and aesthetic) destination. The couple, he tells us, are motoring "somewhere between leisurely and meandering," making their way through the French countryside, on their own schedule, according to their own sanctioned time. In between these moments and movements, the details of Bình's life appear only to disappear.

The logic of the ghost characterizing Derrida's analysis of capital applies equally to the racialized dialectic of affirmation and forgetting that structures Bình's appearance and disappearance within the Euro-American modernity of Stein and Toklas. Like capital, race ultimately *exceeds* the logic of presence and absence, while evading the sequencing of before to after.[28] I would like to describe the paradoxical effacement of Bình's human life-world in between the visible and the invisible as a type of *queer* worlding. As cook and caretaker in the couple's residence and inner sanctum, Bình exemplifies the world division of labor that both institutes and queers the very distinctions separating public and private, as well as the spheres of work and home, labor and affect, productive and reproductive labor. These are the fundamental oppositions upon which the dialectic of European modernity is constructed, but it is only *in between* the time and space of these oppositional terms that we also come to apprehend the contours of Bình's other life-world, a site of affective density where history and subjectivity are remade as a ghostly structure of feeling. Here we come to recognize the in-between as distinct and separate from, indeed beyond but nevertheless within, modernity's dictates of time and space.

"What would it mean," asks Brian Massumi, "to give a logical consistency to the in-between? It would mean realigning with a logic of relation," indeed endowing the in-between with "an ontological status separate from the terms of relation."[29] Paying greater heed to the logic of the in-between in *The Book of Salt* facilitates an understanding of how it comes to accrue its own ontological status, its own ontological consistency, separate from the liberal humanist terms of relation that frame but cannot fully determine it. Brought together with the epistemological effects of historical catachresis, the in-between gives way not only to alternate ways of *knowing* but also, and equally important, to alternative ways of *being*, indeed of *becoming*, in the world. Through this simultaneous realignment of epistemology and ontology, a queer "worlding" of lost and forgotten desires comes to exceed the dialectic of enlightenment, the dialectic of affirmation and forgetting in *The Book of Salt*.

Mirroring

Bình eventually takes up with one of Stein's winsome acolytes, Marcus Lattimore, a gentleman from the American south but not, as Lattimore avers, a "southern gentleman."[30] In the course of the novel, we learn that Lattimore is a man of dubious racial origins. Passing through 27 rue de Fleurus, he also passes for white, his black mother having sold away his birthname; he gains financial security for her silence.[31] Likewise, his on-again-off-again relationship with Bình slips in between the cracks of an Enlightenment compulsion to evaluate and interrogate, to organize and know. Hired by Lattimore to be his Sunday cook, Bình is outsourced as a borrowed servant by Stein and Toklas for only one instrumental purpose: their desire to identify, to taxonomize, and to name—that is, to turn sameness into a manageable difference, and to turn difference into a manageable sameness. "Is Lattimore a Negro?" Stein asks Bình. This, Bình tell us, "is what they [Stein and Toklas], in the end, want to know."[32] And here the question of liberal humanism's racialized past in the colonial slave societies of the New World, and its ghostly return in the present of 1930s Old World Paris, appears as an open secret, an institutionalized regime of passing and privilege, produced but passed over by historicist disciplining.

Let me turn to one last scene from *The Book of Salt*—Bình's initial encounter with Lattimore in the famous Stein Salon. Of Lattimore, Bình recalls:

> I will forget that you entered 27 rue de Fleurus as a "writer" among a sea of others who opened the studio door with a letter of introduction and a face handsome with talent and promise. You stood at the front of the studio listening to a man who had his back to me. I entered the room with a tray of sugar-dusted cakes for all the young men who sit and stand, a hungry circle radiating around GertrudeStein. After years of the imposed invisibility of servitude, I am acutely aware when I am being watched, a sensitivity born from absence, a grain of salt on the tongue of a man who has tasted only bitter. As I checked the teapots to see whether they needed to be replenished, I felt a slight pressure. It

was the weight of your eyes resting on my lips. I looked up, and I saw
you standing next to a mirror reflecting the image of wiry young man
with deeply set, startled eyes. I looked up, and I was seeing myself
beside you. I am at sea again, I thought. Waves are coursing through
my veins. I am at sea again.[33]

For Bình, this mirror image does not produce a reflection of the self-
same. Moreover, it does not present what, after Jacques Lacan, we are
accustomed to describing as the poststructuralist advent of the "I is an
other," one mocking and coherent, trapped on the other side of the
looking glass.[34] This disjunctive mirror image is not simply about the
ways in which individuated, egoic subjectivity is given over to *méconnais-*
sance, a temporal mode of anticipation that Jane Gallop observes is
oriented toward the future perfect tense, the what-will-have-been of the
mirror stage, or as Lacan puts it, the "what I shall have been for what I
am in the process of becoming."[35]

Instead, Bình's reflection brings together two disparate spaces in the
salon, as well as the two disconnected lovers occupying them, aligning
Bình and Lattimore beside each other in the mirror image. By displaying
a curious and handsome Lattimore reflecting an astonished Bình (a "wiry
young man with deeply set, startled eyes"), Truong indexes through this
mirror image an alternative space and time, another human life-world
within the hallowed space of the Stein salon. In Truong's reconfigured
mirror stage, the temple of high modernism does not reflect on itself.
Difference does not return as sameness. Historical understanding is thus
transformed into a process of what Ranajit Guha describes as capturing
"an image caught in a distorting mirror."[36] In Bình's distorted mirror
stage racial difference endures as that which remains irreducible to the
dialectic of enlightenment, a human life-world other to the space and
time of "the young men who sit and stand, a hungry circle radiating
around GertrudeStein."

As Bình slips from the simple past to the past progressive and finally
into the present—"I *looked* up . . . I *was seeing* myself beside you . . . I *am*
at sea again"—he carves out through these grammatical shifts a *racial-*
ized space and time that he and Lattimore share. This alternative modernity summons the epistemology of the oceanic, shifting our attention to the sea as history, from "roots" to "routes," in Paul Gilroy's
famous reading of the black Atlantic—indeed, working to queer the
black Atlantic.[37] This is a queer diaspora in which the gentleman from

the American South and the Vietnamese servant-cook can both appear, despite their very disparate class positions; it is a racialized space and time they can collectively inhabit and share within and beyond the sanctioned time and space of Bình's Mesdames. For, as Bình reminds us, the weight of Lattimore's eyes on his lips transports him to the sea, which as he later tells us, becomes the alternative space and time of belonging itself: "[At] sea, I learn that time can also be measured in terms of water, in terms of distance traveled while drifting on it. When measured in that way, nearer and farther are the path of time's movement, not continuously forward along a fast straight line. When measured this way, time loops and curlicues, and at any given moment it can spiral me away and then bring me rushing home again."[38]

This space and time of non-mimetic racial identity is radically other to standard poststructuralist understandings of the mirror stage as a narcissistic self-other dialectic, which underpins the fracturing of Western subjectivity and consciousness. From a slightly different perspective, we might say that calibrated against Lacan's future perfect, the what-will-have-been of Bình's mirror stage in the what-was of Stein's modernity questions how race is managed and effaced not just in the development of Enlightenment liberal humanism, but specifically through modernism's vanguard and oppositional stance to this very tradition, one dependent on and developed during the height of European colonialism. We might say that what Truong presents us with here is a reconfigured mirror stage in which the spectrality of race emerges as the repressed image of liberal humanism itself.

From a different angle, we might ask how the fracturing of Western subjectivity and consciousness, of which Stein's high modernism is a paradigmatic example, is made possible precisely through this colonial detour, through the forgetting of both Asia and Africa. As an Asian American, postcolonial, and queer text, The Book of Salt insists on a contemporary investigation of race as a comparative project across what Fernand Braudel calls the longue durée.[39] In such an investigation, the U.S. is not configured as a point of arrival in a teleology about immigrant assimilation and settlement. Neither is it valorized as a melting pot or a rainbow coalition undisturbed by cleavings of race, gender, sexuality, and class. Truong does not romanticize the shared or imagined intimacies among Bình, Lattimore, Stein, and Toklas. (Indeed, Lattimore later abandons his young lover after convincing Bình to steal for him one of Stein's unpublished manuscripts, the ironically titled "The Book of Salt.") Instead, Truong highlights their contingent and ever-shifting intersections, facilitating in the process a more sustained consideration of the histories of exploitation and domination that unevenly bind Asian indentureship and African slavery to Euro-American modernity.

The Book of Salt thus demands a critical conversation among ethnic, postcolonial, diasporic, area, and queer studies, one bringing together the intimacies of four continents through scrupulous attention to questions of sex and sexuality. Exerting particular pressure on the processes of historicism, the problematics of queer diasporas in Truong's novel illustrates what Carla Freccero describes as "the affective force of the past in the present, of a desire issuing from another time and placing a demand on the present in the form of an ethical imperative."[40] In this manner, Truong's novel resists any simple slide—any development "continuously forward along a fast straight line"—from modernism to postmodernism as either a political or an aesthetic movement. Instead, it insists on not just a material and psychic but also a formalist investigation of the ways in which the shift from modernism to postmodernism is constituted through disavowed and sublated colonial histories of race. In short, Truong's ghostly matters rearrange conventional understandings about the dialectic pairing of the modern and postmodern, as well as its constitutive dissociation from the colonial and postcolonial. This disappearance and forgetting is the historical foundation of our colorblind age and its racialization of intimacy.

What, we might further consider, is the relationship between the *aesthetic* inscription of Stein as the doyenne of literary modernism in her time and the current *political* inscription of Stein and Toklas as the iconic lesbian couple of historical modernism in our time? Given the temporal lag between these two historical inscriptions, how is it that the once debased status of Stein and Toklas as Jewish lesbians in early twentieth century Paris can now serve to underwrite the current folding in of normative gay and lesbian U.S. citizen-subjects into the authorized time and space of the nation-state? In other words, without discounting the radicality of Stein and Toklas in their time, we still need to ask how they are conscripted today as the poster children for queer liberalism. What possible pasts and what possible futures must be denied in order for this particular narrative of queer freedom and progress to take hold? Indeed, how does queer liberalism not only depend on but also demand the completion of the racial project, the triumph of a colorblind U.S. society as an achieved and settled past? At a moment when discourses of colorblindness evacuate all racial content in favor of a re-ascendant form of the abstract individual—the liberal human—*The Book of Salt* insists on a consideration of what remains unassimilable, unrecognizable, and untold in the making of the political and aesthetic realm of Euro-American modernity.

At the same time, *The Book of Salt* resists any simple affirmation of racial identity or any easy positivist recovery of a lost and effaced racial past. It asks how we might move beyond the dominance of the visual register itself, one overdetermining so many of our contemporary debates on race and the politics of recognition. By creating a mirror image of non-mimetic racial identity—Bình and Lattimore's asymmetrical reflection in the mirror stage of Stein's modernity—Truong opens up a queer terrain of racial belonging outside the authorized terms of dominant representation. She unfolds, that is, a viewing practice that obviates the unremitting demand for mimetic fidelity to universal Euro-American aesthetic and political ideals. At the same time, she refuses to substitute such demands with authenticity, with the visibility of race and racial difference. Instead, Truong conceptualizes an alternative time and space—other forms of racial knowing and being—that are more than just a negation or reversal of the dominant terms of relation. She focuses on the politics of our lack of knowledge, the more extensive forms of disappearance and forgetting that configure the aesthetic and political story of modernism in Stein's time and colorblindness in ours.

Bình and Lattimore's relationship—their history—is of another time and space. It is a history not of affirmation but a history of disappearance, a history of ghosts. The cook's Mesdames come to represent the iconic modern lesbian couple of the early twentieth century, paving the way for queer liberalism today as the latest incarnation of "the rights of man." Bình and Lattimore's relationship cannot assume the lineaments of modern subjectivity or identity. Theirs is a private without a public; through a similar logic, the history of Ho Chi Minh will come to be a public without a private. (As one of the dominant historicist narratives available to decolonization, Marxist revolutionary discourse comes to repress queerness, much as queer liberalism comes to repress race.) While Bình's Sunday pleasures with Lattimore mark a sphere of intense intimacy rivaling that of his bourgeois Mesdames, it is consigned to Benjamin's dustbin of history, stretching back to coerced colonial migrations of black slaves and Asian coolies, and reaching forward into the ubiquitous circulations of migrant labor under the contemporary shadows of global capitalism. Bình and Lattimore index the intimacies of four continents, but their ghostly presence also signals the incompleteness of their temporal and spatial transformation under historicist disciplining of time and space.

And so they must wait.

Closet as Waiting Room

The Book of Salt proffers a critique of historicism by exploring the time and place of the colonial in the modern. *Happy Together*, in turn, extends this line of analysis by focusing our attention on the time and place of the postcolonial in the global.

Happy Together, Wong Kar-wai's sixth feature film and the only one of his productions to be shot outside of Asia, is an eloquent disquisition on the contemporary conditions of an underclass of queer Asian migrant laborers hustling in the global system. Wong's film is a compelling investigation of the material as well as the psychic conditions that make queer diasporas inhabitable or—perhaps more accurately in the case of Lai and Ho—uninhabitable. *Happy Together*, which earned Wong the Best Director Award at the Cannes Film Festival, has garnered well-deserved critical acclaim, yet few reviewers or scholarly critics have focused on the sexual politics of its queer diaspora.

Indeed, many commentators eschew issues of sexuality altogether, describing Wong's portrayal of homosexuality as incidental to the film's central emphasis on emotional deadlock. They note that Wong Kar-wai avoids "cultish gay stereotyping"; that Ho and Lai are "lovers who happen to be homosexual"; that "what was widely pre-billed as a gay-themed movie is only peripherally concerned with such matters."[41] *Boston Globe* critic Jay Carr observes that the film is not "concerned so much with sexual politics as with the existential tedium attached to love's movements from embers to ashes."[42] And writing for *Daily Variety*, Derek Elley aptly summarizes this pattern, contending that although "the universe in which the main characters move is exclusively male, the abstract feelings the movie evokes . . . are transfigured to a universal, sexually neutral level."[43] I would like to suspend for a moment these summary pronouncements on the "existential" or "universal, sexually neutral" nature of Lai and Ho's impossible relationship. Such judgments abstract homosexual particularity in the name of universal (heteronormative) love and disconnection, as well as beg the politics of sexuality and culture as they travel across different global spaces. Furthermore, they level disparities of race and coloniality that underwrite the project of liberal humanism and the contemporary emergence of queer liberalism—its racialization of intimacy and its domesticating of same-sex relations.

What might be at stake were we to think about homosexuality not as peripheral, but as central, to Wong's film and to disparities of race and (post)coloniality that mark neoliberal governmentality in our current moment? Like Bình in *The Book of Salt*, Lai and Ho do not—indeed, cannot—appear within dominant modes of knowing or being that frame the modern (gay) subject and its history of consciousness. Under this threat of racial disappearance, *Happy Together* illuminates other epistemic and ontological coordinates. Through its queer diaspora, Wong's film scrambles our normative cultural and narratological expectations. In *Epistemology of the Closet*, for instance, Eve Kosofsky Sedgwick describes the closet as "the defining structure for gay oppression in [the twentieth] century."[44] In *Happy Together*, however, there is no closet from which to emerge. There is no familiar scene of "coming out," no unveiling or shedding of a past lie in order to embrace the truth of (homo)sexual identity and belonging. Stranded in Argentina, there is no familial or social structure into which the indigent Lai and Ho can come out.

In this regard, it is useful to contrast *Happy Together* with Ang Lee's 1993 film *The Wedding Banquet*.[45] A more recognizably gay film, *The Wedding Banquet*'s entire narrative drive, conflict, and resolution is organized around Wai-tung's (Winston Chao) coming out to his family and the reconciliation of his "modern" Western homosexual lifestyle in New York with his lover Simon (Mitchell Lichtenstein) to the "backward" traditional culture of his Chinese parents. Unlike *Happy Together*, Lee's film configures the closet as the defining structure for gay oppression across the globe, while simultaneously revealing it to be a site for the emergence and development of minority subjectivity and racial identity—as the waiting room of history from which the gay Asian subject must struggle to emerge. In Lee's film, the question of queer family and kinship becomes a racial metric for the not-yet of modernity's now. In other words, Wai-tung's sexual development, his cultivation and claiming of a homosexual identity and agency, becomes a barometer for Chinese modernity and progress itself—that is, the what-will-have-been of Wai-tung's coming out to the what-was of gay and lesbian liberation in the West.

Mark Chiang describes *The Wedding Banquet*'s underlying parable as one that realigns national (Chinese) patriarchy with transnational (post-modern) patriarchy through the flexibility of global capital.[46] The narrative resolution of Lee's film hinges on the ability of the wealthy Taiwanese Wai-tung to produce a male heir, a task accomplished precisely by the exploitation of the undocumented mainlander Wei-wei's (May Chin) reproductive labor.[47] (It would not be a stretch to describe *The Wedding Banquet* as an uncanny exemplar for the politics of transnational adoption and the exploitation of reproductive labor I explore in my next chapter.) With the birth of his son, Wai-tung is able to reconcile the paternal (Chinese) mandate with the liberal rhetoric of cosmopolitan queer family and kinship in a multicultural age.

The Wedding Banquet thus functions as a prescient harbinger for the evolution of queer liberalism in our global moment, one in which a queer planet would be "worlded" by the epistemology of the closet. In Wai-tung's narrative of (homo)sexual liberation as racial progress, the gay Asian entrepreneur can be thus posited as queer liberalism's model minority. Given such conditions, it is little surprise that Wai-tung must be legally enfranchised as a (nominal) U.S. citizen-subject: "My truth is that I am a gay American." His legal status, in fact, compels the plot of the film: in exchange for the promise of marriage and legal recognition, Wei-Wei submits to her continued subordination under an increasing international gendered division of (reproductive) labor.

In contrast to *The Wedding Banquet*, *Happy Together* does not engage in this type of narratological development. In Wong's film, the epistemology of the closet as the imaginary waiting room of history is fundamentally scrambled: there is no positing of gay identity; there is no claiming of legal rights and recognition through liberal political enfranchisement; there is no assertion of social belonging through queer family and kinship; there is no participation in the free market—indeed, there is no shopping at all. In the opening shots of *Happy Together*, we are thrown directly into the film, confronted by Lai and Ho's naked and entangled bodies in a moment of heated sexual exchange. This extra-diegetic moment, outside the time and space of the film's main plot, eschews conventional narratological development of anguished (homo)sexuality. Moreover, it is not a pastoral scene of budding romantic love but an erotically charged scene of graphic anal intercourse, the most explicit sexual encounter between Lai and Ho in the entire film.

Consummated within two and a half minutes of the opening credits of *Happy Together*, the scene is filmed in a grainy black and white. The

Graphic Intercourse: Lai and Ho in a moment of sexual bliss. From *Happy Together*, directed by Wong Kar-wai.

camera frame sways from side-to-side, like a rectangular porthole of a rocking ship. The affective intensity of this sodomitical encounter serves to mark an Edenic moment of sexual union from which its protagonists fall and are ejected into the main plot of *Happy Together*: an interminable cycle of abandonment, breaking up, and "starting over."[48] Unlike *The Wedding Banquet*, there is no recognizable scene of coming out in Wong's film, though in the face of this delirious and graphic opening sequence, we might say that the film itself "comes out" to the audience itself as anything but sexually neutral. In contrast to *The Wedding Banquet* and *Lawrence v. Texas*, *Happy Together* is less concerned with same-sex intimacy and domesticity than with same-sex *sodomy* and the *impossibility* of domesticity.

The inability of critics, I suggest, to detect any significance in the queer diaspora of *Happy Together* stems from the film's persistent eschewal of the dominant aesthetics and politics of queer liberalism. From the very opening moments of *Happy Together*, Wong throws us into an alternative life-world, placing us aesthetically at odds with conventional cinematic expectations of time and space and politically at odds with dominant modes of knowing and being. To the extent that globalization has produced a recognizable gay identity on the world stage, it has organized this liberal consciousness as a supplement to late capitalism and in accordance with strict divisions between capital and labor, underwriting conjugal domesticity, privacy, and intimacy. What makes the queer diaspora in *Happy Together* exceptional and, in this sense, unrecognizable, is that Lai and Ho are aligned not on the side of queer liberalism, i.e. on the side of global capital and citizenship. They do not participate in the commercial scene of global gay life as self-possessed modern liberal subjects of rights and representation. Rather, like Wei-Wei, they are aligned on the side of undocumented gendered migrant labor.

Lai and Ho represent a diasporic underclass of service providers, "servants of globalization," who track flows of global capital through low-wage and unskilled work.[49] As such, they demand a rethinking of queer studies in a more global frame, as well as a more sustained analysis of the connections between the politics of transnational feminism and the emerging field of transnational sexuality. In its attention to the problems of transnational (homo)sexuality, *Happy Together* marks the ways in which the financialization of the globe under neoliberal mandates unfolds a new (post)colonial order in the wake of decolonization, a gendering between the global South and the global North that cripples the possibility of an operative civil society in the former, while shifting priorities in the latter "from service to the citizen to capital maximization." In Spivak's estimation, it "then becomes increasingly correct to say that the only source of male dignity is employment, just as the only source of genuine female dignity is unpaid domestic labor."[50]

Lai and Ho represent a migrant proletariat class in the periphery who code as "unpaid domestic labor," a population whose movements in the global system do not trace an East-West or a South-North pathway; this is a priviledged route of global elites from the Third World to the First World, the traffic from a developing to a (post)industrialized nation-state. In the case of *The Wedding Banquet*'s Wai-tung, economic privilege comes together with sexual self-determination to shape a narrative of (neo)liberal subjectivity and agency, a teleological development from a repressed sexual past to a future of queer freedom and progress. In *Happy Together*, Lai and Ho's movement in the global system cannot be characterized through such a discourse of development. Indeed, their travel from Hong Kong to Buenos Aires traces an alternative South-South movement, a migration from one developing region to another, and a passage from one postcolonial or, better yet, one decolonizing space to another.

Lai and Ho depart for Argentina not just as an attempt to "start over" their flagging relationship. They also leave Hong Kong because Lai has stolen money from his father's business associate. This sum of capital cannot be repaid, rendering absurd numerous critics' descriptions of the couple's journey as "expatriates," "vacationers," or "tourists."[51] As undocumented migrant labor in Argentina, a country that has undergone tremendous turmoil under neoliberal structural adjustment programs, Lai's series of menial jobs—as a doorman at Tango Bar Sur, as a dishwasher and a cook in a Chinese restaurant, as a butcher in a local abattoir—is a succession of declining returns. In turn, Ho's on-again-off-again employment as an exotic hustler, selling himself to First-World tourists, might be described as the other side of the same economic coin. Lai and Ho cannot appear—cannot be visible agents—in these circuits of global capitalism, gay or otherwise. Their presence draws insistent attention to the ways by which contemporary practices of racial exploitation and (post)coloniality continue to suffuse late capitalist social relations under the shadows of neoliberal governmentality and globalization.

The universalizing of homosexuality in *Happy Together* as "sexually neutral" and as "existential tedium" by various reviewers might be characterized as the historicism of our global age. These judgments not only belie a story of development as (sexual) freedom but also situate the epistemology of the closet as the imaginary waiting room of history, marking the ways in which (homo)sexuality continues to serve as a metric of civilization and racial developmentalism. This is a logic that Lai and Ho interrupt. Like Bình, they two are rendered ghostly through this process, demanding in turn their own epistemological and ontological coordinates. From this perspective, the problem of queer diasporas and sexuality in *Happy Together* is not peripheral, but indeed central, to the question of (neo)liberalism and (homo)sexual development in Wong's film.

Tango and the Autonomy of Affect

I have discussed some of the material circumstances of the movements of Lai and Ho in the global system. What is the psychic scaffolding of— the psychic structure of family and kinship underpinning—their impossible relationship? How does Wong encourage us to rethink psychoanalysis and the Oedipal outside the mandates of queer liberalism, outside the dialectic of tradition and modernity, and outside the closet as imaginary waiting room of history?

The impossibility of their beleaguered relationship finds its internalized form in the couple's exquisite psychic deadlock. Stranded in Argentina, Lai and Ho come to embody the most severe example of the Wongian principle that physical movement and psychic movement are antipathetic.[52] The two cannot be happy together, and they cannot be happy apart. Separating shortly after their aborted journey to Iguazu Falls, Ho is beaten by a disgruntled trick, his hands broken and his face battered and bruised. Once again, he returns to Lai, who installs him into his dingy La Boca apartment in order to tend to his wounds. Care, however, in this instance means psychic stasis and the closing down of

Kitchen Tango.
From *Happy Together*.

the world. "Something I never told Ho Po-wing," Lai admits to us in a later flashback and voiceover, "is that I didn't want him to recover too fast. Those days he was sick were our happiest together." Such is the psychic deadlock underwriting their world of smoldering cigarettes and hidden passports: One is happy only when the other is sick; as one gets better the other must fall ill. Although these scenes are filmed from every conceivable angle, the dreary apartment remains cramped and unchanged from beginning to end.

This problem of psychic immobility is nowhere more evident than in the couple's aborted tango. About a third of the way through *Happy Together*, as Ho slowly recovers from his injuries, he attempts to teach Lai to tango, a series of frustrating lessons and steps beginning one day in the cramped space of their studio apartment and ending one evening in the communal kitchen outside their stairwell. Here, like the opening scene of *Happy Together*, tango marks the indeterminate passing of time and space in between capitalist systematization of labor and wages. Bathed in the excessive glow of the fluorescent kitchen lights and accompanied by the haunting music of Astor Piazzola, the couple steps forward and then back, back and then forward. In the end, Lai and Ho move nowhere and, at their most physically intimate, Chris Doyle's elegant camerawork slows their saturated image to a virtual standstill. Locked in an eternal embrace, their time in the space of the communal kitchen grinds to a halt.

This tango sequence reprises a series of formal, avant-garde aesthetic devices that mark what I would like to describe as the *psychic* time and space of the in-between in *Happy Together*. In a series of time-elapsed shots, Lai and Ho are visually frozen, juxtaposed against the rapidly shifting time and space of a Buenos Aires landscape, thumping to its own tempo and beat. In each of these sequences, two different struc-

Cigarette Break.
From *Happy Together*.

Taxi Reunion.
From *Happy Together*.

The Beat and Grind of
Buenos Aires. From
Happy Together.

tures of time and space emerge simultaneously, with Lai and Ho coming to occupy their own alternative human life-world "in between."

As a dance form, tango is given over to this system of doubling, as well. On one hand, the highly structured nature of tango, defying Lai's cognitive capacities to master it, reflects the couple's incompatibility. On the other hand, the excessive affect produced by Lai's and Ho's dance of desire continually exceeds the structural and conceptual limits of tango's protocols. Marking its own history and structure of feeling, it demands, in Elizabeth Freeman's words, "a historiographic method that would admit the flesh, that would avow that history is written on and felt with the body, and that would let eroticism into the notion of historical thought itself."[53] The persistence of the couple's queer desire not only produces tantalizing scenes of sexual longing but also simultaneously indexes, I would suggest, the extra-diegetic moment of sexual frisson that opens Wong's film. Although their tango insistently points to this impossible return—a yearning to recapture that ineffable moment before the couple's tragic fall into life as well as the main narrative of the film—affect might nevertheless be described here as a kind of poststructuralist supplement to the structure of the dance.

A relation of motion and stasis, the affective intensity of their tango marks an alternate human life-world for Lai and Ho, a what-could-have-been, struggling for material expression and psychic form.[54] Unlike emotion, Massumi observes, which is "qualified intensity, the conventional, consensual point of insertion of intensity into semantically and semiotically formed progressions . . . [an] intensity owned and recognized," affect is ultimately "unqualified."[55] Its excessive logics defy emotion's terms of symbolic inscription. Hence, the "autonomy of affect" comes to serve in *Happy Together* as a ghostly marker of the in-between, highlighting an alternative epistemological and ontological framing of Lai's and Ho's now. Indeed, I would suggest that the (post)structure of queer feeling marking the couple's tango opens upon another terrain of social and psychic relations altogether. Ultimately, it points to other ways of thinking about the incest taboo and its structures of displacement. It helps us to think alternative conceptions of family and kinship not just within but beyond the structures of the Oedipal—a poststructuralist account of family and kinship.

Starting Over

How might we imagine a post-Oedipal structure that would make the psychic lives of Lai and Ho possible and livable, a habitable psychic terrain on which their social relations could survive? How might "Anti-Oedipus" function as a kind of ethics?

These questions return us to the issue of "starting over," which dominates the couple's relationship from the beginning to the end of Wong's film. Moments after the opening sequence of the film, we follow Lai and Ho on an aborted trip to Iguazu Falls, a return to origins that remains predictably unfulfilled. Lost and stranded on the dusty roads of Argentina, Lai and Ho quarrel, and then quarrel again. The scene ends with Lai's voiceover about the couple's failed journey and separation: "I never did find out where we were that day. I do remember that he said that days with me were boring, that we should end it. If we were we to meet again one day, we might start over. Actually, for him, starting over has two different meanings."

To "start over"—"由頭來過"—is a Cantonese colloquialism that translates literally as "from the head over again." This corporeal metaphor, absent in the English translation "starting over," suggests an image at once physical as well as psychic. Physically, to start over signifies a literal return, a going back to the beginning, a return to the starting line. But it also simultaneously marks an ostensible departure, a willful attempt to move forward in a new manner that would bring one to another place or effect a different outcome or relation. The physical indeterminacy of the phrase also characterizes the psychic ambivalence of starting over. For Lai and Ho, starting over necessarily signifies both the beginning and, therefore, the end of a relationship. For the two lovers, does starting over mean going back to the beginning, going back to the starting line, or returning to a point of origin? Or does starting over mean an attempt to move forward from their place of fixity, to create new pathways and displacements that would open up breathing room for alternative possibilities in their psychic and social lives?

I would like to explore this issue of starting over in relation to the incest taboo—to its structures of kinship and to its principles of displacement. According to structuralist anthropologists, the incest taboo initiates a series of crucial displacements that organize family and social life. Claude Lévi-Strauss observes that, in its most elemental form, a kinship structure is synonymous with a particular incest taboo (or set of taboos).

The incest taboo is not a biological imperative but a cultural interdiction forcing one to displace away from a forbidden object of desire and into a social network of reciprocity and exchange. Marking the transition from "nature" to "culture," the incest taboo functions as a social law, creating and regulating family and kinship relations through specific sexual prohibitions. By outlawing particular sexual relations between members of kinship groups, the incest taboo is meant to ensure the stable reproduction of culture across generations. In short, it "worlds" the subject by forcing him or her to inhabit a particular position within a familial and kinship structure, one guaranteeing social recognition, economic coherence, and political legibility. For Levi-Strauss, marriage is the most basic form of exchange in the elementary structures of kinship and, in this system, women are considered the most precious of "gifts," bartered and exchanged between a network of fathers and brothers.[56]

The regulation of kinship in this manner continues to enable the political organization and domination of public and private life, stigmatizing "illegitimate" forms of family from "legitimate" and state-sanctioned social norms and ideals. While the incest taboo initiates an exogamic mandate for reciprocity and exchange, it is important to emphasize that displacement can assume historically contingent and variable forms. In other words, while the incest taboo might describe a universal phenomenon of social exchange, the nature of its prohibitions and the pathways of its social displacements can vary, and have certainly varied across historical periods. As Gayle Rubin observes, the incest taboo cannot be explained away as a biological imperative preventing genetically close mating. Rather it must be seen as imposing the social imperative of exogamy and displacement "upon the biological events of sex and procreation," as being motivated by the demand for peaceful coexistence with and among one's potential neighbors and enemies through scripted rituals of displacement and exchange.[57]

Running alongside this anthropological account of displacement and exchange is the psychoanalytic story of how each human being is psychically thrown into a particular structure of kinship, a psychic structure overdetermined by the laws of Oedipalization. In this account, the incest taboo demands a primary displacement from the mother, a displacement that opens up room in our psyches for new objects of desire, for other creatures and things. A traditional Freudian account of Oedipal displacement comes in the form of the little boy's loss of his mother as a prohibited object of desire. The little boy's displacement from his maternal origin is legislated by the Oedipus complex and its particular incest taboo, constituted not only through the father's interdiction of the son's desire for the mother as sexual object, but also by the heterosexual orientation of the little boy's identifications and desires as he searches for her suitable replacement.

Stitching together Oedipal and anthropological accounts of kinship, Rubin observes in her groundbreaking article, "The Traffic in Women," that the "precision of the fit between Freud and Lévi-Strauss is striking. Kinship systems require a division of the sexes. The Oedipal phase divides the sexes. Kinship systems include sets of rules governing sexuality. The Oedipal crisis is the assimilation of these rules and taboos. Compulsory heterosexuality is the product of kinship. The Oedipal phase constitutes heterosexual desire. Kinship rests on a radical difference between the rights of men and women. The Oedipal complex confers male rights upon the boy, and forces the girl to accommodate herself to her lesser rights."[58]

According to Rubin, the Oedipus complex appears to be a psychoanalytic mirror to traditional accounts of kinship in structural anthropology. The Oedipus complex is meant to organize social relations of kinship through its psychic division of the sexes, its heterosexual imperative, and its privileging of the little boy's needs and prerogatives over those of the little girl. While the elementary structures of kinship seem to be neatly reflected in the psychic image of Oedipus, there is nothing inevitable or absolute about this pairing. How might we rethink this privileged connection in a supplemental rather than analogical framing, so as to imagine how we might come to inhabit the world differently, through other forms of psychic displacement and affiliation?

Jacques Lacan's poststructuralist re-reading of Freudian psychoanalysis directs our attention to the ways in which the little boy's displacement away from his mother in the Oedipal scene is, in fact, a secondary rather than primary displacement. For Lacan, the subject's primary displacement comes not through the loss of the mother but through the fall into language. When we enter language, we lose the fullness of our being. Language alienates us from our plenitude. The displacement of the subject into language, into the symbolic world of meaning, demands the sacrifice of being, the forfeiture of presence, the loss of the "here-and-now." Forever idealized and sought after, the here-and-now is retroactively erected as the origin of our desires, the impossible what-has-been that we can never recapture or recuperate.

Importantly, Lacan's poststructuralist re-reading of Freud configures maternal forfeiture as a secondary loss retroactively projected onto this primary loss, our fall and displacement into language. When this secondary, nameable loss—the loss of the Oedipal mother for Freud's little boy—is coupled with this primary, ineffable loss—the sacrifice of being through alienation in language—desire is set into motion. We become aware of the world through the language of desire and through our drive to recapture this lost object of desire in the guise of other creatures and things. Here, Oedipus and its structures of family and kinship provide the code through which subjects interpret their sense of loss, orienting their desires and identifications accordingly. Family and kinship structures function, in other words, as a kind of social language by which we experience, express, and frame loss in terms of both sanctioned and prohibited social formations. As many feminist commentators point out, although Lacan often conflates these two losses, there is nothing inevitable about their connection. There is nothing predetermined between the loss of being and the loss of the Oedipal mother. In short, the maternal does not have to make good on the alienating effects of language.[59]

Lacan's poststructuralist account of language opens up a space for rethinking the politics of kinship, the incest taboo, and (heterosexual) desire—indeed, it demands a poststructuralist account and accounting of kinship. Lacan's theories underscore a crucial point concerning the historically contingent nature of Lévi-Strauss's incest taboo and its politics of displacement. When the secondary loss of the Oedipal mother (Freud) is conflated with the primary loss of being (Lacan), a crucial slippage between structuralism and poststructuralism occurs. Instead of insisting on a poststructuralist account of language and kinship, which would refuse to privilege the Oedipal as inevitable or desirable, we come instead to reify Oedipal forms of family and kinship as an inexorable structural mandate and a foregone conclusion. In other words, we foreclose a poststructuralist reading of language and kinship, aligning the Oedipus complex instead with structuralist accounts of language and kinship. Judith Butler observes that when the study of kinship was combined with the study of structural linguistics, the "exchange of women [was] considered as the trafficking of a sign, the linguistic currency that [facilitated] a symbolic and communicative bond among men."[60] To recast these particular positions of kinship as symbolic is "precisely to posit them as preconditions of linguistic communicability and to suggest that these 'positions' bear an intractability that does not apply to contingent social norms." In this manner, structuralist accounts of kinship burden us with the legacy of Oedipus, a legacy establishing kinship as "always already heterosexual" and "certain forms of kinship as the only intelligible and livable ones."[61] Oedipus becomes the only way of being in the world.

The Story of the World

But Oedipus is not the only story of being in the world. Wong's film most certainly does not follow this anthropological and psychic script. The implicit privileging of the Oedipal through structuralist accounts of language and kinship obviates any critical understanding of the various ways by which loss might be symbolized through any number of possible desires, the various ways in which loss is already psychically lived today outside Oedipal spheres of family and kinship. *Happy Together* is one such poststructuralist account of family and kinship. Lai and Ho insist upon the historically contingent and variable forms that the incest taboo can take—indeed, has already taken—beyond the psychic boundaries of the Oedipal and the material boundaries of neoliberal governmentality and globalization.

Lai and Ho confound traditional Oedipal notions of kinship in their very rearticulation of its terms. So impossible is their relationship in its psychic fixity that, in the final analysis, we might say that Lai and Ho come to constitute their own incest taboo. The two do not displace away from a normative Oedipal scene of maternal loss and forfeiture as much as they must displace away from each other. We might say, in other words, that the incest taboo does not take shape through a privileged Oedipal scenario as much as it emerges from the two men themselves. From this perspective, Wong presents other pathways of displacement and desire by which one can psychically enter the world, other forms of "starting over" instituted through an alternative set of social and psychic exchanges.

The couple's loss of plenitude and displacement of desire gains its symbolic traction in relation to the ineffable sexual bliss that marks the extra-diegetic opening sequence of Wong's film. Eccentric to the main narrative of *Happy Together*, this Edenic moment, shot in black and white, concludes by dropping the couple unceremoniously into the main plot and predicament of the film, their interminable cycle of breaking up and starting over. This moment of excess and plenitude acquires its symbolic significance only retroactively through a queer (post)structure of feeling that marks the flesh and shapes their tango as a psychic trace of this impossible desire. Lai tells us in another voiceover: "Ho Po-wing always says 'Let's start over.' And it gets to me every time. We had been together for a while and had broken up often. But for some reason, whenever he says 'Let's start over,' I always find myself back with him. We left Hong Kong in order to start over. We hit the road and ended up here in Argentina."

A utopia of presence from which they are summarily thrown onto the highways and alleyways of Argentina, the opening sequence represents a fall from being they cannot ever recapture. While they re-experience this initial sacrifice through a series of interminable repetition compulsions—their tango, their sexual cleavings, their break-ups, and their startings-over—the two must finally enter the world by displacing away from each other and by symbolizing their loss finally in a different manner to that of the Oedipal. Lai begins this journey into the world through a displacement from Ho that not only marks a psychic clearing and new beginning for him, but also the end of Wong's film.

The triangulation of the couple's relationship by the young Chang (Chang Chen), a man who "sees" through his acute skills of hearing, marks another critical space of epistemological and ontological bearing. Imploring Lai to speak his unspeakable loss—his impossible desire for Ho—onto the magnetic tape of his voice recorder, Chang travels to Tierra del Fuego, carrying the burden of Lai's affective disenchantment. There, at the ends of the earth, Chang dispatches Lai's sorrow—his enigmatic sobs—into the world, thus providing another pathway, another set of psychic displacements and coordinates for his friend to start over.[62]

The psychic deadlock of Lai and Ho draws insistent attention to alternative configurations of the incest taboo outside the normative structures mandates of the Oedipal. Wong's film thus might be seen as a different type of coming out narrative: it is a coming out into the world, a "worlding," through other forms of psychic displacement. In this regard, Happy Together might also be considered as a coming apart of normative Oedipalized forms of family and kinship, as an interruption of the privileged social narrative of neoliberal globalization, exemplified by the gay Asian migrant-clone of queer liberalism, Wai-tung. Through its queer diasporas, Happy Together charts other ways of thinking about psychoanalysis and poststructuralism, a decolonized psychoanalysis attentive to alternative structures of family and kinship. Wong's film charts different psychic pathways into the light of subjectivity, into the "unexpected revelations of scenes of spring" designated by its Cantonese title, *Cheun Gwong Tsa Sit* (春光乍洩).

Lai's displacement and final separation from Ho marking the conclusion of *Happy Together* facilitates this "unexpected revelation," this emergence into the world, demonstrated by his obligation to surrender the one he first loved in order to make room in his psyche for other creatures and things. "The loss of our first love-object is always tragic," Kaja Silverman writes, "but it is the precondition for care. Only if we pay this exorbitant price early in our lives can things and other people 'matter' to us. Indeed, the case could be stated even more starkly: only because we are thrown into a kinship structure can there *be* a world."[63] Psychoanalysis has often acknowledged that normalization is invariably disrupted by that which cannot be fully disciplined by its regulatory norms. However, it has rarely addressed how new forms of family and kinship can and do invariably arise on the basis of the incest taboo.[64] The queer diaspora of Lai and Ho provides us with one such compelling disquisition.

The very end of *Happy Together* recounts Lai's attempt to return to Hong Kong and reconcile with his estranged father. Predictably enough, *Happy Together* does not end in Hong Kong with Lai's anticipated paternal reunion. The return to origins does not belong, finally, to this particular figure or to this particular place. Instead, *Happy Together* concludes in Taipei, with Lai in transit. On the night of Deng Xiaoping's death, and only five months before Hong Kong's return to Chinese sovereignty, Lai goes to the Taipei night market to search for Chang's family. This motley crew provides an alternative set of psychic coordinates for Lai to start over and move elsewhere.[65] That is, by affiliating with another man's filial unit, Lai and Wong Kar-wai suggest that the turn back to an original scene of loss and impossible desire is made possible only by this move forward, through an alternative structure of family and kinship, and through another time and space outside the prohibitions and mandates of blood descent. As Silverman reminds us, we are "not in the world merely by the virtue of being born in it." To the contrary, "we are only really in the world when it is in us—when we have made room within our psyches for it to dwell and expand. The preposition 'in' is thus in this case less spatial than affective."[66]

Into the World: "Unexpected Revelations of Scenes of Spring." From *Happy Together*.

The final image of *Happy Together* is shot from Lai's perspective on Taipei's new elevated railway system. In the neon glow of the bustling metropolis, and as the soundtrack "Happy Together" plays for the first and final time, the train hurtles forward, and the world moves into Lai as Lai moves into the world.

THREE

The Language of Kinship

⚫ ⚫ ⚫

TRANSNATIONAL ADOPTION AND

TWO MOTHERS IN *FIRST PERSON PLURAL*

Urban professionals want it all, including dogs and children, whether or not they have the time to care for them. Thus usual modes of handling household tasks often prove inadequate. We can call this type of household a "professional household without a 'wife'," regardless of whether its adult couple consists of a man and a woman, two men, or two women. A growing share of its domestic tasks are relocated to the market: they are bought directly as goods and services or indirectly through hired labor.

—SASKIA SASSEN, "Global Cities and Survival Circuits"

Two Mothers

Deann Borshay Liem's documentary on transnational adoption, *First Person Plural* (2000), recounts the filmmaker's 1966 adoption from a Korean orphanage by Alveen and Donald Borshay, a white American couple in Fremont, California, as well as her discovery of her birth mother in Kunsan, Korea, some twenty years later.[1] With the hopes of alleviating the clinical depression from which she has suffered since college, Borshay Liem decides that she must see her two families together, in one room, in the same physical space. And so she orchestrates an excruciating reunion between her American parents and her Korean family, a journey of recuperation and return to origins compelled as much by fantasy as by fact. Midway through *First Person Plural*, however, Borshay Liem halts her narrative of reunion to offer this painful disclosure. Looking straight into the camera lens, she bluntly admits: "There wasn't room in my mind for two mothers."

I begin the chapter with this statement of a *psychic* predicament: the dearth of space in Borshay Liem's psyche for two mothers. I start here because I am struck by the complicated ways by which female subjectivity and maternal blame become the site for the working out of a host of material and psychic contradictions associated with the practice of transnational adoption. A practice in which infants are entangled in transnational flows of human capital, transnational adoption is a post–World War II phenomenon associated with American liberalism, postwar prosperity, and Cold War politics. In the late twentieth century, it has proliferated alongside global consumer markets to become a popular and viable option not only for heterosexual but also, and increasingly, for homosexual couples and singles seeking to (re)consolidate conventional structures of family and kinship in the face of declining birthrates in the West.[2]

Through this contemporary emergence of new family and kinship relations, we come to recognize transnational adoption as one of the most privileged forms of diaspora in the late twentieth century. Yet the figure of the transnational adoptee has until very recently been noticeably absent in diaspora and immigration studies, in Asian and area studies, and in ethnic and queer studies.[3] This omission presents us with an interlocking set of critical questions: Is the transnational adoptee an immigrant? Is she, as in those cases such as Borshay Liem's, an Asian American? Even more, is her adoptive family Asian American? How is the otherness of the transnational adoptee absorbed into the intimate space of the family? How are histories of imperialism and globalization, as well as disparities of race, gender, class, and nation, managed or erased within the privatized sphere of the domestic?

Attempts to answer these questions often result in uncertainty and confusion, and such difficulties suggest that transnational adoption must be analyzed not only in terms of private dynamics of family and kinship relations, but also in regard to larger public histories of colonialism as well as contemporary practices of late capitalist exploitation and domination. Amy Kaplan, in the context of new Americanist studies on U.S. empire, argues that "imperialism as a political or economic process abroad is inseparable from the social relations and cultural discourses of race, gender, ethnicity, and class at home."[4] The vexing issues invoked by transnational adoption suggest that it might be usefully considered in relation to Kaplan's formulation. In this chapter, I explore transnational adoption as a paradigmatic late twentieth century phenomenon situated at the intersection of imperialist processes "over there" and social relations "over here." The chapter considers how late capitalist modes of flexible production and accumulation, in which the practice of transnational adoption must be situated, come to exemplify uneven access to the public sphere and participation in civil society, as well as unequal claims to privacy, intimacy, parenthood, family, and kinship. The chapter also examines how such problems shed light on seemingly contradictory processes of globalization in the face of (re)ascendant discourses of nationalism and the scaling back of civil rights and liberties in the U.S. nation-state.

It is crucial to investigate the material implications and effects of transnational adoption. It is equally important however, as Borshay Liem's maternal predicament suggests, to explore the psychic dimensions of the practice. While we have a small but growing body of scholarship today analyzing the political economy of transnational adoption, we lack a sustained analysis of its psychic range and limits. This chapter considers both the political and the psychic economies of transnational adoption. I first situate transnational adoption in the evolving politics of family and kinship relations in the late twentieth century. Through an analysis of a John Hancock commercial that depicts a white lesbian couple from the U.S. adopting a Chinese baby, I examine the historical conditions and contradictions of the practice that make new social formations of family and kinship thinkable. Ultimately, I argue that, as a contemporary example of the forgetting of race—and of the racialization of intimacy—transnational adoption must be linked to the increased outsourcing of not just domestic, but reproductive labor to the global South. The practice must also be indexed to the concomitant expansion of new forms of labor and value under the shadows of global capitalism. Finally, it must also be analyzed as a new form of passing in our putatively colorblind age. Unlike previous historical incarnations of passing that demand the concealment of racial (or sexual) difference—consider the case of Lattimore in *The Book of Salt*—here we witness not the suppression of difference, but the collective refusal to see difference in the face of it. In this regard, transnational adoption helps to mark the resurgence of an abstract individualism meant to shore up neoliberal claims to colorblindness in our multicultural and post-identity age.

In the second part of this chapter, I elaborate upon the psychic structures that support these new social formations and make them inhabitable and reproducible, or perhaps more accurately in Borshay Liem's recounting, unlivable and barren. Offering a theory of racial melancholia as well as a reading of Freud's essays on femininity and the negative Oedipus complex, I explore the language of kinship—the problem of Oedipal origins and destinations in regard to the psychic genealogy of Borshay Liem's maternal dilemma. As was discussed in the previous chapter, the language of kinship is saturated with, although by no means exhausted by, the mandates of the Oedipal. Like Lai and Ho in *Happy Together*, the figure of the transnational adoptee illuminates the ways in which loss and displacement is lived in relation to, alongside, or outside the Oedipus complex, insisting that we work not just within but finally beyond this privileged psychic structure. If *Happy Together* delineates the variable forms that the incest taboo and displacement has already taken, *First Person Plural* challenges us to imagine other pathways of affiliation, as well as other objects of desire, beyond the sanctioned parameters of the Oedipus complex. In short, Borshay Liem's film demands a poststructuralist reordering of psychoanalysis that could accommodate the possibility of two mothers.

The autobiographical experiences depicted in Borshay Liem's documentary represent a singular set of experiences that might at first seem exceptional to the heterogeneous experiences of different transnational adoptees and their families. Nevertheless, I hope that my analysis of *First Person Plural* will not only resonate with the social and psychological issues of these various groups, but also provide some new theoretical approaches to reframe and to broaden current discussions exploring this phenomenon, especially from the transnational adoptee's perspective.[5] At least since the National Association of Black Social Workers (NABSW) issued a position paper in 1972 advocating the adoption of black children only by black families, there has been a long-standing and contentious debate concerning the politics of transracial adoption and race matching. One the one hand, detractors describe the transracial (and asymmetrical) adoption of black children by white parents as "cultural genocide." On the other hand, advocates of the practice compare prohibitions against transracial adoption to anti-miscegenation laws embedded in a "legacy of white supremacy and Black separatism."[6] Yet, throughout all these debates, little collective attention has been paid either to the politics of race or to the psychic predicaments arising from transnational adoption of Asian children by white parents. While transnational adoption implicates some of our most deeply held values concerning family and kinship, as well as some of our most deeply held beliefs about community and belonging under liberalism, there remains a dearth of critical vocabulary to explore the juncture of private and public in the practice.

The adoption of a child, domestically or from abroad, is obviously a material and affective enterprise of great magnitude. In unpacking its political implications and psychic effects, I do not want to be construed as either an advocate or adversary of transnational adoption. Instead, the relentless moralizing that characterizes too much of our contemporary debates on the erosion of "family values"—of traditional white, middle-class parenthood, the nuclear family, and the psychological (that is, properly Oedipalized) development of the innocent child—must give way to a sustained discussion of both the ethics of multiculturalism in a colorblind age and the emergence of what I call the new global family. It is in this spirit that I offer a sustained analysis of transnational adoption's material contours and affective crossings; for without such examination, we will have few ways to understand, and few therapeutic resources to alleviate, the psychic pain associated with Borshay Liem's striking—indeed, heartbreaking—confession. How might the transnational adoptee come to have psychic space for two mothers? And what, in turn, would such an expansion of the psyche mean for the sociopolitical domain of contemporary family and kinship relations and the politics of queer diaspora?

Two (White) Lesbians and a (Chinese) Baby

In the past decade, a distinct theoretical vocabulary has arisen in the fields of Asian and Asian American studies to describe transnational shifts, on the side of both capital and labor, in conventional orderings of family and kinship. The late twentieth century has witnessed the increasing proliferation of cheap and flexible Asian migrant labor across the globe—in the form of free trade zones, global sweatshops, and human trafficking—as well as the concomitant expansion of Asian immigration into spheres of transnational and global capitalism. Mail order brides, domestic servants, comfort women, and sex workers are some of the more significant terms in a global economy associated with the exploitation of Third World women in an ever-increasing international gendered division of labor supporting First World middle-class families in the global North. In contrast, satellite people, parachute kids, reverse settlers, and flexible citizenship are some of the more prevalent concepts connected to the rise of a distinct Asian transnational capitalist and managerial class. How do we situate another emergent term—the transnational adoptee—in relation to these social constellations of exploitation and privilege? On which side—capital or labor—does the adoptee fall? Indeed, how does the adoptee's presence complicate such binaries? Finally, what would be at stake if we began to rethink the political economy of contemporary global migration through expanded notions of labor and value and by rendering visible the *affective* labor that accompanies the gendered movement of bodies from the global South to the global North?

All these questions must be considered in the context of the historical emergence of queer liberalism outlined in chapter one of this book. That is, to the extent that U.S. gay and lesbian citizen-subjects are no longer eccentric to conventional structures of family and kinship because of their ongoing participation in the transnational adoption market, queer liberalism and the politics of queer diaspora assume a critical significance in relation to one another. The crossing of queerness and diaspora—of sexual and racial formation in the global system and the domestic landscape of the U.S. nation-state—is especially vivid in the adoption of Chinese infant girls by Western couples and singles. A John Hancock commercial aired on network television in 2000 illustrates the social and political stakes of such a queer diaspora. First broadcast during the U.S. women's gymnastics championships, then re-edited for the Olympics and World Series, the commercial depicts a white American lesbian couple at a major U.S. airport with their newly arrived Chinese baby girl.[7] Interspersed between shots of busy white immigration officers, a close-up of the U.S. flag, and throngs of anonymous Asian faces restlessly waiting to gain entry into the country, we spy the couple with their nameless infant waiting patiently in line. The commercial then moves to a close-up of the trio.

"This is your new home," whispers the dark-haired lesbian as she rocks the sleeping infant. "Don't tell her that; she's going to want to go back," the other, a gangly blonde, jokes. "Hi, baby," the blonde says, as her partner asks, "Do you have her papers?" "Yeah, they're in the diaper bag," she responds. As the scene cuts away to a black screen, on which the words "Mutual Funds, Annuities, Life Insurance, Long Term Care

Insurance" appear, the dark-haired lesbian is heard in a voice-over stating, "Can you believe this? We're a family." The commercial cuts to her placing a tender kiss on the baby girl's head, as a second black screen appears with the words, "Insurance for the unexpected / Investments for the opportunities." A third black screen with the John Hancock logo comes into view as we hear a final off-screen exchange between the couple: "You're going to make a great mom." "So are you."

Given the long U.S. history of Chinese immigration exclusion along with bars to naturalization and citizenship, and given highly controversial public outcries and legal challenges to gay and lesbian parenting and same-sex marriage, we must pause to wonder exactly what John Hancock, one of the world's largest financial services companies, is seeking to insure. How does this depiction of transnational adoption and circuits of (human) exchange not only resignify past and present histories of exploited Asian immigrant labor but also situate the adoption of Chinese baby girls by an emerging consumer niche group—white lesbians with capital—as one of the late twentieth century's most privileged forms of immigration?

The John Hancock commercial suggests that, through her adoption and crossing over an invisible national boundary, a needy Chinese object is miraculously transformed into an individuated and treasured U.S. subject, one worthy of investment—that is, economic protection (capital accumulation), political rights (citizenship), and social recognition (family). In the face of immediate right-wing outrage at the commercial, a John Hancock spokesman, defending the company's advertisement, stated that "however a child comes into a family, that child is entitled to financial protection, and John Hancock can help."[8] As such, we need to consider how the rhetoric of financial protection functions as moral justification for increased access to (legal) rights and recognition precisely through the ever-greater accumulation of (economic) property. Indeed, the John Hancock commercial suggests that family is not only whom you choose but also on whom you choose to spend your capital, illustrating another instance of the global restructuring of capitalism and family.

Here, the emergence of queer family and kinship depends on the faithful reproduction of the heteronormative conjugal family, as well as acquiescence to the rationalization of the market and the logic of capital under which it functions. Under this logic, property and rights are conflated as something for particular lesbian and gay populations to enjoy, including at this juncture child and family, parenthood and pri-

Busy Immigration Officers.
From "Immigration,"
John Hancock Financial
Services advertisement,
directed by Hill Holiday.

Entering the U.S.
From "Immigration."

The "Yellow Horde."
From "Immigration."

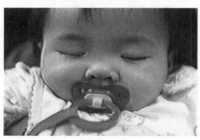

The Nameless Baby.
From "Immigration."

The Family Trio:
Two (white) Lesbians
and a (Chinese) Baby.
From "Immigration."

vacy, and citizenship and national belonging as possessions to be protected and insured. As I discussed in chapter one, the historical emergence of queer liberalism is marked precisely by the ways in which privacy and intimacy underwriting queer family and kinship become racialized property rights unequally distributed among gay and lesbian populations.[9] While property creates new queer subjects for representation, it simultaneously reinforces traditional liberal divides between public and private, between whiteness and otherness. As such, these (white) lesbians with capital are positioned as the idealized inhabitants of an increasingly acceptable and assimilated same-sex version of the heteronormative nuclear family, one in which "financial protection" is inextricably bound together with political citizenship and (a racialized) social belonging as the prerequisites for queer family and kinship.

Anthropologist Ann Anagnost suggests that, for white, middle-class subjects in the era of global capitalism, the position of parent has become increasingly a measure of value, self-worth, and "completion."[10] Indeed, I would suggest that the possession of a child, whether biological or adopted, has today become the sign of guarantee both for family and for full and robust citizenship, for being a fully realized political, economic, and social subject in American life: "Can you believe this? We're a family." The desire for parenthood as economic entitlement and legal right—transnational adoption requiring immigration visas, along with the termination and transfer of parental rights for naturalization and citizenship—not only by heterosexuals but also, and increasingly, by homosexuals seems to stem in large part from an unexamined belief in the traditional ideals of the nuclear family as the primary contemporary measure of social respectability and value. This enjoyment of rights is, of course, ghosted by those queer and diasporic subjects—unacknowledged lovers, illegal immigrants, indentured laborers, infants left behind—consigned to outcast status and confined to the margins of globalization. Like Bình, Lai, and Ho, they have attenuated—and often no—legal claims to family, home, citizenship, or nation.

Legally, U.S. citizenship is granted on the basis of birthplace (*jus solis*) or descent (*jus sanguinis*), deriving from parent to child. (U.S. citizenship is, of course, also possible through the third method of naturalization.) What does it mean that, in our present age, full and robust citizenship is *socially* effected from child to parent and, in many cases, through the position of the transnational adoptee, her visible possession and spectacular display? In this regard, what does it mean to ask, consciously or unconsciously, that the transnational adoptee operate as a guarantee for her parents' access to full social recognition and rights to participation in the public sphere and civil society? Indeed, given the long history of Asian immigration exclusion in the U.S. and elsewhere in the West, how is it possible that this Chinese baby girl could effect such a remarkable transformation? The John Hancock commercial illustrates how capitalism colonizes sentiment around idealized notions of family and kinship in order to sell its financial products and services to newly emergent queer, global families. We must wonder, along with Anagnost, how the figure of the child can function "so relentlessly in U.S. political rhetoric as emblematizing the current state of emergency, even as public support for the needs of children is rapidly eroding?"[11] From this perspective, we need to consider in what ways this version of the queer family and kinship might be poststructuralist and, ultimately, to what political ends.

The baby's need for entry papers ("Do you have her papers?" "Yeah, they're in the diaper bag"), insists that we consider the transnational adoptee an immigrant, thus realigning her with the anonymous Asian crowds from which she is individuated, an individuation that emerges from the dross of the diaper bag. At the same time, this transformation insists on the possibility that the transnational adoptee is a form of embodied (though spectralized) value, a special kind of property straddling both subjecthood and objecthood, both capital and labor. Her movement across invisible national boundaries, East to West and South to North, places the transnational adoptee in a queer diaspora, on the threshold of a tenuous subjectivity continually threatening to undo itself, to unmask the history of its commodification (a point to which I will return below).

If the adoptee's miraculous political, economic, and social transformation obscures the commodification of baby girls as a gendered form of embodied value, bought and sold in the global marketplace, what cultural alibis about Chinese otherness and gender abuse must be produced so as to efface the history of these transactions? How do generalized narratives of salvation—from poverty, disease, and the barbarism of the third world—often attached to narratives of transnational adoption, displace global and local histories of colonialism, military intervention, capitalist exploitation, racism, and gender subordination? In this particular crossing of queerness and diaspora, what kind of global and local histories must be managed and erased?

The movement of the transnational adoptee from "over there" to "over here," and from public charge to private family, individuates her while simultaneously working to encrypt colonial histories in the domestic space of intimate family and kinship relations. Through this occlusion, the public and political are contracted into the domain of private life, and this contraction makes more collective forms of political analysis and activism seem untenable or extreme. This sphere is what Lauren Berlant, analyzing the conservative regulation of family values, heteronormativity, and good citizenship during the Reagan-Thatcher era, has labeled the "intimate public sphere."[12] Significantly, as Borshay Liem's documentary underscores, global and domestic histories of empire and race contracted into the intimate public sphere of the reconstituted white heteronormative nuclear family are often psychically displaced. They re-emerge in psychic life, symptomized by the dilemma of two mothers.

Labor and Value in a Global Age

Before turning to my discussion of two mothers in *First Person Plural*, I would like to consider what kind of effaced histories of colonialism and forgotten histories of race might be recalled in the practice of transnational adoption in order to analyze more fully its global and domestic implications. The following brief historical sketch is crucial to link transnational adoption not just to humanitarian or religious narratives of love, altruism, salvation, and redemption, but also to specific histories of colonialism, capitalist exploitation, immigration exclusion, racism, and gender domination.

Transnational adoption has a long genealogy in the United States, which is embedded in the politics of race and in nationalist anxieties concerning slavery, manifest destiny, miscegenation, segregation, and integration. This history ranges from the forcible removal of children from Native American reservations and their placement in Indian schools, to the more recent boat lifts and air lifts of Cuban and Vietnamese "orphans" after the rise of Fidel Castro's revolutionary government (1960–1962) and the fall of Saigon (1975). Linda Gordon's *The Great Arizona Orphan Abduction*, to examine one brief example, chronicles early twentieth century Catholic Charities' placing of Irish orphans from the New York Foundling Hospital with Mexican mineworker families in Clifton and Morenci, Arizona Territory.[13] In October 1904, over the course of four days, white vigilante squads bearing arms and determined to save a group of forty of these orphans from the dark-skinned and "dirty" Mexicans forcibly kidnapped them, redistributing the children to Anglo families. The events sparked a series of legal battles among which was the filing of a civil suit in the Arizona Territorial Supreme Court by the New York Foundling Hospital, in an attempt to regain custody of the children. The Hospital lost its suit and ultimately appealed to the U.S. Supreme Court, which refused to consider the case. From one perspective, the case could be considered a telling legal decision about the historical color-coding of the borderlands. It helped to consolidate notions of whiteness and respectability in the early-twentieth century U.S. through what we might describe as an early instance of transnational adoption and the vexed production of Mexican racial otherness.

While Gordon folds her account into a longer domestic history of U.S. race relations, Ann Laura Stoler points to colonial histories of adoption practices in relation to the production of white respectability and discourses of civilization. As increased numbers of illegitimate children of mixed parentage populated gray zones along colonial divides, adoption became ever more critical. In India and Indochina, as well as the Netherlands, public welfare, assistance, and orphanages, Stoler writes, were "designed not only to keep fair skinned children from running barefooted in native villages but to ensure that the proliferation of European pauper settlements was curtailed and controlled."[14] Taken together, both Gordon's and Stoler's scholarship provide a historical backdrop for an account of the contemporary emergence of transnational adoption from Asia, tracing its genealogy to the immediate aftermath of World War II.

A humanitarian response by a prospering North America to a wartorn Europe, transnational adoption found its original post-war incarnation in the emigration of European orphans from Germany and Poland to the U.S. It was only after the Korean War (1950–1953), however, and under the shadow of Cold War politics, that the largest wave of transnational adoptions was to take place. Since then, South Korea, with the assistance of Western religious and social service agencies, has expedited the adoption of over 200,000 South Korean children, approximately 150,000 of whom are now residing in the United States and 50,000 of whom are currently living in Western Europe, Canada, and Australia. Until 1991, South Korean children constituted the largest number of transnational adoptees to enter the United States on an annual basis, with South Korea now having the longest continuous foreign adoption program in the world.[15] Transnational adoptions from South Korea have been followed by adoptions from other Asian countries (such as Vietnam, Cambodia, and China) in which the U.S. has had either a notable military presence or strong political and economic interests, or both. In 2006, out of a total of 20,679 orphans coming into the U.S., China (6,493), Guatemala (4,135), Russia (3,706), and South Korea (1,376) ranked highest in U.S. transnational adoptions.[16]

Scholars in postcolonial and transnational feminism link the historical emergence of war brides, mail-order brides, comfort women, and sex workers to foundations of military prostitution and the commodification of Third World female bodies for First World male consumption and pleasure.[17] From this perspective, these phenomena make explicit what is often only implicit or absent in traditional analyses of transnational adoption, the majority of adoptees being baby girls. Parents adopting infants in China are expected to make a cash contribution of between U.S. $3,000 and $4,000 to the orphanage from which the child is selected. These costs are now partially underwritten by many private corporations as well as by the U.S. Government. In 2002, the tax credit for expenses relating to adoption increased from $5,000 to $10,000.[18]

While many feminists have been reluctant to associate the "purchase" of a wife with the "heroic" act of saving a (female) child, transnational adoptions occur predominantly in areas where not only women but also nations themselves cannot care for their own children. Numerous national and international declarations on the rights of children demand that poverty alone should not justify the loss of parental authority.[19] Legal scholar Twila L. Perry asks us: "Could it be argued that, rather than transferring the children of the poor to economically better-off people in other countries, there should be a transfer of wealth from rich countries to poor ones to enable the mothers of poor children to continue to take care of their children themselves?"[20] Dissociating transnational adoption from the historical and economic legacy of war brides, mail-order brides, comfort women, and sex workers thus obscures an understanding of this practice as one of the more recent embodiments of gendered commodification; it is an enduring symptom of an increasing international gendered division of labor, emerging under the shadows of colonialism and now sustained through the practices of global capitalism.

We might approach this question of gendered commodification from another angle, from the perspective of international human rights discourse. As Leti Volpp observes, the post-war discourse of human rights has lately emerged as a technique deployed to measure the progress of states, becoming both the normative language of how injustice is measured and a means through which powerful nation-states might discipline weaker ones. This disciplining, Volpp observes, "often relies on a relation posed between gendered violence and human rights violations, whereby the denial of women's human rights represents the pathological cultures of repressive states."[21] By configuring women as symbols of so-called rogue nation-states, women, women's rights, and violence against women lose their specificity, becoming part of a larger political discourse concerning international relations, sovereignty, global governance, and hegemony: witness, for instance, both President George W. Bush's and Laura Bush's justification of American military intervention in Afghanistan on the grounds of, among other things, the need to liberate Afghan women from the oppressive Taliban regime once supported by the U.S. Government.

While the figure of sexually violated third-world women with little agency—and even more graphically the innocent third-world child sold into sexual bondage—serves as the paradigmatic victim of human rights abuse, it is crucial to underscore that the figure of the third-world woman is ascribed agency precisely at the moment she "freely" relinquishes her child into the global system (or alternately "chooses" to abandon her).[22] Susan Coutin, Bill Maurer, and Barbara Yngvesson note how the language of choice and free will, as well as the rhetoric of donation and gift, animate the discourse of transnational adoption, often serving to cover up and cover over the inexorable disparities in a global system of gendered commodification and exchange that cannot be equalized. As the authors point out, choice is "part of the morality tale that animates Western stories of self and of nation."[23] And nowhere is the rhetoric of choice more important than in the intimate realm of family and kinship relations.

Thus, one might examine how such rhetoric works to conceal the ways in which the reproductive labor costs of the global North are now being increasingly outsourced to third-world women in the global South. In the 1990s, more specifically, harsh immigration laws and restrictions targeting illegal immigration—along with state initiatives such as California's infamous 1994 Proposition 187—sought, among other things, to outsource the reproductive labor costs of the working class. In our contemporary moment, however, it is the reproductive labor costs of the managerial class that are being increasingly outsourced to the global South, as well as being reconfigured through advanced reproductive technologies such as artificial insemination, in vitro fertilization, and surrogacy.[24] These costs are increasingly borne by the subaltern figure of the Third World birth mother, who cannot speak.[25]

Shifting perspectives to the field of Asian American studies, we might consider how transnational adoption from Asia fits both within a gendered postwar pattern of privileged immigration—war brides, mail-order brides, transnational adoptees—and within nineteenth-century histories of anti-Asian immigration, including bars to naturalization and citizenship. The period from 1882 to 1943 is often cited as the official years of Asian exclusion. However, the Page Law of 1875, largely banning female immigration from China to the United States, might be a more appropriate historical date to mark the *gendered* form in which racialized exclusion of Asian immigrants from the U.S. nation-state took place.[26] In this regard, the privileged migration of Chinese baby girls today marks not only a striking reversal of this gendered history of racialized exclusion but also an emergent form of Asian American subjectivity, with considerable implications for Asian American studies, community, and politics. Indeed, it suggests how the transnational adoptee might be considered a proper subject of Asian America, while demanding an epistemological consideration of Asian American identity not reliant on an assumed (blood-line) kinship or a naturalized story of immigration, assimilation, and settlement.

How do we account for this resignification of the gendered history of the Page Law: through the contemporary phenomenon of transnational adoption? How might we rethink conventional paradigms in the field relating to racial domination, gender subordination, and the exploitation of labor? The historical period from the late nineteenth century to World War II—the era of the Asian exclusion and Yellow Peril—is one during which a rapidly industrializing U.S. nation-state produced cheap and flexible labor both through the creation of the illegal (Asian) immigrant outside the rights and privileges of citizenship, and through exclusion laws meant to isolate these communities within their ethnic enclaves and curtail their accumulation of capital.[27] If the transnational adoptee can be described as an Asian American immigrant, but one whose embodied value remains hidden, then we need to rethink questions of labor and value in our contemporary political economy. What kind of work is the transnational adoptee performing for the family and the nation?

Here, in order to investigate how the transnational can supplement histories of race and racial formation in the construction of U.S. domesticity, we yet again need to shift our historical approach. Due to declining birth rates in the postwar period, greater access to abortion and reliable methods of contraception, and an easing of the stigma against women bearing children outside of marriage, fewer white children are now available for domestic adoption.[28] As a result, white parents who are reluctant or unwilling to adopt black children domestically (or fearful of child custody battles with birth mothers), have turned increasingly to transnational adoption as an alternative source for the (re)consolidation of family and kinship.[29] From this angle, the Asian transnational adoptee serves to triangulate the domestic landscape of black-white race relations. Indeed, she might be described as performing a type of crucial ideological labor: that of shoring up of an idealized notion of family and kinship, of making good the white heteronormative nuclear family that might otherwise be unavailable or difficult to attain via the domestic adoption market.

Hence, transnational adoption need not be understood as historically disparate from the pre-WWII period of Asian *alien* and Asian exclusion, with its bars to naturalization and citizenship. In the postwar period of the Asian American *citizen*, the practice of transnational adoption expands traditional accounts of the exploitation of wage labor into areas of consumer capitalism meant to effect a different type of labor power and value. We might describe this form of labor power not as productive labor, in the traditional Marxian sense, but as consumptive labor. Miranda Joseph argues that consumptive labor "is productive, but it is organized very differently from productive labor: it is not organized, procured, or exploited as wage labor."[30] Instead, as Joseph observes, in the shift to global capitalism and its modes of flexible production and accumulation, consumptive labor serves to produce and to organize social community as a supplement to capital.

In slightly different terms, we might say that this phenomenon forces us to recognize new forms of labor and value in a global age. That is, the consumption of the transnational adoptee by parents in the global North completes the ideal of newly emergent multicultural families as a supplement to capital precisely through the exploitation of the child's affective, rather than wage, labor. In other words, while Third World women from the global South have traditionally been exploited for their wage labor in the manufacturing sector, their emotional labor and care work in the domestic sphere, and now their reproductive labor as birth mothers, the exploitation of the transnational adoptee is largely an emotional affair. She helps to consolidate the *affective* boundaries of the white, heteronormative middle-class nuclear family. From this per-spective we might shift the dominant discourse in U.S. exceptionalism of the immigrant as someone who desires America to consider how the U.S. nation-state, as Siobhan Somerville writes, "selects its own objects of desire and produces them as citizens."[31]

Scholars in transnational feminist studies have noted that, in the context of domestic care in the middle-class family household, affective labor (whether coming from white wives or from hired help) is not recognized as work, since the commodification of love and concern falls somewhere between family and work, private and public, but often is regarded as neither one nor the other. These proliferating forms of labor and value become extremely difficult to quantify or to qualify, and are the source of debate for evolving notions of property (see Introduction). The practice of transnational adoption reconfigures this discussion by focusing on the figure of the child as another source of hidden labor and value. As Viviana Zelizer notes, the moment that children are no longer of value in the traditional labor market, they paradoxically become both "priceless" and "commodified."[32] In this regard, the transnational adoptee becomes emblematic of both gift and goods as she moves from East to West, and from the space of public orphanage to the domain of private family. Shifting our attention from the exchange of women in Lévi-Strauss's elementary structures of kinship as that supreme gift creating both kinship and social alliances, transnational adoption posits the exchange of children not as a reciprocal process for the creation and expansion of social relations, but as an extremely one-sided affair in which the rhetoric of gift and the appropriation of the commodity overshadow the consolidation of the privileged middle-class family.[33]

Hence, in the context of transnational adoption, consumptive labor is racialized, producing and shoring up the social and psychic bound-aries of the white heteronormative nuclear family in the global North, guaranteeing its affective integrity through the child's completion of its sanctioned ideals. Under the mandates of this affective imperative, we need to consider how transnational adoption might underwrite powerful regimes of racial, sexual, and economic containment. In constructing a cultural identity for their adoptee, for instance, how do parents utilize discourses of both multiculturalism and colorblindness to absorb racial difference into the intimate space of the family? How are ideals of abstract individualism being invoked to manage, aestheticize, reinscribe, and finally deracinate culture of all meaningful difference?

The practice of transnational adoption suggests that Asian baby girls are, more easily than black children, folded into the imagined community of the white heteronormative middle-class nuclear family. And this folding in, effacing its forgotten racial history, marks the emergence of a new politics of passing in our colorblind age, one demanding analysis of the "colorblindness" of labor, one insisting upon a consideration of new forms of labor and value in regard to family, kinship, and the racialization of intimacy in our global age. All the more then, we need to consider how the stereotype of the hard-working, agreeable, and passive Asian girl, ever eager to please, works to smooth over political problems, economic disparities, and cultural differences.[34] How is racial difference absorbed into a larger narrative of neoliberal multiculturalism, which is based on the rhetoric of choice, the ideal of abstract individualism, and the premise of race constantly appearing as disappearing?

These problems demand a deconstructive rereading of the Asian American model minority myth, one whose genealogy is said to date both from the Cold War necessity to produce good (anti-Communist) Asian subjects, and to the reformation of the 1965 Immigration and Nationality Act, with its subsequent initiation of a professional brain drain from Asia. How do war brides, mail-order brides, comfort women, sex workers, and transnational adoptees collectively challenge, broaden, and reorient traditional accounts of the transformation of Asian alien into Asian American citizen? Juxtaposing this gendered history of Asian immigration, as well as comparative white-black-Asian race relations, to the discourse of model minority illustrates how global histories of gendered commodification do, in fact, affect and effect domestic genealogies of race, racialization, citizenship, and belonging. It draws attention the spectralized value of the transnational adoptee, marking a contemporary crossing of flexible accumulation with the global production of new racialized communities—newly emergent global families— constituted precisely through the politics of colorblindness and the racialization of intimacy. Such a politics is not focused on social justice, material redistribution, or substantive equality but on economic privilege, competition in the free market, and the privatization of family and kinship as political right and entitlement. In this current state of emergency, what are the psychic costs and burdens of these significant contradictions? What is the psychic scaffolding that makes transnational adoption an inhabitable or uninhabitable condition of existence? How can the psychic life of race and colorblindness be described? Let us return to the psychic dilemma of two mothers.

Psychic Diasporas

For the transnational adoptee, where does history begin?

In the opening minutes of *First Person Plural*, we are given several conflicting answers to this question. The filmmaker presents a complex montage sequence that combines family photographs, her adoptive father's home movies, which include scenes of Borshay Liem's arrival at the San Francisco airport on March 3, 1966, and her own footage, shot thirty years later, of her American parents and siblings watching these home movies and recalling their feelings about her arrival. The sequence begins with Denise, Borshay Liem's sister, explaining the excitement of getting a sister, "someone to play with," as she puts it. "I remember getting my hair done to go pick you up at the airport, and I was really jazzed about that," she tells us, an image of her younger self in front of the bathroom mirror flashing up before us. But despite her excitement about picking up Cha Jung Hee, her new little sister from Korea, Denise's investment in feminine self-display reflects a narcissistic logic that underlies the Borshay family's initial encounter with their eight-year-old adoptee. Unlike Binh and Lattimore's asymmetrical reflection in the mirror stage of Stein's salon, this mirror stage of the Borshay family is capable of reflecting only upon itself, capable of entertaining only its own wishes and desires. With a chortle, Denise readily admits: "I think mother went up to the wrong person. Yeah, I think we didn't know until we checked your name tag or something who told us who you were. It didn't matter. I mean one of them was ours."

Here, the language of ownership and possession, along with the assumed exchangeability of the variously tagged adoptees disembarking from the plane, constitutes a clear violation of the exclusive bond thought to exist between mother and child, a bond thought to exist outside the logic of the market.[35] This violation opens immediately upon the terrain of an unacknowledged commodification. Significantly,

"Mirror, mirror on the wall." From *First Person Plural*, directed by Deann Borshay Liem.

Deann's "acquisition" by the Borshay family is accompanied by the simultaneous erasure of Cha Jung Hee's Korean identity and past through the dismissal of her prior family and history. "You know, to us an orphanage meant that you had no family," the adoptive white mother Alveen Borshay later explains. "This way you were going to have a family." Suggesting that Borshay Liem's history only begins with her entry into their particular family unit, Denise concludes: "From the moment you came here, you were my sister and we were your family and that was it. And even though we look different—different nationality or whatever—we were your family."

Echoing Alveen's and Denise's sentiments, Donald Borshay's account of that fateful day is remarkably similar. Although the father recalls a momentary emotional wrinkle after Borshay Liem's initial arrival, this problem is quickly smoothed out through its concerted repression and willing away: "I remember very clearly your first meal," Donald recalls. "Mother prepared something that was very nice. And we were sitting at the table and you just kind of dropped your head and the tears started to come down. No words were spoken. Mother could see what was happening, and she simply took you away from the table and you were excused and from then on it was perfect."

"From then on it was perfect." I have spent some time detailing the various recollections of the "from then on" moment of Borshay Liem's arrival in the United States. I do so because these comments collectively illustrate the ways in which Borshay Liem is commodified as an object to be enjoyed while, in the same breath, her Korean past is effaced and denied, a forgotten history repressed and passed over. In Denise's, Alveen's, and Donald's recollections, history proper begins only at the moment of Borshay Liem's arrival "over here," the privatized language of family and kinship working to overwrite histories of militarization and suffering as well as the particularities of Cha Jung Hee's past in Korea.

Alveen admits quite forthrightly that her initial desire to adopt Deann stemmed from watching Gary Moore commercials on NBC television. These advertisements, depicting the plight of Korean War orphans, outlined the "Foster Parents Plan," to which Alveen cathects as a substitute for the church from which the family has become estranged. "Daddy had gone into real estate and was doing really well," Alveen recounts, "and I said we should do something for somebody because life has been really good for us, and I watched the TV and Gary Moore came on." One cannot describe Alveen's attachment to Cha Jung Hee, the foster child Donald and she initially sponsor from afar, as anything but sincere and enthusiastic (albeit unreflective) American liberalism. Still, this narrative of liberal benevolence cannot be easily reconciled with Borshay Liem's painful past. Public histories of colonialism, civil war, social conflict, and abject poverty in Korea cannot be easily connected to the domestic sphere of the prosperous American home.

Moreover, while there is no such thing as a motherless child, the opening sequence of *First Person Plural* highlights the management of Borshay Liem's past history through the vicissitudes of nomination, through the problem of her proper name. Sent to the United States at eight years old, Borshay Liem has a series of proper names and identities that are erased through her multiple exchanges. "My Name is Kang Ok Jin," Borshay Liem begins in the opening lines of *First Person Plural*. As her face flashes onto the screen and fades into an eerie solarized silhouette, she continues: "I was born on 14 June, 1957. I feel like I've been several different people in one life. My name is Cha Jung Hee. I was born on 5 November 1956. I've had three names, three different sets of histories. My name is Deann Borshay. I was born 3 March 1966, the moment I stepped off the airplane in San Francisco. I've spoken different languages, and I've had different families." First "Kang Ok Jin" and then deliberately substituted for another child, "Cha Jung Hee," by the Korean adoption agency, "Deann Borshay" is finally born on 3 March 1966, not by her Korean birth mother, but by her arrival on the San Francisco Jetway. Ultimately, through the animating desires and projections of her American family, she enters what they consider to be her history proper. Indeed, to the extent that adoptees are born *legally* at the moment of the transfer of parental rights from the (absent) birth mother to adoptive parents—with the rewriting of the adoptee's birth certificate to reflect this exchange and new family genealogy—there is no maternal origin to which they can return. As far as the law is concerned, the birth mother and "back there" no longer exist.

It is important to note that the repression of Borshay Liem's past is carried out not only as a collective family project but also, and more importantly, through the *strict management of the adoptee's affect*. That is, the contraction of Korean history into the privatized boundaries of the white American family is finessed through the management and control of Borshay Liem's emotional life. The silent tears that mark her traumatic arrival and the negation of her past is a language of affect—a feeling of kinship—that cannot have symbolic life or recognition. These

Three Names, Three Histories. From *First Person Plural*.

tears must necessarily be refused, as Donald Borshay does indeed first deny and then excuse them, such that Borshay Liem has little psychic recourse to work through her considerable losses.[36]

How might we begin to analyze Borshay Liem's affective losses? A number of years ago, in response to a series of Asian American student suicides at the university where I was teaching at the time, I co-wrote with Shinhee Han an essay entitled "A Dialogue on Racial Melancholia."[37] In this article, we analyze Freud's theories of mourning and melancholia as presenting a compelling framework to conceptualize registers of loss and depression attendant to the conflicts and struggles associated with immigration, assimilation, and racialization for Asian Americans. As described by Freud, melancholia—in contrast to his concept of normal mourning, where libido is eventually withdrawn from a lost object to be invested elsewhere—is a pathological mourning without end. As Freud's privileged theory of unresolved grief, melancholia delineates a psychic condition whereby certain losses cannot be avowed and, hence, cannot be properly mourned. In our argument, racial melancholia describes both social and psychic structures of loss emerging from Asian immigrant experiences that can be worked through only with considerable pain and difficulty.

Here it is important to emphasize that the immigration process is based on a structure of loss. In "Mourning and Melancholia," Freud describes the lost object as embodying a person, place, or ideal. When one leaves a country of origin, voluntarily or involuntarily (as in the case of transnational adoptees), a host of losses both concrete and abstract must be mourned. To the extent that lost ideals of Asianness—including homeland, family, language, property, identity, custom, status—are irrecoverable, immigration, assimilation, and racialization are placed within a melancholic framework, a psychic state of suspension between "over there" and "over here." In Freud's theory of mourning, one works through and finds closure to these losses by investing in new objects and ideals—in the American dream, for example.

However, to the extent that Asian Americans are perpetually consigned to foreigner status and continue to be considered eccentric to the U.S. nation-state, and to the extent that ideals and standards of whiteness remain unattainable for them, it might be said that Asian Americans are denied the capacity to invest in new people, places, and ideals. This inability to invest in new objects is a crucial part of Freud's definition of melancholia. Racial melancholia thus describes a psychic condition by which vexed identification and affiliations with lost objects, places, and ideals of Asianness, as well as whiteness, remain estranged and unresolved.

In *First Person Plural*, we witness the numerous ways in which Borshay Liem's past is repressed, the continuous ways in which her racial difference and past history are managed, denied, and forgotten, so that she cannot mourn what she has lost in Korea. Furthermore, the documentary portrays Borshay Liem's frustrating and impossible identifications with ideals of whiteness that remain perpetually elusive. Speaking about her vain attempts to mimic the "American ways" of her siblings, Denise and Duncan, Borshay Liem presents us with a series of home movies documenting her tortured development into adolescence: Deann sitting amidst her white dolls; Deann dressed up like a Korean doll; Deann the prom queen; Deann with her towering white high school boyfriend; Deann as a perky college cheerleader.

In an especially harrowing episode recounted by her mother, a young Borshay Liem is shown in a home movie combing the very blond hair of a doll. In a disturbing voice-over commentary that could easily be described as an Asian version of Toni Morrison's *The Bluest Eye*, Alveen tells Borshay Liem, "You said, 'Mother, my ears always stick out. I hate that.' I said, 'Honey, that can be fixed if you want,' and you wanted." At this point, Donald Borshay chimes in, "So we went to the plastic surgeon in San Jose . . . and when they went to take the bandages off, then you began to cry." Again, the family is faced with an overflow of tears— an overflow of affect—that is met with bafflement and thus remains outside the parameters of symbolic inscription.

Throughout the documentary, we witness in everyday acts, gestures, and offhand comments by her entire family, the active production of Borshay Liem's Korean otherness, accompanied by its simultaneous reinscription and containment, a whitewashing and effacing of this difference through what I have been calling the racialization of intimacy. In the opening minutes of Borshay Liem's documentary, her brother Duncan, in what can be described only as a simultaneous tone of self-congratulation and discomfort, tells her: "You didn't come from my mommy's womb. You don't have the family eyes, but you've got the family smile. Color and look doesn't make any difference. It's who you are. You're my sister." And in response to Deann's admission to Denise that "I always thought you had the perfect eyes. It was always frustrating because I couldn't get my eyelashes to look like yours," the latter immediately retorts: "People would see us or whatever and they'd say 'Is that your sister? You guys look just alike.'"

Duncan's and Denise's statements collectively underwrite the tenets of an emergent multiculturalism under neoliberalism—the acknowledgment and dismissal of difference—that provides a contemporary twist to what Homi Bhabha earlier described as the irreducible failure of mimicry: *"Almost the same, but not quite . . . Almost the same but not white."*[38] This imperative to conform—what Deann describes as the impulse to "create a collage of things and [make] myself over to fit all the little things I had seen"—implicates Deann's desire to blend in as well as her siblings' simultaneous acknowledgement and refusal of such efforts. This dynamic underscores a new form of passing in our putatively colorblind age, which is less about the concealment of difference than about our collective refusal to acknowledge it, as I noted above. From a slightly different perspective, we might describe this new logic of passing as marking the coming together of a prior history of the Asian model minority stereotype, as "whiter than white," with a neoliberal multiculturalism under which race only ever appears as disappearing, a racial politics that acknowledges difference only to dismiss its importance. In short, this coming together installs the law of colorblindness under the sign of an anti-racism, whose stuttering logic goes something like this: *we are all different, but we are all the same, too . . . but it doesn't really matter.*

Freud maintains in "Mourning and Melancholia" that melancholia emerges from a pathological disposition and can be distinguished from regular mourning by its inability to end.[39] In "A Dialogue on Racial Melan-

Ideals of Whiteness:
White Dolls.
From *First Person Plural*.

Ideals of Whiteness:
China (Korea) Doll.
From *First Person Plural*.

Ideals of Whiteness:
Prom Queen.
From *First Person Plural*.

Ideals of Whiteness:
High School Sweetheart.
From *First Person Plural*.

Ideals of Whiteness:
Cheerleader.
From *First Person Plural*.

The bluest eye.
From *First Person Plural*.

"Identical" twins.
From *First Person Plural*.

"Identical" twins.
From *First Person Plural*.

cholia," Han and I contest Freud's distinction between mourning and melancholia. If experiences of immigration, assimilation, and racialization in the United States are fundamentally determined both through the forced relinquishing of lost but unspeakable Asian ideals and through foreclosed investments in an idealized whiteness, then we might justifiably describe racial melancholia as a normal everyday group experience for Asian Americans. This insight places Asian American subjectivity and racial melancholia on the terrain of conflict rather than damage. In this respect, racial melancholia might be better described as a depathologized structure of feeling, pointing to those unidentified affects marking emergent group formations and identities.[40] Operating less as an individual than a group dynamic, racial melancholia for Asian Americans and transnational adoptees involves not just mourning or melancholia, but a continual negotiation between mourning *and* melancholia.

Significantly, this negotiation is often and even exclusively configured within Asian American cultural politics as an *intergenerational* and *intersubjective* negotiation. That is, problems and contradictions arising from Asian American immigration are often interpreted in terms of master narratives of intergenerational cultural conflict between parents and children, between older and younger generations. The tendency to reduce all social issues, including those resulting from institutional racism and economic exploitation, to first-generation versus second-generation cultural struggles, threatens to displace them from the public domain and into the privatized space of the family.[41] In the process, it effaces what are necessarily public histories and conflicts, absolving the state and mainstream community from responsibility, from proper political address or redress.

While pointing out this palpable danger, I would like to emphasize in the present analysis of transnational adoption the elimination or attenuation of this intergenerational and intersubjective process, the loss of the communal nature of racial melancholia. As a collective social unit, the family cannot recognize Borshay Liem's racial melancholia: Borshay Liem's losses remain unaffirmed and unacknowledged by those closest to her, by her own family, by those most affectively immediate to her. This is the striking difference concerning the ways in which racial melancholia is often negotiated collectively within Asian American immigrant families, in contrast with the ways in which it is often negotiated in isolation by the Asian transnational adoptee. Earlier, I asked whether the transnational adoptee, as well as her adoptive family, was Asian

American. To the extent that Borshay Liem's adoptive family recognizes her as a racialized subject—while not recognizing themselves as such—we witness an emotional cleaving of great consequence in the intimate space of the family. This failure of recognition serves to redouble the effects of racial melancholia, severing Borshay Liem from her family unit, affectively segregating her, and ultimately forcing her to negotiate her losses in silence and isolation. In short, what should necessarily be an *intergenerational* and *intersubjective* negotiation of loss is transformed into an *intrasubjective* negotiation of loss in its inexorable singularity. This is the feeling of kinship—the psychic life of race and the racialization of intimacy—that haunts Borshay Liem in this documentary of affect.

"There was an unspoken contract between us, which we had all agreed upon, that I was an orphan with no family ties to Korea," Borshay Liem later explains, referring to the public language of contracts and exchange to pierce the bubble of the private nuclear family. In an emotional voice-over, one hand covering over her mouth as she speaks, Borshay Liem offers this painful insight: "I belonged only to my American parents. It meant I didn't have a Korean history or Korean identity . . . I think being adopted into my family in some ways brought a lot of happiness for both me and for my parents, my American family. But there was also something that was—there was also a lot of sadness that we couldn't deal with as a family. And a lot of that sadness had to do with loss." She adds, "I was never able to mourn what I had lost [in Korea] with my American parents," attempting to explain the years of clinical depression from which she suffered after leaving her family and Fremont to attend college at Berkeley.

What is especially disturbing here is not just the fact that the family cannot recognize Borshay Liem's racial melancholia, that they cannot easily conceive of her adoption as involving loss, or that they cannot easily imagine her arrival in the United States as anything but an unequivocal gain. Equally distressing is the fact that Borshay Liem's clinical depression marks a sphere of intense sadness, an excess of and excessive affect that is (mis)read by those involved in her psychic plight as ingratitude. Such interpretations only serve to exacerbate her enduring feelings of disloyalty and shame. What, after all, could be less grateful on the part of an adoptee than depression?

Hence, what is justifiably felt to be a happy event from the point of view of the Borshay parents and siblings comes to overdetermine the adoptee's affect and feelings of kinship. Deann's melancholia is countered by an overpowering joy on the part of the other family members, such that their collective emotional will comes to overwrite her affective states and experiences. In the end, Borshay Liem tells us, "I forgot everything. I forgot how to speak Korean. I forgot any memory of ever having had a family, and I even forgot my real name . . . the only memories I have of my childhood are the images my father filmed while growing up. I relegated my real memories into the category of dreams."[42]

For Borshay Liem, racial melancholia involves the overwriting of all her childhood memories of and affective ties to Korea. In this regard, the psychic predicament of the transnational adoptee might be described as the containment of her emotional agency. Indeed, though I earlier described the practice of transnational adoption as one of the most privileged forms of diaspora and immigration, Borshay Liem's experiences also underscore it as a process largely devoid of affective self-determination. In her attempts to mourn the unspeakable losses initiated by her (involuntary) exchange, the transnational adoptee might also be said to function under an affective embargo, making it particularly difficult to negotiate her melancholia and transform it ever gradually into mourning. Here, I am delineating a profound form of racial melancholia, which, in Borshay Liem's words, reduces memories to dreams and agency to fantasy.

Ultimately, it is only the mother who notices this affective discrepancy. Reviewing some thirty years later the family movie of her arrival on the San Francisco Jetway, Alveen discovers Borshay Liem's stricken facial expression. In a voice-over accompanying this visual segment, she admits to her daughter, "When you arrived—little stoic-face and bundled up in all those clothes—we couldn't talk to you. You couldn't talk to us. I realize now that you were terrified. Because we were so happy, we just didn't think about that." Alveen's delayed recognition and acknowledgement of Borshay Liem's terror some thirty years after the fact creates what I would like to describe, borrowing a term from Walter Benjamin, a "dialectical image."[43] This dialectical image joins together two disparate times and spaces, shocking us out of an account of history as the way-it-really-was and creating an alternative story and historical narrative. In *First Person Plural*, the emotional clash between the Borshay family's affective joy and the young adoptee's obvious terror is transformed into a repetition compulsion, becoming a return-of-the-repressed, psychically negotiated between daughter and mother.

Their joy, her terror.
From *First Person Plural*.

Here, let us remember that adoption, especially in our contemporary moment, is not only bound up in the outsourcing of reproductive labor to the global South, but also with questions of faltering maternity, failed reproduction, and proper mothering. To the extent that adoption, rather than having no children, is often viewed as the last alternative to biological reproduction, the bond between adoptive mother and child is continually overdetermined. In the case of transnational adoption, these issues become especially problematic because of the child's tenuous place within the biologized ideal of the nuclear family and blood-line kinship. Because the racialized difference between the white mother and Asian daughter can elicit comment, because it can become something demanding explanation, the maternal bond often appears as something unnatural and in need of support.[44] "Some people would ask and others would kind of look," Alveen tells Borshay Liem, "and you knew they were wondering, but we didn't care." Given the challenge to negotiate racism and alterity within the intimate public sphere of the white family, Alveen's reaction follows a logic of colorblindness that wills away difference even as it installs the traumatic effects of its denial in Borshay Liem's psyche. The mother is not just responsible for removing Borshay Liem from the dinner table; she is literally burdened with handling her daughter's disjunctive affect. Ultimately, she is blamed for the daughter's psychic predicament: "Emotionally," Borshay Liem concludes, "there wasn't room in my mind for two mothers."

Let us unpack this mother-daughter dilemma more carefully.

The Negative Oedipus Complex

In traditional Freudian psychoanalysis, as I discussed in the previous chapter, the little boy displaces away from the mother (the incest taboo) and affiliates with the father (an Oedipal identification), agreeing to defer his desires by finding a mother substitute later in time. In this origin story of male subjectivity and gender privilege, history begins with the mother. Here it is important to recall that, for the little girl, Freud's narrative of infantile displacement and affiliation also places the maternal figure at the origin of the subject's history. Unlike the little boy, the little girl's process of maternal separation is fraught with difficulty and hesitation. Describing the little girl's psychic development, Freud offers an account of two mothers—the phallic mother and the lacking mother—one giving over to a genealogy of unrelenting recrimination and blame. Summarizing his views on the riddle of female subjectivity, Freud writes in his 1933 essay, "Femininity":

> A woman's identification with her mother allows us to distinguish two strata: the pre-Oedipus one which rests on her affectionate attachment to her mother and takes her as a model, and the latter one from the Oedipus complex which seeks to get rid of her mother and take her place with her father. We are no doubt justified in saying that much of both of them is left over for the future and that neither of them is adequately surmounted in the course of development. But the phase of the affectionate pre-Oedipus attachment is the decisive one for a woman's future: during it preparations are made for the acquisition of the characteristics with which she will later fulfil her role in the sexual function and perform her invaluable social tasks. It is in this identification too that she acquires her attractiveness to a man, whose Oedipus attachment to his mother it kindles into passion. How often it happens, however, that it is only his son who obtains what he himself aspired to! One gets an impression that a man's love and a woman's are a phase apart psychologically.[45]

Commentators typically gloss Freud's famous lament—"that a man's love and a woman's are a phase apart psychologically"—as the notion that women direct toward their sons or children the "love which their husbands desire for themselves."[46] What accounts for this cleaving and generational displacement? What psychic mechanism, in turn, forces the little girl to shift her affectionate attachment to the pre-Oedipal mother so as to identify, ever so reluctantly, with a debased and lacking mother and to invest her desires with the unforgiving figure and the name of the father?

According to Freud, the castration crisis and the subsequent penis envy it activates in the little girl work to alienate her from an affectionate attachment to the pre-Oedipal mother, what Freud elsewhere labels the "negative Oedipus complex." In surrendering the negative-Oedipal mother to identify with the symbolic mother of lack, the little girl is not just exiled from activity into passivity but also forced into an impossible psychic trajectory of contempt toward this figure, and finally toward herself. "The suppression of women's aggressiveness which is prescribed for them constitutionally and imposed on them socially," Freud observes, "favours the development of powerful masochistic impulses, which succeed, as we know, in binding erotically the destructive trends which have been diverted inward."[47] Here, Freud delineates the emergence of the normative female subject as not just profoundly masochistic but melancholic. The little girl is a subject not only melancholically estranged from the loved phallic mother and the pleasurable passion she once represented but also narcissistically wounded in her masochistic identification with the lacking mother. In short, she can neither mourn the loss of, nor come to terms with, the realities of this once pleasurable figure.

From another perspective, the legacy of the little girl's severed history with the negative-Oedipal mother is one in which the affectionate bonds to the phallic non-lacking mother are melancholically transformed, from intense love to magnified hate, resulting in an impossible, masochistic love, such that it becomes, Freud observes, "very striking and [may] last all through life."[48] In covering up the passionate bonds of attachment between the little girl and her loved mother, the castration crisis establishes the conditions for the emergence of the symbolic mother of lack, what Freud calls the positive-Oedipal mother, whom the little girl blames for her "mutilated" condition, her "castration" and her lack of a penis. This is an endless cycle of vilification. For every daughter who comes to blame her mother for her subordinate position is also implicating herself through this vexed identification. Should she become a mother herself, she is liable to equal treatment, forced to relive this psychic censure and hostility from the receiving end. This affective process explains how the little girl comes to have no psychic room in her mind for two mothers. More precisely, it explains how the little girl comes to have no psychic room for the non-lacking, negative-Oedipal mother, yet have psychic space and contempt for the positive-Oedipal mother and the diminished world she comes to represent in her fallen state.

How does this paradigm manifest itself, specifically in terms of Borshay Liem's maternal predicament? How are the negative and positive Oedipus complexes negotiated between the bodies of two mothers—the Korean birth mother and white adoptive mother? What should be immediately clear in Borshay Liem's psychic predicament is that the negative and positive Oedipus complexes necessarily map out both a sexual and a racial divide. This racial divide creates a set of distinctions between Koreanness and Whiteness that must also be traced back to a kind of castration crisis, in which the latter category emerges as the privileged and governing trope. For the Asian transnational adoptee, whose racialization is both produced and denied at once by her adoptive white family, issues of recrimination and blame become remarkably complicated. How might these ugly feelings come to be mitigated?

Melanie Klein's theories of reinstatement and reparation of the mother to a world of loved internal objects grant a crucial understanding of Borshay Liem's psychic dilemma. Klein tells us that psychic stability and health depend upon a subject's ability to align and test continually the real mother against her phantasmatic images, both good and bad. In "A Contribution to the Psychogenesis of Manic-Depressive States," Klein describes a psychic state in which the good and the bad mother are pulled so far apart that a process of dissociation emerges:

> In some patients who had turned away from their mother in dislike or hate, or used other mechanisms to get away from her, I have found that there existed in their minds nevertheless a beautiful picture of the mother, but one which was felt to be a *picture* of her only, not her real self. The real object was felt to be unattractive—really an injured, incurable, and therefore dreaded person. The beautiful picture had been dissociated from the real object but had never been given up, and played a great part in the specific ways of their sublimations.[49]

Klein delineates a psychic mechanism of loss by which a beautiful picture of the good mother is created and maintained precisely as a defense against a supposedly real mother figure thought to be irreparable—an "injured, incurable, and therefore dreaded person." For the purposes of our present discussion, we need to ask how the infant might deal with anxiety and loss in order to repair, recover, and reconcile a beautiful picture of the good mother with the real mother. What must be psychically jettisoned—and what kinds of sublimations become necessary—for the reinstatement of such a beautiful picture?

In "A Dialogue on Racial Melancholia," Han and I found that, in the case of Asian American immigrant children, race and sexuality must often cleave—that racial difference must often be dissociated from the figure of the real mother—in order for a beautiful picture to emerge. For the transnational adoptee, however, who is the real mother? And how might a beautiful picture of her look? In the case of Borshay Liem, psychic negotiations of good and bad must necessarily be brokered across two *racialized* bodies, the Korean birth mother and white adoptive mother. "I had a particular difficulty talking to my American mother about my Korean mother . . . I didn't know how to talk about my mother with my mother because she was my mother," Borshay Liem states confusedly at one point.

For Borshay Liem, in other words, the question of who the real mother is oscillates wildly, such that blame and recrimination spill upon the terrain of an unrelenting melancholia and masochism, for which the reinstatement of any beautiful picture becomes highly constrained. At one point in the documentary, Borshay Liem admits that even though "it was as if I had been born to them somehow," she cannot, as an adult, accept Alveen and Donald Borshay as her parents. (Of course, we must also remember that Alveen is the actual mother who both lives through and negotiates Borshay Liem's recriminations and blame.) Ultimately, Deann feels as if she must choose one family over the other, one mother over the other. Hoping to alleviate these feelings of disloyalty, Borshay Liem confesses, "I felt if I could actually see them come together in real life that somehow both families could then live within myself. So I asked my parents to go to Korea with me."

However, Borshay Liem's attempt to repair the images of her two mothers, through her long-anticipated reunion with both women, illustrates the difficulty of her psychic dilemma, to bring racial otherness together with a beautiful image of the maternal. Borshay Liem's attempts to achieve psychic integration are met by her two families with confusion, resistance, and a lack of understanding about the absolute need to move beyond the singular notion of the real mother. In fact, much of Borshay Liem's reunion in Korea is spent trying to determine who the "real" mother really is. As such, the initial internalized trauma of Borshay Liem's transnational adoption, and her separation from the

Korean birth mother, is not just externally reenacted but redoubled. After her initial rejection of the adoptive white mother, Borshay Liem is, in turn, rejected by *both* mothers.

"You look like your mother," Alveen tells Borshay Liem upon their arrival at the family's residence in Kunsan, Korea. Alveen's ironically gracious relinquishing of Borshay Liem to her Korean birth mother is met with equally "gracious" ambivalence and resistance. "She [the birth mother] says it's natural because she's her daughter," the translator first relates. "Yes," Alveen responds. But then the translator adds, turning to Borshay Liem: "She [the birth mother] says that although she is your mother, she only gave birth to you so you should really love and do everything you can for your adoptive parents . . . She wants you to be happy with your parents, your adopted parents." Hearing this imperative, we see Borshay Liem wince, as tears begin to flow again. Having initially rejected her white mother (and father), Borshay Liem is rejected.[50]

According to her Korean brother, who speaks on behalf of the Kang family (the father having died years before), Borshay Liem was sent away for a "better life." "It's not that important anymore," he rationalizes. "We are not very proud of what happened. She really needs to consider the cultural differences between us. Only then will she understand us. We have been apart for thirty years. It would be easier to close the gap between us if we spoke the same language. However, our cultural differences are difficult to overcome." Describing her adoption as an alienation from her "native" Korean culture and a net gain of a "better life" for Borshay Liem in the U.S., the Korean brother's attitude is similar to that of Donald Borshay's, insofar as neither man is capable of recognizing Borshay Liem's emotional wounds, needs, and desires, or capable of acknowledging the tangible and intangible losses in her transnational exchange. Tellingly, Borshay Liem does not state that there wasn't room in her mind for two fathers.

In *First Person Plural*, affective responsibility is highly gendered, a psychic dynamic of which the mothers are not only aware, but also for which they are both finally held accountable. "She [Borshay Liem] is filled with heartache," the Korean birth mother recognizes, "so I am very sad." The Korean birth mother is "unable to express" this sadness in adequate ways, having "no words to describe the agonizing years" after she relinquished Borshay Liem for adoption. But the Korean birth mother, like Alveen Borshay, must tend to the affective dissonance of the event and assume blame for the situation, which helps to fuel an endless cycle of recrimination. The Korean birth mother thanks the white adoptive mother for raising Borshay Liem, and in this way her sorrow and gratitude become, in the words of Alveen Borshay, "our joy." As such, Borshay Liem's reunion and fantasy of return to diasporic origins disturb the notion of completion and closure, revealing in the process the asymmetry separating women in Third World nations who relinquish their children from those in First World nations who receive them. This racialized asymmetry between First and Third World, global North and South, comes to underpin the gendered dilemma of maternal melancholy and masochism delineated by Freud's negative Oedipus complex. Here, the endless cycle of maternal vilification is constituted by racial disparities that force a rethinking of the category of the "real" mother, as well as the "good" and "bad" mother, as the good and bad *racialized* mother in Klein's theories of object relations.[51]

Psychically pushed and pulled away by both her Korean and her American mother, Borshay Liem is unable to create space in her mind for two mothers. While there is a proliferation of multiple sites of the real in this constrained reunion, there is nevertheless absolute psychic fidelity on the part of everyone involved that the position of the real mother can only be singular, not multiple. Indeed, Borshay Liem's maternal predicament ultimately renders the question of the real impossible. That is, Borshay Liem ultimately does not have space in her mind for any real mother at all. In slightly different terms, while she cannot have room in her mind for two good mothers, she does indeed have ample room in her mind for two *bad* ones. The Korean birth mother is blamed for abandoning her to her fate in the U.S.; the white adoptive mother is blamed for being unable to mirror or acknowledge her emotional and racial predicaments. Hence, Borshay Liem cannot reinstate a beautiful picture of either mother, rendering Klein's dynamic of maternal reparation and recovery extraordinarily tenuous. Rejected by both mothers, she too must reject them.[52]

The singularity of the real mother, as well as the question of maternal blame, continues to haunt Borshay Liem through the very end of *First Person Plural*. Confessing that, with her American parents in the room, she felt more like a "temporary visitor" with her Korean family, Borshay Liem admits that "the only way I can actually be closer to my Korean mother is to admit that she's not my mother anymore. The only way to be close to her is to acknowledge that she hasn't been my mother for over thirty years, and that my other mother has been my mother for—in a way my real mother." Borshay Liem's speech expresses the will to move forward from a place of psychic fixity, the need to choose between the two mothers. But her wish is riddled with ambivalence, as she continues to be haunted by the notion of singularity, origin, and return. Responding to Alveen Borshay's statement, "after all, that's your real mother [the Korean mother]," Borshay Liem attempts to broker a truce, stating slowly and cautiously, "I think . . . you're my real mother." "Well, I feel that way," Alveen Borshay responds, "I really do." Again, there is a certain asymmetry between Alveen and Deann, a cleaving between affect and language, a break between their feelings of kinship. That is, while Alveen can *feel* like Borshay Liem's mother, Borshay Liem can still only *think* this possibility.

Moreover, Borshay Liem's statement about feeling like a "temporary visitor" in Korea returns us to the rhetoric of hospitality, the problem of host and guest that comes to overshadow Borshay Liem's psychic existence on both sides of the Pacific. Toward the end of the documentary, Borshay Liem discloses this childhood fantasy: "When I was younger, I think I held onto this fantasy that if I was good enough in my new home and good enough with my American parents—that if everything was perfect and that I behaved properly and did well in school and all of that—that I would somehow be sent back to Korea to be with my Korean family." Her rhetoric of the guest invokes refugee discourses that characterize much of the history of Cold War politics in the Asian-Pacific, particularly Korea and Vietnam.[53] This rhetoric connects transnational adoption with U.S. political and military affairs concerning the containment of communism, while linking it to a contemporary discourse of asylum seekers under international human rights discourse and treaties.

To be legally recognized as a refugee proffers certain privileges in the form of relief and assistance different from those received by other migrants seeking entry into the nation-state.[54] Indeed, refugee status in the U.S. is adjudicated by immigration judges on a case-by-case basis, and is understood as an exception to immigration law and policy governed by Congress. This trope of hospitality and benevolence, bestowed and withdrawn at the will of the host, describes well the material conditions and psychic predicaments of the transnational adoptee. As a privileged immigrant in the diaspora, Borshay Liem nevertheless continues to feel haunted by a sense of psychic insecurity, the hope of return and its impossibility. What she must eventually discover is that there is no home to return to, a psychic quandary embodied in the impossible question of the "real."

This question of the real—of the fidelity to the singular and the origin—is the kernel of the psychic dilemma of two mothers. Even more, it is the key to imagining a poststructuralist theory of family and kinship predicated not on Oedipal origins but on anti-Oedipal destinations. This moving beyond fidelity to the singular, this moving forward from the intransigence of the real, is complicated by two powerful and compelling fantasies of return for the transnational adoptee: the return to the birth mother and the return to the place of origin. The politics of queer diasporas thus draws attention to these impossible desires for the real mother or the real motherland. These intersecting discourses of return underwrite a personal narrative of self-realization, completion, and closure that, as *First Person Plural* illustrates, is unattainable, inciting only further fragmentation and displacement in its persistence. In returning to Korea for her family reunion, Borshay Liem is forced to acknowledge the fact that confronting the past is always double-edged, challenging any sense of recoupable stability. She is forced to confront, that is, a notion of return that does not support authenticity and racial belonging, heteronormativity and blood-line kinship.

Following this family reunion, Borshay Liem admits that she has given up "that childhood fantasy of returning to my family," of "somehow be[ing] sent back to Korea." She recognizes her need "[to] develop another relationship, a different relationship with my Korean family." Curiously, the conclusion of *First Person Plural* does not endorse such a moving forward. Rather, the documentary ends with Borshay Liem's marriage ceremony and the birth of her son, Nick. The sentimental resolution to Borshay Liem's social and psychic predicaments is a normative Oedipal structure legislating only one privileged place for mother, father, and child. Hence, Borshay Liem's resolution to the dilemma of two mothers does not finally move her beyond notions of the singular or conventional structures of Oedipal family and kinship. Rather, this marriage allows her to create and inhabit a compensatory nuclear family structure of her own, to make good on what she believes she never possessed. Borshay Liem's marriage to her Korean American husband, Paul Liem, also highlights and complicates questions of ethnic purity and return to racial origins. The final image in *First Person Plural* is delivered in the ironic form of a family photo of this naturalized Oedipal trio.

Oedipal trio.
From *First Person Plural*.

Girl Love

I would like to conclude this chapter by way of my own return to the negative Oedipus complex. In "Girl Love," Kaja Silverman reminds us of Freud's insistence that it is only by accessing a woman at the level of her negative Oedipus complex that a man can love her. "It is in this identification," Silverman quotes Freud, "that she acquires her attractiveness to man, whose Oedipus attachment to his mother it kindles into passion." Silverman observes that "so long as the negative Oedipus complex remains hidden from the female subject herself, she will not be able to respond to the desire it arouses in the male subject."[55] Hence, the melancholy and masochism to which female subjectivity typically leads is based not just upon the impossibility of any reciprocal relationship between the sexes; it is also based upon the loss of the loved mother, the forfeiting of a realm of extraordinary affective intensity, and the closing down of the possibility of any redemptive form of female love and connection. The castration crisis inaugurates this form of pathological sexuality in the little girl who, like her lacking mother, finally becomes a subject who cannot love and who no one else could possibly love.

What would it mean for the little girl to have access to the passionate psychic intensity of her negative Oedipus complex, an affective intensity ultimately demanding, as we observed in the last chapter, its own epistemological and ontological consistency? What would it mean for the little girl, like the little boy, to have equal and reciprocal access to the affective realm of the loved and lost mother, to refuse to devalue her, to repudiate the logic of maternal blame and recrimination? It would mean, of course, that she would have room in her psyche for two good mothers, that she would possess an affective capacity beyond the traditional dictates of Oedipal paradigms. Silverman proposes that this recovery is possible precisely through the symbolic reinscription of the affect associated with the negative Oedipus complex. This recovery—one available to men and to women alike—is facilitated through a signifying process Silverman calls "girl love."

In both *The Interpretation of Dreams* and "The Unconscious," Freud maintains that every signifying act in a given subject's life ultimately refers back to a primally repressed term, which, as we witness in *First Person Plural* and elsewhere, is still primarily the mother. But, while she is configured as our ground of desire, the mother in fact provides the first signifier for a more primordial loss, our fall into language. As discussed in the last chapter, captation by language is a loss that Lacan variously describes as the fading of presence, being, or the here and now. Silverman writes:

> Unlike the other signifiers of the *hic et nunc*, though, she [the mother] has nothing to refer back to. What she stands in for psychically cannot provide this function, since it is precisely what escapes signification. Although serving as the support for libidinal symbolization, the mother is consequently devoid of semantic value. It is not she who gives all of the other signifiers of desire their meaning; it is, rather, *they* who determine what *she* can mean. To go "backward," libidinally speaking, is also not finally to touch "ground;" it is, instead, to apprehend the groundlessness of all signification.[56]

"Girl Love" represents a signifying process whereby one recuperates the loved and lost negative-Oedipal mother not by moving backward toward the recovery of origins, but by moving forward, "to symbolize lack in a way that is utterly our own."[57] It is a signifying process that involves the quickening of disparaged creatures and things, that endows devalued others—the bad Korean mother and the bad white mother—with new and alternative meanings. "There is also nothing primordial about this relationship," Silverman writes. "It does not represent a continuation of the female subject's early love for her mother, but rather its symbolic recovery from a later moment in time, and there is no limit on when that can occur."[58] What I am proposing is not the recuperation of an origin in the recaptured figure of the lost mother or lost place of origin, but the deployment of the affective intensity—of the feelings of kinship—

associated with this loved figure for a forgotten though crucial new form of symbolization. From this perspective, I would like to describe *First Person Plural* as a "documentary of affect." It is, in other words, the film's insistent attention to the dilemma of two mothers, to affective intensity, and to structures of feeling, that presents us with a new language for family and kinship, with new forms of symbolization that mark a post-structuralist account of psychoanalysis at a definitive remove from the Oedipal.

Were it not for the castration crisis, Silverman concludes, we would all, men and women alike, have permanent access to the affective intensity of the negative Oedipus complex. "Girl Love" thus recuperates a lost form of symbolization represented by the negative Oedipus complex, where libidinal openness rather than fixity reigns, and where words rather than binding affect come under the influence of their unconscious desires. By symbolizing lack in highly personalized and alternative forms, we can create psychic space for two good mothers. While our words would still induce the fading of being, they would also induce a kind of second coming. They would not only open psychic space for, but also lend symbolic sustenance to, two good mothers—two *good-enough* mothers, two beautiful pictures—not just the mother of lack but the mother of love, not just the Korean mother or the white mother, but both. The maternal resignification facilitated by "girl love" thus provides a crucial corrective to conservative Oedipal mandates of family and kinship, a politics of affect beyond Oedipus. We return to mother and motherland not by going back, but by moving forward. We do not bring the present into the past. Rather, we bring the past into the present. We keep the past alive in the present by signifying, and quickening through our desire, those creatures and things that conventional culture would disavow and bury.

Throughout *The Feeling of Kinship*, I ask why we have numerous poststructuralist accounts of language, but few poststructuralist accounts of kinship. I have spent some time analyzing the material and psychic contradictions of transnational adoption in *First Person Plural*, for the practice manifests the broader paradoxes of globalization and liberal political enfranchisement—the contemporary crossings of sexuality, race, and national belonging under the shadows of late capitalism. As an instance of globalization and its discontents, transnational adoption opens upon the difficult affective terrain of poststructuralist notions of family and kinship precisely through the problem and possibility of two mothers. While global capitalism has given rise to numerous material reconfigurations of family and kinship, I fear that these new forms of social identity and affiliation do not have any concomitant psychic support. To the extent that the transnational adoptee functions as a guarantee to conventional ideals of the white heteronormative nuclear family, straight or gay, and to the extent that she cannot in turn create space in her mind for two good-enough mothers, the possibility of poststructural kinship is dubious at best. To the extent, however, that transnational adoption allows us to denaturalize powerful Oedipal myths of return, animating the politics of heteronormativity and diaspora, we are left with several possible psychic alternatives and political prospects for a poststructuralist account of family and kinship.

As a contemporary phenomenon, transnational adoption installs racial alterity and otherness in the privatized space of the white American family, even as our national borders continue to be sealed in unprecedented ways, especially after the events of 9/11. The contemporary formation of interracial families from the global North and South represents an opportunity to question and rethink the conservative impulses of both heteronormativity and diaspora. In the context of *First Person Plural*, the disjunctive affect of the transnational adoptee illuminates a painful though potentially productive psychic and social terrain exceeding the privatized boundaries of Oedipal family and kinship. There is no smooth translatability between the psychic demands of the Oedipal and the disjunctive affect of the transnational adoptee. In this regard, we might approach the question of two mothers in transnational adoption as a psychic protest that necessarily erodes the boundaries between the public and private, "over there" and "over here." If, in our colorblind age, the political sphere has been largely contracted into private life, then the practice of transnational adoption, one creating new global families and producing new racial formations at once, provides one crucial site to reengage the politics of race, gender, nation, and capital—one crucial site for a rethinking of the racialization of intimacy and the forgetting of race.

Under the shadows of globalization, this erosion of boundaries separating public from private calls for a broader response to economic exploitation, racist domination, and gender subordination that goes beyond, in Anagnost's words, "merely asserting one's entitlement to be a [transnational] parent."[59] Parents of transnational adoptees should not be held any more or less accountable than the rest of us to the vicissitudes of globalization, the problems of neoliberal governmentality, and the crises of multiculturalism. Nevertheless, the practice of transnational adoption presents a specific opportunity for white middle-class subjects to confront and negotiate difference within the social and affective configurations of the new global family.

Restoring collective history to the process of a transnational adoptee's social and psychic development is crucial to the survival of the new global family. It is also crucial to an ethical multiculturalism that rejects the liberal model of private and public, as well as the ideals of the white heteronormative nuclear family, as the standard against which all social orderings must be measured. Positing such an ethical multiculturalism may not just lead to powerful alliances for a progressive politics, but could conceivably cut across historically constituted divisions of gender, race, and class to create important international and domestic political alliances. For what we witness so eloquently in *First Person Plural* are the ways in which transnational adoption unfolds upon a terrain of kinship that exceeds traditional notions of marriage, family, and social alliances but is embedded in histories of war, nationalism, racism, and gendered violence. In the process, Borshay Liem's documentary also helps us to imagine new psychic structures, new poststructuralist accounts of family and kinship beyond the Oedipal. Reimagining family and kinship, as well as rethinking nation and community in terms of queer diasporas, offers a host of political opportunities, economic responsibilities, and cultural commitments.

Here, let me return to the John Hancock commercial, to the two white lesbians and a Chinese baby, a phenomenon at the very intersection of queer liberalism and queer diasporas. In this crossing lies a nascent possibility, the prospect that this child might grow up to exist in a world where the psychic structure of two—indeed, three, four, five, or perhaps no—mothers of various races could be psychically accommodated. It is crucial to imagine and to live these other social possibilities, these other poststructuralist psychic arrangements.

The next chapter continues to explore these possibilities.

FOUR

The Prospect of Kinship

☙ ☙ ☙

TRANSNATIONAL ADOPTION
AND RACIAL REPARATION

with Shinhee Han, Ph.D.

When I was younger, I think I held onto this fantasy that if I was good enough in my new home and good enough with my American parents—that if everything was perfect and that I behaved properly and did well in school and all of that—that I would somehow be sent back to Korea to be with my Korean family.
—DEANN BORSHAY LIEM, *First Person Plural*

We didn't know that we could never be good enough, so we kept trying to do the impossible.
—JANE JEONG TRENKA, *The Language of Blood*

It is not surprising that the language of the "good enough"— exhibited in the two epigraphs above—permeates the documentaries and memoirs of numerous transnational adoptees, coming to saturate their psychic space, coming to inhabit their conscious and unconscious thoughts. What is perhaps more unexpected is the adoptee's recurring feelings of inadequacy, her frequent displacement of the dynamic of the good enough from mother to daughter—that is, from the (m)other to her self. In Deann Borshay Liem's *First Person Plural*, racial melancholia appears as a psychic effect of not having enough space in one's mind for two good-enough mothers. Even more, though, it might be described as the compounding of such hidden grief precisely through the adoptee's assumption of this dislocated psychic burden, through the conviction that it is she, rather than the mother, who "could never be good enough." Such psychic bonds between mother and daughter are, as Jane Jeong Trenka observes in *The Language of Blood*, written under the sign of the "impossible."[1]

This chapter continues the discussion from the previous chapter on the predicaments of the good enough. It extends our analysis of Melanie Klein and object relations theories concerning reinstatement and reparation of the mother—a prospect of and possibility for kinship beyond the normative boundaries of the Oedipal. I co-authored the following case history and critical commentary about Mina—a transnational adoptee from Korea—with Shinhee Han, a New York-based psychotherapist. This chapter is part of an ongoing collaboration whose larger goal is to illustrate how a more speculative humanities-based approach to psychoanalysis might supplement its clinical applications, and viceversa.[2] In the context of race and racial difference, which remain undertheorized across various disciplinary deployments of psychoanalysis, and now threaten to disappear altogether under a political cloud of colorblindness and queer liberalism, such a critical venture is all the more urgent.

As I discussed in chapter three, transnational adoption involves the intersection of two very powerful origin myths—the return to mother and to motherland. In the case history examined in the present chapter, problems relating to Asian immigration, assimilation, and racialization are absolutely central to the patient's psychic predicaments. First-generation Asian immigrant parents and their second-generation American-born children typically negotiate problems of immigration, assimilation, and racialization as intergenerational and intersubjective conflicts. As we have seen, however, the transnational adoptee often struggles with these issues in social and psychic isolation. In Mina's case, she mourns the loss of her mother and motherland—a repressed past prior to her "official" arrival and history in the United States—as a profoundly unconscious and intrasubjective affair.

Moreover, we witness in Mina how these significant losses trigger a series of primitive psychical responses such that we are forced to rethink Melanie Klein's theories of infancy—of good and bad objects as well as good and bad mothers—in terms of good and bad *racialized* objects as well as good and bad *racialized* mothers.[3] Mina's case history demands a consideration of racial difference as constitutive of, rather than peripheral to, Klein's fundamental notions of splitting and idealization, depression and guilt, reinstatement and reparation. In short, we come to recognize that Klein's developmental positions are also, and at the same time, racialized positions. More specifically, if the productive negotiation of racial melancholia resides in the possibility of creating psychic space in one's mind for two good-enough mothers—the white adoptive mother as well as the Korean birth mother—then we are faced with the significant task of rethinking Klein's theories on reinstatement and reparation as a psychic process that necessarily unfolds simultaneously upon a complex terrain of sexual and racial difference. For Mina, the reparative position ultimately demands the racial reparation of her lost and devalued Korean birth mother. It demands, that is, an accounting of how the good enough might be distributed across a number of maternal figures and racial ideals.

The present chapter concludes by focusing on the ways Mina's case history draws attention to the materiality of the psychotherapist as a racialized subject. In particular, it considers how the transference/counter-transference dynamic between Mina and her Korean American analyst is framed not only by the public fact of their shared racial difference, but also by the public nature of the analyst's pregnancy during the course of the patient's treatment. We examine how Han's pregnancy constitutes her, to reformulate D.W. Winnicott, as a "racial transitional object" for Mina.[4] Along the way, we reconsider Winnicott's theories about "object usage" in relation to Mina's "use" of the therapist to transition into a reparative position for race. Such a transition allows her to resignify her vexed identifications with both a disparaged Koreanness and an idealized whiteness. From this perspective, we come to understand how our everyday interactions with one another—as teacher and pupil, as therapist and patient—might rework the feelings of kinship that support psychic life or, in contrast, the burdens of kinship that make a network of social relations and belonging impossible.

To its very end, Borshay Liem's *First Person Plural* constitutes the real mother as a singular, reified, and entrenched position in which one is forced to invest psychic fidelity. In contrast, the following case history and commentary illustrates how the good enough might be reworked in order to open upon an affective terrain of psychic movement rather than fixity. Ultimately, Mina's story underscores the simple fact that we do not—that we cannot—live our lives under a perpetual cloud of psychic negativity. From this perspective, racial reparation illuminates a process for the reworking of the good enough in regard to a particular figure—the mother—as well as in terms of a network of social relations and ideals—including race and nation—that govern the politics of family and kinship. In this regard, we hope our approach to psychoanalysis, and object relations in particular, might provide a theory for repairing and redressing race and social belonging.

Case Presentation

Mina is a 23-year-old transnational adoptee from Korea. She is a dancer in a renowned New York City ballet company. One of Mina's mentors referred her to me (Han) as she was beginning her first year with the ensemble. Mina carries herself with the natural grace of a ballerina. During our consultations, however, she often sat at the edge of her seat. She is a smart and articulate, though rigid, young woman who sought psychotherapy to understand better the problems in her romantic relationships along with the "whole adoption thing." She believes that the two are somehow connected.

In her presentation Mina recounted that, since age 13, she had had a series of white boyfriends. Every relationship was marked by some degree of abuse, mostly verbal. Furthermore, although she boasts of her "sexual power" over men, Mina believes that she was often coerced into sexual relationships with her partners much sooner than she desired. At the start of her sessions with me, she was not in a relationship because she felt that she needed to "figure out" herself first. Mina had a theory that her birth mother had been a college student who found herself in a precarious and perhaps abusive relationship with a boyfriend. This boyfriend subsequently abandoned her mother when she became pregnant with Mina. Mina spoke angrily about her previous boyfriends and recounted her fantasies concerning the circumstances by which her birth mother had become pregnant. At the same time, Mina blamed herself for consistently choosing "bad" boyfriends. Collectively, these failed relationships have had a negative impact on Mina's self-regard. Despite her formidable artistic talents, she suffers from low self-esteem and often displays excessive intolerance toward others.

During our initial consultation, Mina asked how much I knew about Korean transnational adoption; she also asked "what kind of Korean" I was. She immediately wanted to figure out my attitudes toward adoptees: she wondered if I was adopted, a recent immigrant, born in the

United States, or from an affluent background. She believed that the overwhelming majority of Koreans—in both Korea and the United States—are prejudiced against Korean adoptees. She stated that she does not like Koreans at all. In particular, the Korean nationals with whom she attended dance school "made her sick" with their "Gucci, Louis Vuitton, and Chanel accessories," as well as with their "garish" and "ugly" makeup. She felt especially disconnected from them because they spoke only Korean to one another. "They are in America," she remarked. "Why don't they speak English?" Finally, she accused them of behaving disingenuously. "These girls all have white boyfriends. And they sleep around all the time," she stated. "But they act virginal around other people, as though no one can tell how slutty they really are."

Before I could respond to Mina's statements, she told me that she thought I was a Korean American, but not the type she described. (I am, in fact, a "1.5 generation" Korean immigrant, having moved to the United States when I was 13.) I took this as a warning not to carry my Gucci purse to work. At the same time that I wondered if I were going to be a "good enough" Korean for Mina, I also realized that in all likelihood she did not consider herself a "good enough" Korean for me. I decided to share with Mina my prior experience with Korean transnational adoption, in particular, my specialty as a post-adoption social worker assisting both transnational adoptees and their parents. Skeptically, she replied, "Good." Because of her angry, aggressive, and defensive attitude, I felt unsure whether our relationship would continue beyond the initial consultation. "She's a tough one," I concluded. I reminded myself to be careful, lest Mina group me with those Koreans she hates or, even worse, create a new category of "bad Korean" just for me.

A white couple from Philadelphia adopted Mina when she was 11 months old. She has a younger brother, also adopted from Korea, who is now a first-year student in a small liberal arts college in the Northeast. Mina describes her brother as an "easy-going kid" who does not seem to have many issues concerning his adoption or Koreanness. She is not very close to him. Mina's mother is a freelance journalist who often writes for travel magazines. Although her mother was once a full-time reporter, she quit her office job to raise Mina and her brother at home. Mina describes her relationship with her mother as very close. They talk on the phone at least once or twice a day. She discloses "everything" to her mother, including her boyfriend problems and her adoption issues. While Mina feels that her mother offers solid advice, she also worries that her mother "knows too much" and is consequently biased about these topics. Mina looks and sounds confident when she says that her mother would do "anything and everything" she wants her to do. Mina's father is a professor of applied mathematics. She describes him, in contrast to her mother, as somewhat distant and "clueless" about her life. Both, however, are actively involved in Mina's flourishing dance career and often travel from out of town to attend her performances.

Mina reported that her adoption file contained very little information. She was found in a tattered basket at the doorstep of a church in Inchon City, near Seoul, in South Korea. The minister and his wife took Mina to a local police station. From there she was taken to an orphanage. One week after Mina was found, a young woman visited the church to inquire about the infant left at the doorstep. Mina wonders if this woman was her birth mother. She hypothesizes that her birth mother was perhaps not a college student, after all, but a "poor whore" who lived in a nearby city. And she stated angrily, "Why didn't the bitch leave just a little more information about me? Like, my name and her name! Did she even think to give me a name?" Mina stated that she has two questions for her birth mother if and when she finds her: "What's my name?" and "Why did you give me up?" After these answers are furnished, she claims she wants nothing further to do with her birth mother or Korea. Mina's anger toward her birth mother is palpable. Unlike other transnational adoptees I have previously treated—adolescents and adults who often created idealized pictures of their lost birth mothers—Mina's negative attitude toward hers is remarkably raw and unrelenting.

During the years at her dance academy, Mina's engagement with her adoption issues was often displaced by school demands. She was the only one of her classmates chosen to join her ballet company upon graduation. Mina was surprised by this achievement. Her teachers had been telling her that, while her technique was superb, she needed to work more on her emotional expression. Shortly after joining the ballet company in the fall, she began treatment with me. Four months later, Mina started seeing a young choreographer, Henry, who was already in another relationship. It started off as a friendship, which quickly evolved into a series of romantic episodes. This relationship spun Mina's emotions wildly. Her volatile moods were largely contingent on Henry's continued but failed promises to break up with his girlfriend.

As their tumultuous affair progressed, a distinct pattern emerged.

Mina became increasingly dependent on Henry. She organized her daily schedule around his while also taking care of Henry's everyday chores, his laundry, and the cleaning of his apartment. Gradually Mina grew exhausted and resentful, but she could not bring herself to end the affair. She wondered if her birth mother had found herself in similar circumstances, resulting in her pregnancy with Mina. A few months later Henry abruptly ended the relationship, announcing that he had decided to become engaged to his girlfriend.

At the time Henry broke up with Mina, I was four months pregnant. As I was in my second trimester, the pregnancy had become noticeable to a few patients. I wondered if Mina had perceived my physical change. I was due to give birth at the end of the summer, around the time that Mina was scheduled to return from her summer tour. Before she departed, however, I decided to discuss my pregnancy with her. When I told her, Mina's reaction was very controlled and polite. I asked Mina directly how she felt, and she answered, "Oh, it's fine. You having a baby has nothing to do with my adoption. You're a professional. You'll come back to the office and we will work together as usual."

Despite her initial nonchalance, as my belly swelled, Mina often asked how I was feeling, how much weight I had gained, and if my pregnancy had been planned or was an "accident." "I know nothing about you," she said. "But I know that you are well-educated and independent. So, I don't know if you're having this baby alone, with a man . . . or even a woman." On further exploration of her fantasies about me, Mina added, "I think you're married and this is a planned pregnancy. You wouldn't be so stupid and just get knocked up." It seemed important to Mina that my baby have two parents who would love and care for him and, most importantly, keep him.

As her summer tour approached, Mina wanted to know if we could schedule phone sessions while she was away, "just in case." I reassured her that I would be available until I gave birth. At the moment, I wanted to explore with Mina any possible feelings of abandonment—indeed, any unacknowledged feelings of envy or jealousy toward my unborn child. I feared that my pregnancy might raise doubts about the importance of our relationship as well as Mina not feeling "special enough." But as much as I attempted to raise these issues, Mina deflected all conversation, showing little interest in pursuing such topics. She departed for her summer tour soon after these exchanges.

During Mina's tour, we more or less kept to our weekly sessions over the telephone, until a couple weeks before I gave birth. After giving birth, I took maternity leave and was not in contact with Mina for two months. Upon resuming our sessions in late fall, Mina immediately asked if my baby was a boy or a girl and offered warm congratulations. She then delved into her big news: she had just attended a transnational adoption camp. Following the dance tour, Mina had decided to volunteer as a camp counselor for adopted children from Korea as well as China. There, for the first time, she spent an extended period with other Korean adoptee volunteers who had either found their birth mothers (and families) or were contemplating such a search. As she began to experience a drive to absorb their various stories, Mina also started to reconsider her own search for her birth mother. Mina's shift in attitude made me wonder how much her recent actions were connected both to my having had a child and her subsequent experiences at adoption camp.

That fall, Mina joined both a Korean adoptee support group and a mentoring group for young adopted Chinese girls in New York City. While she expressed considerable envy toward the social and cultural support that the white parents she encountered collectively provided to their Chinese daughters, her feelings toward her own adoptee support group were quite negative. She described them as a "bunch of screwed-up Korean adoptees who are obsessed with their adoptions." Upon further exploration of her attitude, Mina confessed that she fears there is something deeply wrong with her because, like these "screwed-up" peers, she too was adopted and would never be "good enough."

Indeed, throughout her treatment Mina expressed blatant prejudices against not only the Korean nationals at her dance school but also nearly ever other minority group in the U.S.—African Americans, Latinos, Jews, Asian Americans, as well as gays and lesbians. For instance, she characterized African Americans as "those lazy blacks who are all in gangs and only know how to steal and kill." She described Latinos as the "dumbest racial group" and Jews as "those who sniff money all day." As for Asian Americans, she embraced the ostensibly positive model minority stereotype, observing, "At least Asian Americans are academically successful and work hard and don't bother anyone." Finally, gays and lesbians were "abnormal" and "flamboyant" people obsessed with sexual display.

It was very difficult for me to endure Mina's tirades against these various groups. As Mina's prejudices waxed and waned over the course of her treatment, I continued to hold her anger without any direct verbal confrontation. I grew increasingly concerned, however, about the ways my negative counter-transferences might affect her. As I learned more about Mina, though, I began to understand that her bigotry was deeply connected to the fear of being seen by others—and of accepting herself—as a minority. Mina's emphasis from the very beginning of our work together had been, "I'm an American! I have an Asian face but I'm white! My parents are white and I grew up in a white suburb, and I feel most comfortable around white people." Under this tough and brittle exterior, though, Mina felt extremely vulnerable and conflicted about her own racial identity, as evidenced not only by her aversion to Koreans in general but also by her vexed identifications with her new friends as "a bunch of screwed-up Korean adoptees" in particular. Hence, as I began to feel more empathetic and protective toward Mina and her feelings of inadequacy, I made a conscious effort to police my disapproval as it arose.

During that fall, Mina spent more and more time with her new Korean adoptee friends. She reported that most of their conversations revolved around what they all called "the search" (for their birth mothers) and the ways "the search" often provoked intense rivalry around the amount and quality of information uncovered. For the first time, I began to notice Mina's deep and growing struggle with the idea of beginning her own search, one motivated by competitiveness with and a desire to belong to this group. It became increasingly clear that Mina was starting to come to terms with the great psychological difficulties associated with initiating the search process.

During this period, Mina also volunteered to be a spokesperson at a local adoption agency. There she met with potential parents to talk about the "do's and don't's" of transnational adoption. Mina would tell these potential parents to "embrace the culture and language of their children as their own." In our sessions, she began to express new feelings toward her adoptive parents: "I'm so angry at them for not exposing me to Korean things. I told my mom maybe I'm screwed up because I didn't have anything Korean when I was growing up. I asked her why she didn't do this, and she responded that she didn't know why. It didn't occur to her. How can she say that?"

It seems that Mina's de-idealizing of her adoptive mother stems from a feeling that she had intentionally kept Mina away from all things Korean, including her birth mother. In fact, as Mina has become more involved in these various adoption activities, it has become increasingly apparent to me that she has been regressing and is in greater conflict with her adoptive mother. Nonetheless, Mina calls her every morning and evening to complain about being lonely and unhappy. She blames her mother for her agitated state of mind, but at the same time she feels more dependent on her. As a result, her mother has made extra visits to New York.

A year and a half into our sessions, Mina's desire to take action on "the search" congealed. She decided to go to Korea for a big adoption conference during the upcoming summer recess, and she planned to stay afterward to search for her birth mother. Again, Mina expressed great frustration and anger about having such limited information about her adoption. She also had a long list of reservations and anxieties: "How long will it take? Where will I stay—in Seoul or Inchon City? How will I get around when my Korean is barely good enough for ordering food in restaurants? I'll be so lonely. I don't really know anyone there and I don't want to see anyone from the dance school. Who will really help me? How will I know if someone is really genuine or just wants to take advantage of rich Americans?" When I suggested, "It sounds as if you'd feel more secure if I went there to search with you," she smiled and quietly acknowledged, "I guess so." Upon asking her how she felt that I could not go with her, she immediately responded, "Oh no! I wasn't asking or thinking that you could go with me. Besides, you have a baby to take care of."

Trying to refocus our discussion on the issue of her birth mother, I proposed that, if we followed Mina's fantasies about her, she might currently be around my age. Mina looked at me with great surprise and said, "Wow, that could be true. I just never thought of it that way." My comment seemed to introduce to Mina the idea that her birth mother is a real, living person rather than a fantasy. Mina added, "I just always imagined her as a 20-something-year-old girl like me . . . but I guess she isn't anymore." On further exploration, Mina admitted, "I want her to be married but with no kids. I don't want any siblings, not even half-siblings. I don't want to be the one she didn't keep." Mina hoped that her birth mother was okay, "living a normal life, but not too happy." Despite her curiosity about her birth mother's present circumstances, Mina continued to feel angry that her birth mother had not tried to search for her. And she envied those adoptees whose birth mothers had sought them out first. She feared that she had been erased from her birth mother's memory from the moment after she was dropped off at the church doorsteps.

In the following session Mina introduced yet another fantasy, one connected to her stuffed animals. Mina has been collecting ducks since she was a toddler. She takes one female duck, Suzette, with her wherever she goes. Indeed, Suzette has now traveled around the world with Mina on tour (a lucky duck). When Mina was nine, Suzette got "married" to Tommy and gave birth to three baby ducklings. However, Suzette did not like her babies because all they did was whine and cry, demanding constant attention. Suzette pecked and hurt them, and finally she abandoned them. As a consequence, Tommy was left to take care of these "ugly ducklings" along with another duck, Jane. Mina describes Jane as a sort of nanny. It was only recently that Tommy, Jane, and the ducklings have been reunited with Suzette, joining her in Mina's New York apartment. Still, Mina asserts, Suzette "hates" these babies.

Mina told me that she also hates babies because they are such helpless creatures. When I suggested that perhaps she feels that her helplessness as an infant contributed to her birth mother abandoning her, Mina expressed great shock. After some silence, she asked, "How could I not have thought of this possibility? I have been blaming myself all this time without realizing it. My mother gave me up because I couldn't do anything. I didn't have any skills." Mina understood that this is the reason why she had become so independent, so strong willed and intent on taking care of herself and no one else, not even a husband if she later marries.

Reminding Mina about the care she constantly extended to Henry and other former boyfriends, I asked what kind of "skills" she could have possibly possessed as an infant. Mina replied matter-of-factly, "I should have known how to feed myself and how not to rely on my mother; be toilet trained, so she didn't have to change my dirty diapers." She speculated that perhaps she cried too much, and, as a result, her birth mother was forced to give her up. After this "revelation," Suzette stopped abusing her ducklings. Instead, she "bathed and cleaned them up."

Currently, our primary focus is on Mina's preparations for "the search." Mina plans to put advertisements this coming summer in Korean newspapers. In addition, she has brought in her adoption file to share with me, to look for "possible clues." As Mina mentioned earlier, there is little information in the file that we could use to make her advertisement distinctive. Finally, Mina has decided to participate in a Korean television program that reunites lost relatives. She repeatedly states, "I'm all for results. That's all I care about, and I don't care what I have to do to find her." In this regard, Mina requested that I call and talk with the church couple who first discovered her. She has also asked her adoptive mother to go with her to Korea to help with "the search." Mina is determined to find her birth mother and to demand answers about their brief life together. She has become increasingly agitated about her abandonment, and she wants answers.

Commentary: Racial Melancholia

Let us return to a set of questions raised in the previous chapter: Is the transnational adoptee an immigrant? Is she Korean? Is she Korean American? Are her adoptive parents, in turn, immigrants, Korean, or Korean American?

Mina's case history provides some provocative and vexing answers to these questions. Mina does not consciously see herself as an immigrant, a Korean, or a Korean American. She insists that, like her adoptive parents, she is an "American." While she has an "Asian face," she nevertheless feels "white." "My parents are white, and I grew up in a white suburb, and I feel most comfortable around white people," Mina reasons. In fact, Mina despises Koreans as a categorical whole—the "ugly," "garish," and "slutty" Korean nationals at her dance school who speak only Korean to one another, as well as Koreans and Korean Americans who are "prejudiced against Korean adoptees." Indeed, sounding rather like an unreconstructed xenophobe, she espouses an "English-only" attitude toward these disparaged others.

Psychoanalysis teaches us that such extreme feelings of disavowal and hate often represent for the patient unconscious and ambivalent identifications with the excoriated object. In this regard, Mina's struggles with the "whole adoption thing" raise a number of issues concerning immigration, assimilation, and racialization that are consistent with the psychological problems of many Asian immigrants and their second-generation children. Not unlike Mina, these second-generation Asian Americans often exhibit ambivalence toward, or discomfort with, questions of race and racialization—for example, identifying with a dominant white mainstream while dis-identifying with their immigrant parents as racial others.

Departing from these observations, how might we bring some psychic specificity to Mina's case history and to the phenomenon of transnational adoption in general? Let us return to the question of racial melancholia as a depathologized everyday structure of feeling examined in the previous chapter. Racial melancholia provides a powerful theoretical framework to analyze the ungrievable losses associated with everyday experiences of immigration, assimilation, and racialization for Asian immigrations and their second-generation offspring. What must be emphasized in Mina's case, however, like that of Borshay Liem, is the suspension of this intergenerational and intersubjective process, the loss of the communal nature of racial melancholia.

"I'm so angry at them [her adoptive parents] for not exposing me to Korean things," Mina angrily states at a later point in her treatment. "I told my mom maybe I'm screwed up because I didn't have anything Korean when I was growing up." To the extent that Mina's parents do not recognize her as either an immigrant or a Korean/Korean American, and to the extent that Mina herself does not affectively *feel* herself to be an immigrant or a Korean American, the numerous losses relating to her birth, birth mother, abandonment, adoption, and migration remain unacknowledged and unaffirmed by her own family and self. All the more, they remain unaffirmed in the face of the public nature of her adoption. Unlike the Asian immigrant family circumscribed and defined by bloodlines, which is seen if not always felt as an integrated racial unit, the transnational adoptee disrupts the aesthetic continuity of the white nuclear family. She cannot pass, and her presence often draws attention not only to her racial difference but also to the fact of her adoption.[5] In a colorblind age, this difference might be acknowledged or even embraced under the rubric of multicultural diversity. As I emphasize in chapter three, however, histories of race, gender, colonialism, nationalism, and militarization are decidedly effaced by such a dynamic. Racial melancholia thus delineates the encryption of public histories of political, economic, and social conflict into the private space of family and kinship relations—another instance of the racialization of intimacy.

Mina mourns these significant losses in solitude. She negotiates them not intersubjectively, but *intrasubjectively* and *unconsciously*. Furthermore, to the extent that adoptive white parents in general recognize their transnational adoptees as immigrants or racialized subjects, but do not consider themselves immigrants or racialized subjects, in turn, we witness a highly significant affective cleaving within the private space of the white nuclear family. In other words, while transnational adoptees identify with their parents' whiteness, their parents do not necessarily identify with their children's Asianness. Such a failure of recognition—of identification—threatens to redouble racial melancholia's effects, severing the adoptee from the intimacy of the family unit, emotionally segregating her, and obliging her to negotiate her significant losses in isolation and silence.

As Freud reminds us in "Mourning and Melancholia," melancholia is one of the most difficult psychic conditions to treat, as it is largely an unconscious process. One feels justified, he writes, "in maintaining the belief that a loss of this kind has occurred, but one cannot see clearly what it is that has been lost, and it is all the more reasonable to suppose that the patient cannot consciously perceive what he has lost either. This, indeed, might be so even if the patient is aware of the loss which has given rise to his melancholia, but only in the sense that he knows *whom* he has lost but not *what* he has lost in him."[6] Mina knows that she has lost her Korean birth mother, but she does not know what she has lost in her. And through the unspecified and ungrievable nature of this loss, we come to witness Mina's psychic repudiation of the embodied humanity of this lost maternal figure as one psychic effect of racial melancholia. Hence, in attempting to identify a number of crucial developmental issues attendant to the practice of transnational adoption, we might highlight the social and psychic isolation engendered by racial melancholia, which manifests itself in especially acute and unconscious forms for the transnational adoptee.

Here, let us emphasize that Mina's adoptive white mother is a warm and caring person; she is consistently empathetic, conscientious, and responsive. Mina not only discloses "everything" to her, but she also feels that her adoptive white mother would do "anything and everything" for her. For instance, as Mina's treatment evolved over time, and as she has come into greater conflict with both whiteness and her white mother, Mina's mother has been able to hold effectively her daughter's growing rage. She does not retaliate against Mina's frequent and angry attacks but provides increased emotional support by making herself available for extra phone calls as well as by making more trips to New York City. Moreover, she has agreed to go to Korea with Mina in order to search for her birth mother.

The adoptive mother's failures—if they can be labeled as such—are less individual than social. That is, what Mina's case history underscores is the necessity of analyzing her psychic struggles not just in the particular context of her individual family dynamics. Rather, Mina's psychic dilemmas demand an accounting of the larger political, economic, and cultural forces of race, gender, colonialism, nationalism, immigration, and militarization as they are encrypted within the private space of the family, configuring the developmental trajectories of the transnational adoptee and organizing her psychic life.

Racial Reparation

Mina's case history is striking in that the "return" to origins—the return to mother and to motherland—marking her psychic development occurs through the very dissociation of mother from motherland. This process might be analyzed productively in relation to Melanie Klein's notions of infantile development—of splitting and idealization, depression and guilt, reinstatement and reparation. According to Klein, the paramount crisis of the infant's psychic development involves its loss of, and separation from, the mother, a process beginning around the age of 4 to 5 months and initiated through the creation of two internalized images: an idealized image of the "good" mother that the infant seeks to protect and preserve, and a threatening image of the "bad" mother that the infant aggresses and destroys. This splitting and idealization of the mother figure invokes intense anxiety on the part of the infant, spilling onto the psychic terrain of depression and guilt. The infant fears that it has killed not just the bad mother but, along the way, the good mother as well. During this time, if the actual mother provides "good enough," consistent care, the infant slowly learns to trust that she will be nurtured rather than annihilated. In this manner, the infant is able to maintain a "beautiful picture" of the mother, learning to reconcile and adjust its internal images and objects with its external realities and discontents.

Reparation thus describes the psychic process by which the infant negotiates the depressive position by making "good the injuries which [it] did in phantasy [to the mother], and for which [it] still unconsciously [feels] very guilty."[7] Klein defines reparation as an act that encompasses "the variety of processes by which the ego feels it undoes harm done in phantasy, restores, preserves, and revives [dead] objects."[8] It is only after having traversed the extreme violence of paranoid splitting and persecution, only after it has destroyed the mother as hated and loved object, and only after it has responded to its unconscious guilt, that the infant can begin to negotiate the depressive position and come to terms with the havoc it has wreaked. If the infant succeeds in mitigating this violence, then he or she can repair, reinstate, and restore the mother as good object—indeed, as separate subject with agency and will—initiating an object relation not only with her but also beyond her, with the rest of the world and its many creatures. According to Klein, "making reparation" constitutes "a fundamental element in love and in all human relationships."[9]

Klein's reparative process locates a primal violence at the heart of subjectivity and subject formation. Mina's case history illustrates the profoundly racialized character of that violence. In mourning her un-acknowledged loss of mother and motherland, Mina deploys a psychic strategy of splitting and idealization dependent on the segregation of gender and race. That is, she idealizes the white adoptive mother while simultaneously de-idealizing the Korean birth mother. Hence, the re-parative position that Klein associates with the infant's reinstatement is, in Mina's case, a racialized position.

Mina's case history insists that we consider Klein's concepts of good and bad objects as theories about good and bad racialized objects, her concepts of the depressive and reparative positions as theories about *racial* reparation. Indeed, Mina's case history broadly demands consider-ation of how racial difference is figured within primal fantasies of infan-tile development, fantasies that are too often analyzed solely in terms of gender and gendered development. From another perspective, Mina's case history also reveals the racial nature of kinship, the social and psychic processes of (pre)-Oedipal family formations that continue to regulate the symbolic meaning and importance of bloodlines, race, and nation. Mina's "whole adoption thing" implicates a terrain of infantile development and object relations—a primal territory of splitting and idealization, guilt and depression, reinstatement and reparation—that haunts her into adulthood. It casts a long and profound psychic shadow over all her relations with others, romantic or otherwise, and it over-determines not just her sexual preferences but her racial antipathies as well.

In short, Mina's history insists on our rethinking Klein's concept of good and bad mothers through a more refined theory of good and bad *racialized* mothers. As such, psychic health would entail a reparative position for race, one accounting for the unfixing of Mina's racialized idealizations, her racial splitting of the mother, and her segregation of love. It would demand, in other words, the psychic possibility of two "good-enough" racialized mothers—not the white *or* Korean mother but rather the white *and* Korean mother. In contrast to Freud's more developmental stages, Klein's conception of reparation, as a psychic process and position the subject continually negotiates, offers one way of understanding how the loss of mother and motherland, associated with transnational adoption and racial melancholia, might be managed over time. How exactly does Mina negotiate a psychic space between racial melancholia and racial reparation?

In order to consider how Klein's theory of the beautiful picture might help to restore a notion of the good-enough mother across racial registers, it is useful to return to the discussion from chapter three. In "A Contribution to the Psychogenesis of Manic-Depressive States," Klein describes the ways in which some patients deploy psychic mechanisms of splitting and idealization in order to preserve a "beautiful picture" of the mother in the face of a seemingly real object felt to be wholly debased and inadequate:

> In some patients who had turned away from their mother in dislike or hate, or used other mechanisms to get away from her, I have found that there existed in their minds nevertheless a beautiful picture of the mother, but one which was felt to be a *picture* of her only, not her real self. The real object was felt to be unattractive—really an injured, incurable and therefore dreaded person. The beautiful picture had been dissociated from the real object but had never been given up, and played a great part in the specific ways of their sublimations.[10]

The Korean birth mother—the "bitch" and "poor whore"—who abandoned Mina on a church doorstep, without proper explanation or a proper name, comes to assume the status of this unattractive creature, this "real object." She becomes "an injured, incurable and therefore dreaded person."

Such dread opens on the affective terrain of hate and envy. It poisons Mina's relationship to Koreanness, accounting for her radical devaluation of all things associated with the motherland, from her "slutty" Korean classmates at dance school to Korean and Korean Americans who are all "prejudiced against Korean adoptees." So too Mina devalues the other "screwed-up" Korean adoptees she encounters at adoption camp and from her local support group, as well as the Koreans in Korea who will take advantage of "rich Americans" searching for their birth mothers. Mina's dread threatens her therapeutic relationship to the Korean American therapist, who is warned by Mina, from their very first session, not to be like these disparaged others. Equally distressing, it shapes her antipathy and bigotry toward numerous other racialized and minority groups.

If, as Klein insists, the "beautiful picture [of the birth mother] had been dissociated from the real object but had never been given up, and played a great part in the specific ways of their [the patients'] sublimations," then we come to witness in Mina's case history the particular racial forms and defenses that these sublimations assume. Mina's excessive idealization of whiteness and of the white adoptive mother, a figure of limitless plenitude who would do "anything and everything" for her, is coupled with her excessive devaluation of both the Korean birth mother and racial otherness as a categorical whole. In short, Mina sublimates the beautiful picture of the Korean birth mother, displacing it wholly into an idealized whiteness, an idealized white mother who possesses all the qualities—education, privilege, independence, and insight —the birth mother decisively lacks.

The extreme nature of Mina's idealizations and de-idealizations suggests how racial difference can function phantasmatically in primitive processes of splitting, projection, and introjection around the maternal figure that marks the paranoid development of infantile psychic life. Even more, it indicates how for Mina, good and bad objects become racially segregated into "white" and "Korean," and how this splitting forecloses the possibility that good and bad can simultaneously pertain to both maternal figures at once, functioning across racial registers. Only by coming to such an affective position—only by renegotiating a beautiful picture in relation to both whiteness and Koreanness as good enough —can Mina accomplish the difficult task of racial reparation.

Mina is prepared to undertake this formidable venture. For despite her numerous tirades against the Korean birth mother and Koreanness, we can nevertheless detect a beautiful picture—albeit a repressed and unconscious one—of the lost mother and motherland, not fully circumscribed by an idealized whiteness. For instance, in describing the Korean birth mother as a "poor whore," Mina displays a psychic and linguistic ambivalence unfolding along the terrain not just of hate, but love. Through this turn of phrase Mina not only condemns the "bitch" who abandoned her but also establishes a degree of sympathetic identification with this devalued figure—the double meaning of *poor* whore assuming an economic and emotional resonance in relation to the birth mother's imagined plight.

Indeed, throughout the course of her treatment and during her various regressions into racial antipathy, Mina nevertheless displayed a remarkable psychic fidelity to the Korean birth mother. Mina's repeated romantic failures with abusive and unavailable boyfriends, the imagined duplicities of her Korean classmates, her bond with Suzette—the mother duck who "pecked," "hurt," and finally "abandoned" her ugly ducklings—and the deep-seated fear that she is responsible for her own abandonment, all underscore the ambivalent identifications that Mina preserves in relation to the lost Korean birth mother as both loved and hated object, as both good and bad object. Indeed, Mina's recursive assumptions of inadequacy, of not being good enough herself, may indicate that she is taking on the difficult psychic burdens of failure she once ascribed solely to the bad Korean birth mother.

Klein reminds us that extreme feelings of persecution and hate do not necessarily foreclose the possibility of love; indeed, they are in certain cases its very preconditions. Mina's racial tirades could simultaneously indicate a type of psychic desperation, a defense against a feeling of imminent loss, the loss of the good object or of goodness itself. In this respect, Mina's racial persecution anxieties are psychically complex, insofar as they indicate an attempt to preserve not just the ego but the "good internalized objects with whom the ego is identified as a whole."[11] Her excessive idealizations of whiteness can, at the same time, denote that persecution is the main driving force configuring the ego. For as Klein observes, infants "whose capacity for love is strong have less need for idealization than those in whom destructive impulses and persecutory anxiety are paramount."[12]

In short, Mina's affective polarities—her excessive idealization of whiteness and her excessive hatred of Koreanness—might, in fact, belie a great psychic effort on her part to preserve unconsciously the goodness of the lost Korean birth mother, a figure whose existence is felt to be in crisis, if not altogether irrecoverable under the palimpsest of the idealized white mother. Klein writes, "The stronger the anxiety is of losing the loved objects, the more the ego strives to save them, and the harder the task of restoration becomes the stricter will grow the demands which are associated with the super-ego."[13] Mina's case history thus raises the possibility of an ethical death drive at the heart of Klein's theories of infantile development. Such an ethical death drive preserves a space of goodness for the Korean birth mother, while mapping the psychic parameters under which we might begin to theorize a reparative position for race, one involving not only this specific maternal figure but also racial ideals at large.

In our prior work on racial melancholia, we suggest that the melancholic's absolute refusal to relinquish the lost other—to forfeit alterity—at any cost delineates one psychic process of an ethical death drive, in which the loved but lost racial object or ideal is so overwhelmingly important to the ego that it is willing to preserve it even at the cost of its own psychic health.[14] In other words, racial melancholia indicates one way that lost and socially disparaged racial (m)others and ideals live on unconsciously in the psychic realm beyond the normative mandates of the Oedipus complex.

From this perspective, Mina's case history illustrates how processes of incorporation underwriting racial melancholia might have their benevolent and ego-sustaining dimensions, a possibility "Freud overlooks in the effort to link melancholia with the institution of the super-ego."[15] In Klein's account of maternal separation and the incorporation of good and bad mothers, Judith Butler argues, guilt is produced not through the internalization of an external prohibition, as it is in Freud's account of the super-ego in "The Ego and the Id," but through an internal mechanism that seeks to save objects from the ego's own destructive possibilities. For Klein, the infant's psychic experiences pose a mortal threat not just to the loved object but ultimately to its own self as well, its connections to other creatures and things. Reparation thus provides one psychic mechanism of preserving the lost object after, from, and beyond violence, reconstituting and redirecting the negativity of the death drive away from unmitigated guilt and destruction.

In Mina's case history, the death drive might be said to underwrite a type of ethical fidelity to the Korean birth mother as well as Koreanness itself. Such an ethical hold on the part of the melancholic ego becomes the precondition for racial survival, a psychic strategy for living and for living on. In the transferential aspects of melancholic identifications, Freud observes, "is the expression of there being something in common, which may signify love."[16] The redistribution of this love across a field of foreclosed, repressed, and unconscious objects—the desegregation of this love such that Mina can apportion to the devalued Korean birth mother some of the affect she reserves for the idealized white

mother—constitutes one social and political project for racial reparation, returning us to the affective reservoir of the negative Oedipus
complex. In so doing, it also expands the psychic terrain of transnational adoption and alternative family and kinship structures.

Klein is even more emphatic about this paradoxical connection between hate and love, of profound psychic violence, melancholia, and the
death drive as the constitutive basis for (racial) reparation: "But, while in
committing suicide the ego intends to murder its bad objects, in my view
at the same time it also always aims at saving its loved objects, internal or
external. To put it shortly: in some cases the phantasies underlying
suicide aim at preserving the internalized good objects and that part of
the ego which is identified with good objects, and also at destroying the
other part of the ego which is identified with the bad objects and the id.
Thus the ego is enabled to become united with its loved objects."[17]
According to Klein, successful psychic negotiation by patients who exhibit extreme anxieties of persecution or excessive mechanisms of idealization requires that the patients "revise their relation to their parents—
whether they be dead or alive—and to rehabilitate them to some extent
even if they have grounds for actual grievances."[18] Patients who fail in the
work of mourning were "unable in early childhood to establish their
internal 'good' objects and to feel secure in their inner world. They have
never really overcome the infantile depressive position."[19] Perhaps the
most crucial element in Mina's slow psychic evolution—her gradual
move toward a reparative position for the Korean birth mother and
Koreanness—is the transferential relationship that she builds with her
Korean American psychotherapist. As a Korean American therapist, Han
is a figure Mina has specifically sought out for treatment, and one she
ultimately constitutes as a racial transitional object.

Racial Transitional Objects

Winnicott's theory of transitional objects proves especially useful in considering the dynamics of Mina's transference. In "Transitional Objects
and Transitional Phenomena," Winnicott outlines his concept of the transitional object, that "first possession" of the infant—the thumb, the teddy
bear, the tattered blanket—which opens up a "transitional space," an
"intermediate area between the subjective and that which is objectively
perceived."[20] He continues, It "is not the object, of course, that is transitional. The object represents the infant's transition from a state of being

merged with the mother to a state of being in relation to the mother as something outside and separate."[21] The transitional object is neither strictly internal nor strictly external. "It is never under magical control like the internal object, nor is it outside control as the real mother is."[22]

On the whole, transitional phenomena give "room [to the infant] for the process of becoming able to accept difference and similarity," and thus they become the "root of symbolism in time."[23] Transitional phenomena negotiate the invariable frustrations of the infant as it comes to terms with its compromised autonomy in a world of others it cannot fully control. By providing a psychic third space between inner and outer worlds, transitional phenomena permit the psyche to negotiate what were previously felt to be mutually exclusive options: inside/outside; subjectivity/objectivity; unity/separation. Indeed, we might say that transitional phenomena allow the infant the means to negotiate Freud's pleasure and reality principles, the life and death drives, and what Klein described as primitive positions of extreme love and hate, which must eventually be resolved by the integration of the mother as a whole, separate, and good-enough object. The transitional object, as Adam Phillips points out, "is always a combination, but one that provides, by virtue of being more than the sum of its parts, a new, third alternative."[24] This transitional third space is not one of obstacles and fixity, but one of psychic movement and possibility.

Significantly, the fate of the transitional object is gradual decathexis. Over a number of years, Winnicott observes, the transitional object "becomes not so much forgotten as relegated to limbo . . . It is not forgotten and it is not mourned. It loses meaning, and this is because the transitional phenomena have become diffused, have become spread out over the whole intermediate territory between 'inner psychic reality' and the 'external world as perceived by two persons in common,' that is to say, over the whole cultural field."[25] For Winnicott, the domains of play, artistic creativity, religious feeling, and dreaming become those privileged zones of transitional space whereby the recurring burdens of reality are negotiated throughout a subject's life. The task of reality-acceptance is never complete. Winnicott underscores that "no human being is free from the strain of relating inner and outer reality, and that relief from this strain is provided by an intermediate area of experience which is not challenged (arts, religion, etc.). This intermediate area is in direct continuity with the play area of the small child who is 'lost' in play."[26]

Winnicott suggests, in patients who were not started off well enough by their mothers or whose mother were not "good enough," that the fundamental task of the psychotherapy is to open up this transitional space for creative play. Indeed, psychotherapy as a clinical practice might be defined by this one purpose, that it "takes place in the overlap of two areas of playing, that of the patient and that of the therapist. Psychotherapy has to do with two people playing together. The corollary of this is that where playing is not possible then the work done by the therapist is directed towards bringing the patient from a state of not being able to play into a state of being able to play."[27]

While it is clear that Mina draws great sustenance from practicing her art—dancing—it is also evident that such a privileged realm of artistic creativity does not fully allow the successful negotiation between her inner psychic reality and her external world. Mina's dance teachers repeatedly tell her that, although her technique is "superb," her "emotional expression" remains blocked. Moreover, Mina's enactment of her adoption and abandonment fantasies through the parable of her ducks—constituted by the patient as literal transitional objects that remain to be decathected—underscores the extent to which her capacity to play with her racial predicaments and impasses, her ability to negotiate productively her inner and outer realities, is circumscribed. Under such conditions, the role of the therapist is to bring her patient into a state of being able to play such that racial difference can be reinstated and repaired, ultimately to be dispersed over a wide cultural field. Here, we might describe this clinical goal as the pedagogy of racial reparation.

Winnicott's distinction between object relating and object use, between the patient and the therapist in the space of the clinic, further illuminates Mina's psychic and racial predicaments.[28] On the one hand, Winnicott associates object relating with orthodox Freudian notions of transference, with the analyst as blank screen on whom figures from the past (mother, father, siblings) are projected. On the other hand, Winnicott argues, object use not only takes into account the question, "Who am I representing?" but also raises the important question, "What am I being used to do?" In other words, it is not enough to say that the analyst stands in for the mother, unless we specify what particular aspects of the mother (gender or race, for example) are being revived and worked through and for what purposes.

For Mina, issues of object relating and object use come together in crucial ways that are intensified by the pregnancy of her Korean American psychotherapist. The visibility of the analyst's pregnancy, like her race, makes the pregnancy public property between analyst and patient, while intensifying the transference and countertransferences between them. Often, pregnancies can also lead to resistance and reaction formations that place inordinate strain on the therapeutic relationship.[29] It is clear that Mina cannot initially use the lost Korean birth mother, in any productive manner, to negotiate her racial antipathies. The return of this figure, however, in the transferential guise of the pregnant Korean American therapist/mother, instigates a particular set of psychic reactions, allowing Han to become a racial transitional object for Mina. Through these transferences and counter-transferences, Mina is able to move psychically from object relating to object use.

What is the therapist being used to do? She is being used by Mina as a transitional object allowing her to resignify her vexed racial identifications with the lost Korean birth mother, not as a bundle of hated projections, but as a whole person, a thing-in-itself. From this perspective, Mina also might be seen as using the young Chinese transnational adoptees that she mentors as racial transitional objects. Through them, Mina negotiates both her more complicated identifications with her Korean transnational adoptee peers and Koreanness itself—a kind of psychic coalitional identity politics that denaturalizes strict divisions between private Oedipal family dynamics and public discourses of race and racism. At the same time, such a denaturalization opens up a racial space beyond antinomies of good and bad, or black and white. In our colorblind age, it offers the possibility for the collective reworking of racial antipathies and ideals that govern conventional notions of family and kinship, loosening the ties that anchor their sexual and racial moorings.

By disclosing her pregnancy to her patient, the Korean American therapist becomes the good enough Korean mother. Mina's therapist keeps her child but, most importantly, does not abandon her patient in the process. In this regard, she is both a good enough, (private) mother and a good enough, (public) analyst. Han is an educated, privileged, and independent Korean woman, with qualities similar to Mina's idealized adoptive white mother. In Mina's estimation Han's pregnancy is planned, for she "wouldn't be so stupid and just get knocked up." As a racial transitional object, she introduces into Mina's psyche the notion of similarity *and* difference in regard to the figure of the de-idealized Korean birth mother, while simultaneously mitigating the affective extremes characterizing the polarities between bad and good. In short, the therapist allows Mina a way to play with and to reintegrate the bad qualities of the hated (Korean) mother and the good qualities of the loved (white) mother into one figure, opening up a transitional space in which overlapping areas of loss and care might take hold. "You're a professional," Mina avers to the Korean American therapist. "You'll come back to the office, and we will work together then."

By providing a space for Mina to explore any potential feelings of abandonment and jealousy ("Oh, I wasn't asking or even thinking that you could go with me [to Korea]. Besides you have a baby to take care of"), and by suggesting that Mina's Korean birth mother might "currently be around my [Han's] age," the therapist becomes a screen on which the birth mother can take shape as an actual living person rather than a set of fragmented pictures, hated projections, or persecutory fantasies. She becomes, in short, a person with a separate reality. In using the therapist in this manner, Mina is finally able to resignify both her attitude and affect toward the Korean birth mother, such that a beautiful picture might begin to emerge. "I just always imagined her [my birth mother] as a 20-something-year-old girl like me," Mina admits. "But I guess she isn't anymore."

Mina uses the Korean American therapist as a racial transitional object that allows her to renegotiate her attitudes toward the Korean birth mother, Koreanness, race, and racial difference. In the course of her treatment, a significant psychic shift occurs with regard to Mina's ducks: Suzette ceases to abuse her ugly ducklings and has instead "bathed and cleaned them up." Exhibiting such care toward her abandoned ducklings represents for Mina an altered affective capacity, an altered identification with a lost Korean birth mother and, indeed, a lost ideal of Koreanness. Moreover, Mina opens the book of her past. She decides to share with the therapist her adoption file and thus her "unofficial" history prior to her "official" arrival and history in the United States. At the same time, Mina decides to begin a search for the lost Korean birth mother, a search that she does not initiate in isolation, but with the support of others, including her adoptive white mother. Thus, Mina comes to occupy a psychic position in which anger can be negotiated and loss can be repaired such that the Korean birth mother might be reinstated into a world of loved objects. In this manner, Mina sets the psychic stage for her birth mother to emerge as good enough.

The capacity to use the analyst, as Winnicott points out, "cannot be said to be inborn." It is the task of the therapist to abet the transformation from object relating to object use, to "be concerned with the development and establishment of the capacity to use objects and to recognize a patient's inability to use objects, where this is a fact."[30] Analysts, like mothers, Winnicott writes, "can be good or not good enough."[31]

Han's transformation into a good enough mother/analyst allows Mina to constitute her disparaged Korean birth mother and, in turn, her idealized white adoptive mother as good enough mothers too. How does this happen? Mina's transition hinges on several factors regarding the pedagogy of race and racial difference in the space of the clinic, as well as the material importance of the therapist's racialized body in the course of treatment. Arguably one of the most under-theorized aspects of psychoanalytic theory, race cannot be seen as merely additive or symptomatic of more primary psychic conditions. Mina's case history insists on an understanding of race, not just sex and sexual difference, as constitutive of the earliest forms of object relations and subjective development. Her story underscores the ways transnational adoption, as a contemporary social phenomenon, opens onto a psychic terrain of intense splitting and idealization. These are primitive psychical processes that can be understood only through sustained attention to the politics of race and racial difference. In a neoliberal, colorblind, and multicultural age, this racial return must become a central concern for psychoanalytic theory and practice, informing our understandings of how Oedipal paradigms of family and kinship are always riven and bound by questions of race and nation as well.

Mina's case history forces us to revise in fundamental ways Freud's pathological notions of melancholia as an everyday structure of racial feeling, Klein's ideas concerning the paranoid, depressive, and reparative positions as racial positions, and Winnicott's concept of transitional objects and the good enough as possible psychic tools for negotiating the pain of racial history and reality. For Winnicott, the creative and cultural domains are the privileged dominion of transitional space, but we learn from Mina's case history that culture and cultural difference—the rhetoric of multicultural harmony—may also be the source of racial upheaval and unrest, not just the panacea for, but also the poison of, reality.

Mina's case history also suggests that we must consider how hate and envy—Klein's most toxic of psychic positions—may represent to minority patients a form of mental gymnastics to which they must subject themselves in order to preserve and protect their socially disparaged loved objects and ideals, objects and ideals felt to be lost or under imminent social erasure.[32] Mina's intense aversion toward the Korean nationals at her dance academy—young Korean women who, to Mina's unconscious mind, are cherished rather than abandoned by their well-to-do families—might be analyzed in this light for, as Klein reminds us, a "very deep and sharp division between loved and hated objects indicates that destructive impulses, envy and persecutory anxiety are very strong and serve as a defense against these emotions."[33] Klein defines envy as "the angry feeling that another person possesses and enjoys something desirable—the envious impulse being to take it away or to spoil it."[34] For Klein, envy is the most poisonous of psychic states; it is pure psychic destruction. Unlike jealousy, in which the subject feels deprived by somebody else of an object he or she loves, envy focuses aggression not on rivals but on the object itself. Envy entails not only the desire to possess this loved object but also the desire to spoil the goodness of the object with bad parts of the self. In an infant, envy simultaneously involves robbing the good breast of its positive qualities while "putting badness, primarily bad excrements and bad parts of the self, into the mother . . . in order to spoil and destroy her."[35] For Klein, envy thwarts all attempts at reparation. Representing senseless aggression, envy threatens mental development itself, for it impairs the infant's ability to build up the good object, instead opening onto the psychic terrain of the death drive, of deep negativity, antirelational, and anti-life tendencies.

For Mina, however, envy does not reach such extreme psychic heights. Proving instead to be resourceful, if not outright creative, envy in Mina's case history might be described as a kind of melancholic racial coping mechanism in a colorblind age, used to preserve the goodness of the lost (Korean) mother. To the extent that Mina's primitive psychic processes of splitting and idealization segregate the good (white) mother from the bad (Korean) mother along a strictly racialized divide, her story allows us one way of perceiving how envy might not be entirely psychically destructive or socially debilitating, abetting rather than hampering Mina's entry into a reparative position for race. From a slightly different perspective, Mina's envy might be said to facilitate an ethical death drive by which she can spoil just a little bit the goodness of whiteness and the white mother she idealizes.[36] In an age of queer liberalism, this psychic divestment from a long legacy of whiteness as property and privilege proves useful. Through this spoiling of whiteness, Mina can make room in her psyche to begin to repair the badness of the Korean birth mother and Koreanness itself. In other words, through envy's spoilage, Mina can begin to undo and to redress the psychic displacements that configure whiteness as a kind of racial palimpsest masking the lost goodness of the Korean birth mother. In this manner, she learns to resignify and quicken her desire for those lost creatures and things that conventional culture and kinship would disavow or bury.

Mina begins to address and repair her racial melancholia by returning to the light of consciousness the forfeited goodness encrypted in this dreaded maternal figure. In short, she begins to come to terms with not only the lost Korean birth mother but also the goodness that she has lost in her. Thus, Mina unfolds in her psyche the Korean birth mother as a different type of historical subject, one who can come to occupy the space of the good enough. In the process, she simultaneously creates psychic room for the idealized white adoptive mother to emerge as good enough, too. Mina creates a reparative mechanism through which good and bad can overlap and move across racial divides; in the process she reworks the binds and bonds of family and kinship that make certain relationships seemingly impossible.

Admittedly, such an interpretation of Kleinian envy is unorthodox. The racial exigencies of Mina's case history, as well as the disappearing act of race that defines our colorblind age, however, demand such creative infidelity. Ultimately, as Mina discovers a reparative position for race that is productive rather than debilitating, psychoanalysis as a clinical process and a theoretical enterprise also begins to address, in more programmatic ways, the profound legacies and difficult histories of racial pain. It attends to the prospects of kinship and racial reparation as both an individual and a collective endeavor.

FIVE

The Feeling of Kinship

෨ ෨ ෨

AFFECT AND LANGUAGE

IN *HISTORY AND MEMORY*

Emotion is a certain way of apprehending the world.
—JEAN-PAUL SARTRE, *The Emotions: Outline of a Theory*

Language still denies us its essence: that it is the house of the truth of Being. Instead, language surrenders itself to our mere willing and trafficking as an instrument of domination over beings.
—MARTIN HEIDEGGER, "Letter on Humanism"

To articulate the past historically does not mean to recognize it "the way it really was" (Ranke). It means to seize hold of a memory as it flashes up at a moment of danger.
—WALTER BENJAMIN, "Theses on the Philosophy of History"

Feeling in History

Rea Tajiri's video, *History and Memory: For Akiko and Taka-shige* (1991), is a documentary about a young Japanese American woman whose family endures internment during the Second World War.[1] Whereas the young woman's mother has repressed all memories of her internment experience, the daughter has nightmares she cannot explain, recurring images of a young woman at a watering well. The daughter is depressed, and her parents argue over the etiology of her depression. Eventually, the daughter discovers these images are re-enactments of her mother's history in camp. Ironically, the mother has history but no memory, while the daughter has memory but no history. For both mother and daughter, history and memory do not come together until the daughter visits the site of the former internment camp, Poston, nearly forty-six years later. There, she realizes it is her mother's history that she "remembers."

Like *First Person Plural*, *History and Memory* might be described as a documentary of affect. Tajiri's video proposes an alternative historical understanding in which, as Janet Sternburg observes, the "primacy of truths claimed by facticity yields to the equally pressing claims of interior life."[2] The film is an eloquent disquisition on processes of racial melancholia discussed in the previous two chapters.[3] It exemplifies the ways in which historical traumas of loss, grief, and forgetting are passed down from one generation to another unconsciously, how, as Freud remarks in his essay on "The Unconscious," "the unconscious of one human being can react upon that of another, without passing through the conscious."[4] The daughter's psychic predicament illustrates Freud's observations that the most difficult losses suffered in melancholia are unconscious ones, psychic forfeitures that cannot be properly grieved and for which Freud could offer no simple solution or remedy. "[One] feels justified in maintaining the belief that a loss of this kind occurred," Freud writes in "Mourning and Melancholia," "but one cannot see clearly what it is that has been lost, and it is all the more reasonable to suppose that the patient cannot consciously perceive what he has lost either. This, indeed, might be so even if the patient is aware of the loss which has given rise to his melancholia, but only in the sense that he knows *whom* he has lost but not *what* he has lost in him."[5]

Tajiri knows that she has lost something in her mother but, like Mina in our discussion in the last chapter, she is unable to specify the exact nature of this loss or to name this history of forgetting. Hence, through a painful but unspeakable sadness, we come to witness a psychic forfeiture of great consequence, a cleaving between mother and daughter that begs historical explanation. As his privileged theory of unresolved grief, melancholia represents for Freud one of the most pathological and incurable of intrasubjective psychic conditions. Freud typically casts melancholia as an individual predicament, but *History and Memory* decidedly configures this psychic condition as an intersubjective and collective intergenerational struggle negotiated between a mother and a daughter, through their vexed feelings of kinship. In Tajiri's documentary, emotion thus becomes a "certain way of apprehending the world."[6]

In the concluding moments of *History and Memory*, Tajiri offers the following resolution to her psychic predicament. Over an edited sequence of images—a kneeling young woman in a blue dress (played by Tajiri herself), white ruffles poking out from under her sleeves, her hands filling a canteen from a watering well in the desert, her cupped palms scooping the streaming water to splash on her face—the director offers this final voiceover:

> My sister used to say how funny it was. When someone tells you a story you create a picture of it in your mind. Sometimes the picture will return without the story. I've been carrying around this picture with me for years. It's the one memory I have of my mother speaking of camp while we grew up. I overhear her describing to my sister this simple action: her hands filling a canteen out in the middle of the desert. For years I've been living with this picture, without the story, feeling a lot of pain, not knowing how they fit together. But now I found I could connect the picture to the story. I could forgive my mother her loss of memory and could make this image for her.

I would like to reflect for a moment on Tajiri's extended voiceover, a meditation on the ways in which story and picture, as well as history and memory, must finally connect and come together such that Tajiri can forgive her mother her "loss of memory."

This coming together is neither a direct nor a simple affair. As Tajiri moves away from the realm of the social to the domain of the psychic, history, affect, and language become increasingly entangled. Overhearing her mother describe to her sister a simple action, "her hands filling a canteen out in the middle of the desert," Tajiri's recollection comes to assume the form of a haunting image. Less representational than emotional, and marked by the failure of language, this image is dissociated from the traditional protocols of signification and accompanied by an excruciating affective intensity that eludes, while simultaneously demanding, symbolic inscription.[7]

By underscoring the ways in which historical events relating to Japanese internment are transformed into unspeakable private emotion and grief, Tajiri's film draws attention to the public nature of melancholy, extending our discussion of affirmation and forgetting from chapter two into the domain of the psychic, while engaging a recent body of scholarship focused on the public and political life of feeling.[8] In doing so, History and Memory illustrates how the encryption of trauma, to borrow a concept from Abraham and Torok, transforms the collective

"Her hands filling a canteen out in the middle of the desert . . ." From *History and Memory: For Akiko and Takashige*, directed by Rea Tajiri.

event of internment into a private and individuated conflict of kinship, a psychic incorporation that Marianne Hirsch has described in the context of the Holocaust as "postmemory."[9] In the process, intergenerational strife and gendered discord become the displaced sites of national history, serving to obscure the politics of race and nation. Indeed, such an encryption reduces political conflict to cultural questions of filial struggle and opposition. As argued in the discussions of transnational adoption in the previous two chapters, it also abets the psychic proliferation of bad mothers.

In the final analysis, the mother's lost history of the camp finds its social trace in the daughter's recurring image of a young woman "filling a canteen out in the middle of the desert," a persistent though inexplicable picture whose affective pain must be repaired through intergenerational forgiveness. In this regard, Tajiri's maternal predicament returns us to the question of racial reparation introduced in the last chapter. Here, *History and Memory* demands a sustained investigation of racial reparation as not only a private but also a public phenomenon, drawing attention to the processes by which the mother might emerge as good enough and history as "the way it really was" might be reconsidered. In short, Tajiri's documentary expands our discussions of racial reparation, configuring it as an individual and collective dilemma, a psychic as well as a political practice.

Like a fleeting Benjaminian flash, Tajiri's picture of a young woman at the watering well appears at a moment of danger threatening "to disappear irretrievably."[10] For it returns as an image decisively severed from any historical understanding. However, this is not an irretrievable loss.

Ultimately, Tajiri's film illustrates how racial reparation becomes animated through a productive reciprocity between—rather than a binding of—affect and language. Much of poststructuralist thought, as Rei Terada points out, assumes an antipathetic relationship between affect and language.[11] *History and Memory* suggests a different account of this cleaving. It offers a critical vision in which affect and language might not be disjunctive, but instead work collectively to transform our relation both to history and to structures of family and kinship.

From this perspective, we might say that *History and Memory* offers us an extended meditation on the nature of a picture—the ways in which images might come to (re)negotiate a relationship between affect and language in order to underwriting new historical meaning. Tajiri's maternal predicament also returns us to a set of issues raised in chapter two, regarding the dialectic of affirmation (of freedom) and forgetting (of race) that marks the limits of historicism, narratives of liberal progress, and freedom in our colorblind age. In Tajiri's documentary, as in Truong's *The Book of Salt*, history as the way-it-really-was gives over to alternative modes of knowing and being, through which forgotten histories and subjects might come to inhabit the world in a different manner.

History and Memory is part of a growing body of cultural productions about Japanese internment by *sansei* (third-generation) artists born after the Second World War. These include films such as Lisa Yasui's *A Family Gathering* and Janice Tanaka's *Memories from the Department of Amnesia*, and *Who's Going to Pay for These Donuts, Anyway?* Also included are novels and collections of poetry such as Julie Otsuka's *When the Emperor Was Divine* and Lawson Fusao Inada's *Legends from Camp*.[12] Unlike their second-generation (*nisei*) parents and first-generation (*issei*) grandparents, these third-generation (*sansei*) directors and writers did not live through internment.[13] For the most part, their films and novels have been produced and published after House Resolution 422, also known as the Civil Liberties Act of 1988. Signed into law by President Ronald Reagan on August 10, 1988, H.R. 422 not only provided monetary restitution of $20,000 to each surviving internee but also offered a national apology for the "grave injustice done to both citizens and permanent residents of Japanese ancestry by the evacuation, relocation, and internment" of 112,000 Japanese American civilians, two-thirds of whom were U.S. citizens, during the Second World War.[14]

Although the monies were never fully disbursed, the Civil Liberties Act of 1988 also promised to establish a $1.5 billion "public education fund to finance efforts to inform the public about internment so as to prevent the recurrence of any similar event."[15] As Japanese internment and its policies of indefinite detention fade from national consciousness in the face of our current and indefinite War on Terror, Marita Sturken's observations about the political legacy of internment, the bombing of Hiroshima and Nagasaki, and the abnegation of Constitutional protections during the Second World War become increasingly prescient: "What challenges does [Japanese internment] pose to the complicity of memory and forgetting? What would it mean for Americans to remember the names Manzanar, Poston, Tule Lake, Topaz, Minidoka, Heart Mountain, Jerome, Gila River, Amache, and Rohwer in the way that they know the names Auschwitz, Dachau, and Buchenwald?" To begin to memorialize the camps and their survivors, Sturken observes, would entail "[rethinking] the myth of America's actions in World War II, a myth that even now remains resolutely intact," while "[opening] up the question of what constitutes American nationalism and identity."[16]

Today, the Civil Liberties Act of 1988 is commonly heralded as the conclusion to a regrettable but anomalous chapter of American history. But as *History and Memory* so emphatically insists, political reparation and psychic reparation are hardly coterminous. Returning to a history of Japanese internment before her time, Tajiri raises this urgent question: What does it mean to take responsibility for a historical event you never actually experienced? *History and Memory* suggests such responsibility is as much an affective as it is a political affair. Indeed, it suggests that historical inquiry might be motivated by an affective relationship between past and present rather than approached solely as a causal affair. This is all the more so in the face of internment's ostensible historical resolution, and with the great likelihood, as Victor Bascara argues, that the Civil Liberties Act "may go down in history as multiculturalism's last gasp—the last demonstration of an idea that it is the role of the state to bring about social and economic equality."[17]

If the daughter's cure, in *History and Memory*, requires the bringing together of story and picture, history and memory, this bringing together does not involve the recovery of a lost narrative or the restoration of a set of causal, referential events. Indeed, this reciprocal address of emotion between mother and daughter functions under the sign of displacement, indexing histories not of affirmation but forgetting. Conceived in this manner, history is not a set of new representations or corrective visions. To the contrary, history is, in Fredric Jameson's famous formulation, "what hurts . . . [It] can be apprehended only through its effects, and never directly as some reified force."[18] Like *The Book of Salt*, *History and Memory* draws insistent attention to dominant modes of knowing and being under historicist disciplining, all the while considering how affect might come to supplement history as the way-it-really-was by providing another language for loss. Tajiri's affective predicament insists on a notion of history that, in Benjamin's words, "[seizes] hold of a memory as it flashes up at a moment of danger." This appropriation of memory's affective valences ultimately works to expand the signifying capacities of language and to endow forgotten creatures and things with new historical significance and meaning.

Here, affect might be considered a form of history itself, exerting considerable pressure, as Ann Cvetkovich suggests, on conventional understandings of identity and representation, while insisting on a reconsideration of the traditional divide between political and emotional life.[19] Tajiri's affective predicaments highlight the fact that history is not linear, progressive, or resolute; indeed, it is not even past. Hauntingly present, history is, in the words of Cathy Caruth, "referential precisely to the extent that it is not fully perceived as it occurs" and "can be grasped only in the very inaccessibility of its occurrence."[20] Tajiri's affective predicaments, a lingering of emotion on the limits of conventional representation, are ones for which we must learn to take historical responsibility. And it is an ownership of some consequence to the impasses of race and identity politics that we currently face in our colorblind age.

The Non-Visible

I have made a number of claims concerning the relationship between affect, language, and history, the implications of which I would like to unpack more slowly. Let me begin by returning to a detailed analysis of the closing sequence of *History and Memory*, one leading up to Tajiri's final voiceover discussed above.

This closing sequence exemplifies the aesthetic structure of *History and Memory*. Throughout the documentary, Tajiri manipulates image, sound, and text. She frequently overlaps all three simultaneously, but more often than not they remain unsynchronized. In this way, *History and Memory* overwhelms the viewer's capacity to synthesize its numerous visual, acoustic, and textual details. On the level of the visual regime, Tajiri shows clips ranging from classic Hollywood movies and musicals to U.S. Army and War Relocation Authority (WRA) propaganda films. She combines 8mm home movies surreptitiously taken in camp, with more recent home videos, photographs, and maps. All the while, she presents scrolling texts with factual information about Japanese internment, along with scrolling storyboards relating unverifiable family stories narrated from the perspective of an omniscient observer, represented as the ghost of her deceased paternal grandfather.

On the level of the acoustic regime, Tajiri employs a series of voiceover commentaries about her own and her relatives' thoughts and feelings regarding their experiences in camp. She presents an ongoing correspondence with an uncle residing in Holland and engages in a series of exchanges with her parents, aunts, a niece, and a nephew. Throughout, she overlaps these non-diegetic voiceovers with digital sound effects and a number of soundtracks from well-known wartime Hollywood musicals, including Michael Curtiz's Oscar-winning *Yankee Doodle Dandy* (1942).

In the last five and a half minutes of the video, Tajiri engages in a commentary on John Sturges's film *Bad Day at Black Rock* (1955). John J. Macreedy, played by Spencer Tracy, arrives in Black Rock, hoping to deliver to a Japanese American farmer his son's posthumous war medal, awarded for bravery during the Second World War. The farmer Komoko is nowhere to be found. He never appears, "not even a picture," in Tajiri's words. Eventually, we surmise that Komoko has been murdered, the victim of racial antipathy against the Japanese after their bombing of Pearl Harbor. As scenes from Sturges's film are intercut with the recurring image of a young woman at the watering well, the director concludes, "Komoko's disappearance from Black Rock was like our disappearance from history. His absence is his presence. Somehow I could identify with this search, the search for an ever absent image and the desire to create an image where there are so few."

Following this declaration, however, Tajiri does not present us with an "image where there are so few," that is, with a representational image of an absent but imagined Komoko. Rather, she follows this sequence with a black screen, on which the following scrolling text appears after a short pause:

NEW YORK TIMES
AUGUST 28, 1990:
ASSEMBLYMAN GIL
FERGUSON, REPUBLICAN

ORANGE COUNTY, CALIF.,
SEEKS TO HAVE CHILDREN
TAUGHT THAT JAPANESE
AMERICANS WERE NOT
INTERNED IN
"CONCENTRATION CAMPS",
BUT RATHER WERE HELD
IN "RELOCATION CENTERS"
JUSTIFIED BY MILITARY
NECESSITY.

Two years after the passage of the Civil Liberties Act of 1988, and after the ostensible political "resolution" to a regrettable chapter in U.S. history, we witness an ongoing battle over the historical meaning of Japanese American internment that continues to be fought over in the present. After Tajiri presents this, we hear a voiceover dialogue between daughter and mother. Again, the camera shows neither Tajiri nor her mother. Instead, it displays a series of seemingly random, though loosely connected, objects that serve to bind the two women together: rocks and plants in the mother's Chicago garden; a logbook of internees from Poston; a wooden bird given to Tajiri's mother by Tajiri's grandmother; and a tiny scrap of tarpaper from a Poston barrack.

Over each successive image, Tajiri's mother narrates a story about the lingering psychic effects of internment and her recurring dreams of California, where she lived as a young girl prior to her incarceration in the concentration camp. Although she has resided in Chicago for over forty years, the mother speaks of strange feelings of transience, of "living temporarily in Chicago," a city to which her family was relocated after being released from Poston. Legally, the mother is a U.S. citizen. Nonetheless, the rhetoric of the refugee finds uncanny resonance in the mother's psychic predicaments. Again, we are forced to consider the supplemental functions of the political and the psychic. We are forced to rethink, that is, the category of the refugee not only as a formal legal designation but also as an emotional state—a condition of "internal exile," to borrow a suggestive phrase from Victor Burgin.[21]

Next, we hear a voiceover by Tajiri's nephew, who reads from a movie review he published in the *Chicago Tribune* of Alan Parker's *Come See the Paradise* (1990). The film features Dennis Quaid and Tamalyn Tomita, and superimposes a romance plot, concerning the dramas of interracial

TAUGHT THAT JAPANESE

AMERICANS WERE NOT

INTERNED IN

"CONCENTRATION CAMPS",

BUT RATHER WERE HELD

The meaning of internment: an ongoing battle of history. From *History and Memory: For Akiko and Takashige*.

love, over the historical events of internment. As Tajiri presents us with a sequence of interspliced images from Parker's movie and the WRA documentary footage of Japanese evacuation and relocation, the nephew reads:

> This week's movie is *Come See the Paradise*, about a Japanese American family interned in U.S. concentration camps during World War II. Actually, this one is kind of personal for me because my grandmother, her family, and the family of my grandfather, who was in the U.S. Army, were all in the camps too. I don't have any good stories though, because my grandparents never really told me about it. I was thinking of throwing in some impressive facts, like about the memo President Franklin Roosevelt received before creating the camps that explained why they weren't necessary. Or about how no Japanese were ever convicted of anti-U.S. sabotage. But I thought they would bore you. Did they? I also thought that I might get on Dennis Quaid's case for playing the virtuous white guy who audiences can relate to and, of course, gets the girl. And after all, the director Alan Parker is the same guy who made *Mississippi Burning*, the civil rights film that pretended that white FBI agents helped out. I was even thinking of calling the movie *Come See the Parasites*. But then I figured that, being half white myself, maybe I don't have that moral authority, so I guess nastiness is out, too. I guess I could just go for the straightforward review. The film was pretty much sentimental mush, but it was well-done professional mush. Ratings. I'm not giving it a star rating, but I'll say this: not as good as *Godfather III* but better than *Death Stalker III, Warriors from Hell*.

"Alien Roundup" (War Relocation Authority). From *History and Memory: For Akiko and Takashige.*

"Alien Roundup" *(Come See the Paradise)*. From *History and Memory: For Akiko and Takashige.*

Interracial love child
(War Relocation
Authority). From
*History and Memory:
For Akiko and Takashige.*

Interracial love child
(*Come See the Paradise*).
From *History and
Memory: For Akiko and
Takashige.*

pick it up. It is a gum

wrapper. She peels away

the foil and puts it in her

pocket.

(Trans)national alliances and failures: divided allegiance. From *History and Memory: For Akiko and Takashige*.

With the conclusion of the nephew's voiceover, the penultimate scene of *History and Memory* begins. Over a slow cinematic pan across sets of railroad tracks that transported the Japanese internees to their desert jail at Poston, Tajiri offers two simultaneous stories about (trans)national alliances and failures. In a voiceover, she reads a letter written by her uncle, whose self-imposed exile in Holland begins soon after his discharge from the U.S. Army. At the same time, over the visual footage of the Poston railroad yard, Tajiri projects a scrolling text that portrays another story of divided allegiance:

Voiceover: Uncle's Letter	*Scrolling Text*
You asked what I thought I gained or lost from the Evacuation—gained, very little, except a unique situation that a very tiny percentage of the American public had ever experienced. What I lost was my faith in the American Constitution. And it is for that reason that I left the U.S. forty-three years ago, a year after I returned from the War.	They are walking down the street, the boy and his mother. On the ground she sees something. She stops to pick it up. It is a gum wrapper. She peels away the foil and puts it in her pocket. When he sees a wrapper he stops and does the same. Later at home, he finds a whole collection of tinfoil balls which she saves and sends to Japan.

These two overlapping narratives—connecting internment and the aftermath of the Second World War with the devastating atomic bombing of Hiroshima and Nagasaki—illustrate the personal and private consequences of war and public violence. It underscores the complicated political affiliations and emotional conflicts that mark the cleaving of homeland from nation, a nexus of conflicting political and psychic demands that continually exceeds the Manichean binaries of friend versus enemy, Asian versus American—indeed, constituting the impossibility of the category of "Asian American." Tajiri's parable about mother and son encodes the political and psychic dynamics mirroring the filmmaker's own cleaving from her mother. The collecting and mailing of tinfoil balls to Japan illustrates the deflected manner by which histories of violence are melancholically encoded, passed down from one generation to the next not through monumental acts of brutality or abuse but unconsciously, through what Michel de Certeau describes as "the practice of everyday life."[22] Equipped with these accumulated insights and images, we witness the final scene of *History and Memory*: Tajiri's concluding voiceover and haunting image of her mother at the watering well.

I have spent a number of pages describing the last five and a half minutes of *History and Memory* in the hopes of conveying the complex, often disconcerting, viewing experience organizing the formal aesthetics of Tajiri's video. Unlike many conventional documentaries, Tajiri's film does not represent history as a progressive, chronological narrative, systematically moving from cause to effect, from before to after. *History and Memory* eschews protocols of what Bill Nichols describes as documentary filmmaking's "discourses of sobriety," its "distinct [forms] of literalism," and its mimicking of the "canons of expository argument."[23] In their place, Tajiri presents us with a complex argument concerning the supplemental relationship between political and affective histories of Japanese American internment that cannot be easily reconciled with dominant U.S. or Japanese American accounts of the event. Thus, she offers a meta-critique of the project of historicism itself, of history as the way-it-really-was. If the cacophony of visual, acoustic, and textual details overcrowding Tajiri's film might be read as the debris of historical wreckage, accumulating at the feet of Benjamin's angel of history, Tajiri's documentary asks how we might begin to sort through this catastrophic detritus to make new historical sense.[24]

Here, I would like to connect Dipesh Chakrabarty's concept of the hermeneutic tradition discussed in chapter two to my analysis of affect in Tajiri's documentary. Associated with Heidegger, the hermeneutic tradition produces what Chakrabarty calls "'affective histories,' [and] finds thought intimately tied to places and to particular forms of life." The hermeneutic is based on "a loving grasp of detail in search of an understanding of the diversity of human life-worlds."[25] It exists in distinct contrast to an analytic tradition that seeks to posit the empirical as the basis of historical truth and to level human specificity by abstracting heterogeneity and particularity into a universal narrative of Euro-American historical consciousness. Demanding that its subjects perform routine feats of self-abstraction and disincorporation, the analytic sublates difference by annihilating the contingent particulars of the body, emptying it into the homogenous time and space of modernity's now.

History and Memory's complex aesthetic structure calls attention to the persistent tensions between the analytic and the hermeneutic traditions, as a problem both of the visual and of the status of a picture. In expressing her "desire to create an image where there are so few," Tajiri grapples with the false seductions of the analytic: the impulse to recover Komoko in the field of representation, the language of the empirical, and the domain of the visible. In other words, the analytic contract promises that a hitherto excluded Japanese American subject and Japanese American history might be reclaimed and restored into a historical narrative of U.S. liberalism, freedom, and progress through the production of new representations and "corrective" images. Peter Feng describes *History and Memory*'s "busy" aesthetic as a type of Bakhtinian heteroglossia, a dialogizing practice marking the clash between dominant representations, such as ubiquitous images from Hollywood cinema and Asian American counter-representations that are consigned to the margins of the visual field.[26] Evaluating Tajiri's "desire to create an image" along these lines, the battle for history becomes a conflict organized around the referential tenets of an analytic tradition sustained through a set of universalizing binaries: visible/invisible; presence/absence; inclusion/exclusion; positive/negative.[27]

The creation of images "where there are so few"—the restoration of a recuperated Japanese American subject into the picture of U.S. national history—underwrites liberal notions of freedom and progress whereby visibility is legitimated as the mark of presence and inclusion, more so of justice. This process endorses a project of racial liberalism and identity politics abstracted into the empty, homogenous time of our colorblind age. It threatens to universalize the story of Japanese American internment as an unfortunate swerve on the otherwise straight road to democracy and racial assimilation.[28] This dialectic of affirmation (of freedom) and forgetting (of race) demands a progressive narrative, not only of self-correcting democracy, but also of a homogenizing image of internees as loyal and docile American patriots deserving of redress. In the process, it overwrites any affective or cultural ties with Japan, as Tajiri's story of the Uncle in Holland and her parable of tinfoil balls so poignantly underscore.

In her reassessment of Japanese American internment, historian Mae Ngai writes about the perverse and unpredictable effects of the WRA assimilationist policies in camp, with a particular focus on the loyalty questionnaire instituted for the military draft of service-age men as well as the programs for the renunciation of U.S. citizenship and repatriation to Japan. Ngai observes that the alleged disloyalty of "no-no boys" (those that refused the military draft) and renunciants disrupted pristine images of unwavering Japanese American loyalty and enduring patience under democratic duress. Yet, at the same time, it also complicated this political image of divided loyalties by injecting other personal motivations into the historical narrative, including the desire to keep families together under the threat of imminent separation:

> To be sure, the duress of internment, insensitivity and miscalculation by the WRA, parental pressures, and the coercive atmosphere created by the extreme nationalists were all factors that contributed to the renunciants' actions. But there is another factor, not acknowledged in the literature, that should make us more cautious about how we assess Japanese Americans' attitudes toward citizenship: the influence of dual nationalism. The renunciants were not exclusively patriotic citizens of the United States who were but temporarily confused. Rather, they held complicated, divided loyalties, a set of allegiances that sustained commitment to life in America alongside affective and cultural ties, even patriotic sympathies to Japan. They may have considered the Hoshi Dan and Hokoku Seinen Dan to be extremists, but they did not necessarily believe it was abhorrent to support Japan. It may seem bizarre that people would fight to stay in a concentration camp, but Japanese Americans were not crazy to think that white Americans despised them. For otherwise loyal American citizens, repatriation to Japan was not unthinkable in the context of war and internment.[29]

Such complex motivations cannot be easily reconciled with the narrative of benevolent assimilation championed by the WRA, which seemed "to believe that Japanese Americans would cooperate with, if not welcome, their reformation, unaware of its essentially coercive character. Other liberals, if not enthusiastic about internment, nevertheless believed that Japanese Americans proved their Americanness in the camps," underscoring the idea of how an "unfortunate incidence of war [was turned] into a positive social good."[30]

Such an affirmation of liberal progress all too easily dovetails with the historicist logic of a fixed past leading to an inevitable present: the what-was of Japanese internment in the what-is of U.S. democracy, freedom, and progress. This is all the more so in the face of internment's ostensible political resolution: the national apology and monetary reparation that mark the definitive writing of Japanese American internment into the past of U.S history. In short, such an account underwrites the WRA's notions of the camps as laboratories of "benevolent assimilation," as "planned communities" for an "Americanizing Project," however misguided or improbable the idea of a democratic concentration camp might seem. The concentration camp thus becomes, in Ansel Adams's words, merely "a detour on the road to American citizenship," rather than a continuing and enduring symptom of racial division and forgetting that structures the U.S. nation-state, U.S. national identity, and the legacy of liberal humanism.

With the sanction of the WRA, Adams published *Born Free and Equal: Photographs of the Loyal Japanese Americans at Manzanar Relocation Center* (1944). He pictured the camp's landscape not as a state of exception—a site of indefinite detention—but as a site for democracy: "the huge vistas and the stern realities of sun and wind and space symbolize the immensity and opportunity of America."[31] In this manner, the aberrant time and exceptional space of the concentration camp becomes incorporated and absorbed into the homogenous, empty time and space of the U.S. nation-state. Constituting the concentration camp, in Chakrabarty's terms, as the imaginary waiting room of history, internment becomes an accelerated political process for the incorporation of Japanese Americans into a U.S. body politic, placing them into an ironic narrative of progress without freedom. Adams's affirmation of such a perverse picture of Manzanar cannot account for histories of forgetting. Moreover, such a picture of Manzanar cannot account for the ways in which "ever absent images" constitute the very conditions of possibility through which liberal binaries of inclusion/exclusion and visible/invisible emerge and obtain their epistemological coherence. To return to our discussion from chapter two, such a historicist perspective forecloses the what-could-have-been that inhabits and saturates the emergence of the now.

In a film that presents such a proliferation of sound, image, and text, it would not be unreasonable to suggest that Tajiri does indeed "desire to create an image where there are so few," and to account for this lost and forgotten history. Yet, at every turn, the filmmaker expresses epistemological doubt at such a representational enterprise, which reinforces rather than problematizes the terms by which history is deployed to further historicist and causal narratives of freedom and progress. For, in the same breath in which she expresses her determination "to search for an ever absent image and [her] desire to create an image where there are so few," Tajiri also denaturalizes this referential impulse by emphasizing that Komoko is not in fact absent from history, but that his very "absence is his presence."[32] By drawing attention to the process by which Komoko's absence constitutes the dialectic of visibility and invisibility that structures the representational coherence of the political domain and its politics of identity, Tajiri returns us to the realm of the in-between. Picturing absence through this aesthetic strategy, she relocates history to the domain of the affective, to the realm of ghosts, and to the space of the "non-visible."

Emerging in between the dialectic of visibility and invisibility, the non-visible indexes the realm of forgetting, which demands its own epistemological coordinates and ontological consistency. The in-between thus marks losses that can only be indexed by acts of haunting and imagination. It looks toward the past not as a mode of recuperation and referentiality but toward horizons of being and becoming—"a doing in futurity," to borrow José Muñoz's concept of a queer politics oriented away from pragmatism, rights, and recognitions, and toward a more phenomenological approach to queer politics and history as a "thing which is not yet here."[33]

Tajiri begins *History and Memory* by offering us a succinct four-tiered philosophy about the relationship between pictures and history. Accompanied by archival film footage of land and aerial bombings from the U.S. and Japanese military, cinematic clips from Fred Zinnemann's film *From Here to Eternity* (1953), and finally a blacked-out screen, Tajiri delivers a voiceover that shifts us progressively away from the analytic and empirical to the hermeneutic and spectral:

[1] There are things which have happened in the world while there were cameras watching, things we have images for. [2] There are other things which have happened while there were no cameras watching, which we re-stage in front of cameras to have images of. [3] There are things which have happened for which the only images that exist are in the minds of the observers present at the time. [4] While there are things that have happened for which there have been no observers except for the spirits of the dead.

Tajiri's final category, "spirits of the dead," brings us to the threshold of haunted history. But while ghosts and spirits might provoke disbelief or suspicion, they are not, as Chakrabarty remind us, "dependent on human beliefs for their own existence."[34] They do not rely upon our collective recognition to validate their ways of knowing or their modes of being. Their time is not our time, and the writing of their histories demands a certain epistemological and ontological humility. They demand a plurality of times and spaces existing together, a disjuncture of the present with itself.

The spirit of Tajiri's dead grandfather, who relates from beyond the grave the literal disappearance of the family house in California, while its owners are imprisoned in Poston, marks a history of forgetting, a history of loss, and a history of "absence as presence" that defies analytic vision. (The family never learns what happened to the house.) The figure of the ghost thus troubles modern historical consciousness and its traditional claims to agency. It introduces the what-could-have-been as that privileged category through which history becomes both haunted and an alternative historical understanding emerges into a horizon of being oriented toward a doing in futurity.

In this manner, the what-could-have-been in *History and Memory* comes to inhabit and saturates the emergence of our colorblind now, all the while slipping away from the dialectics of visibility and invisibility that governs the politics of recognition, the logics of the empirical, and the temporal march of historical progress from past to present. These are histories of forgetting and loss that defy conventional representation and symbolic inscription. Ultimately, they must be channeled through the realm of affect in order to gain epistemological and ontological traction.

Weaving the disjunctive time and space of the affective through official historical accounts of Japanese internment, *History and Memory* underscores the difficulty of animating a hermeneutic practice within and beyond the dominance of the analytic. Even more, by focusing on the psychic predicament between mother and daughter, Tajiri's video emphasizes how the battle for history becomes embedded on the level of the intersubjective as a question of wounded kinship. Ultimately, Tajiri asks how we might begin to rework the demands of historicism through the realm of affect and through the domain of forgetting and the non-visible.

"I remember having this feeling growing up that I was haunted by something, that I was living within a family full of ghosts," Tajiri tells us. "I could remember a time of great sadness before I was born. We had been moved, uprooted. We had lived with a lot of pain. I had no idea where these memories came from, yet I knew the place." Indeed, later in *History and Memory*, Tajiri returns alone to Poston, the site of the Colorado River Tribal Indian Reservation, and searches for the house where her mother had once lived. Through some "intuition or internal divining rod," Tajiri recounts, "she had indeed found the spot," the barrack where her mother and her mother's family had once been imprisoned. There are, as Tajiri shows us throughout *History and Memory*, different ways of knowing and being that cannot be written under the sign of the analytic, and I am precisely interested in Tajiri's notions of knowing and not knowing outside the acceptable boundaries of the analytic and inside the hermeneutic spheres of affective life.

Here, I would like to describe *History and Memory*'s aesthetic strategy —Tajiri's deployment of picture as affect—as a kind of negative dialectics, one refusing the sublation of binary terms (e.g. visible/invisible) into ever-higher levels of liberal reason, development, freedom, and progress. By juxtaposing unexpected events, spaces, and objects from past and present, *History and Memory* creates numerous sets of emotional analogies that index the space of forgetting and loss, the space of the in-between: Spencer Tracy's search for Komoko with that of Tajiri for her mother's history; the wildflowers that adorn Komoko's grave with those found in her mother's Chicago garden; the wooden bird found in her mother's jewelry case with the photograph of her grandmother in a Poston wood carving class, discovered by accident one afternoon twenty-five years later in the National Archives; the abandoned space of the Poston internment camp with Colorado River Tribal Indian reservation; the nephew's linking of Japanese internment with the struggles for black empowerment; the "canteen" in the desert with the "canteen" at the Salinas Race Track where the mother's family was first evacuated—these are all dialectical images in Walter Benjamin's sense. They are objects and images taken out of their conventional temporal and spatial contexts, dislodged and ejected from sanctioned historicist narratives of cause and effect. "Historicism contents itself with establishing a causal connection between various moments in history," Benjamin writes. "But no fact that is a cause is for that very reason historical."[35] Placed in sudden juxtaposition with one another, these displaced objects serve to "blast open the continuum of history," disturbing the pageant of historicism, of cause and effect, written and endorsed by the victors.[36]

It is important to emphasize that these dialectical images are not historically transparent; they do not reflect a given totality. In this sense, they are not analogies or resemblances in the traditional sense of the concept—of likenesses or similarities. Rather, they are displaced connections in which the positing of a correspondence depends upon not just formal structural analysis, but also the apprehension of difference—of a break, a displacement, an absence. This is the methodology of queer diasporas. Most importantly, these dialectical images are driven together by affect, lending Benjamin's critique of historicism and his theories concerning the aesthetics of shock a specifically *emotional* character.

These emotional analogies join Tajiri's present with forgotten moments from the past, carving out a space for what-could-have-been in the now, through a practice of what I would like to call *affective* correspondences. In doing so, they refuse the writing of internment into the past. Rather, they keep the past affectively alive in the present, providing a site for the reconstitution of melancholia's social residues, by configuring affect as a tool for political disenchantment and social reform. In this way, affect becomes the site of history as a doing in futurity. It becomes a site of both individual and collective repair, of collective racial reparation. Affect thus comes to supplement the political, allowing Tajiri to "grasp the constellation which [her] own era has formed with a definite earlier one."[37] The aesthetics of shock is transformed into a historical practice of not cause and effect but rather *cause* and *affect*.

Dialectical images: "Flowers for Kimoko's grave." From *History and Memory: For Akiko and Takashige.*

Dialectical images: "Wildflowers in Mother's Yard 1989." From *History and Memory: For Akiko and Takashige.*

Tajiri sustains through these affective correspondences an open and ongoing, rather than fixed, relationship with the past, bringing its fleeting ghosts and specters into the now. These correspondences are always there. They are not visible, however, until we have liberated their images from the sanctioned historical narratives in which they are embedded. Syntagmatic relationships underwritten by the pageant of historicism prevent us from seeing figural ones, and it is within the latter, rather than the former, that the practice of history should reside. In this manner, Tajiri offers us the possibility of socializing melancholia, assuming a collective relationship with forgetting and loss. Unlike political reparation, which seeks to write history into an eternal image of the past, Tajiri's deployment of affect—what I am describing as psychic reparation—supplies a "unique experience with the past," promising to change the "specific character" of the past by generating an altogether different analogy.[38] These affective correspondences contain within them an explosive potential to reassemble the empty, homogeneous time and space of the now, in which "time stands still and has come to a stop."[39] That is, they do not just connect the mother's past to Tajiri's present but, in turn, encourage us to connect Tajiri's past to our present: Japanese internment, for instance, to indefinite detention; the exceptional spaces of Poston and Manzanar to Guantánamo Bay; New York's "Ground Zero" to that of Hiroshima and Nagasaki.[40]

In doing so, they promise to break the repetition compulsion of history—the continual political rehearsal of history as the way-it-really-was, the continual suspension of civil liberties, racial profiling, and the forgetting of race in the name of national security and citizenship. Over time, the detritus of unacknowledged correspondences grows ever higher at the feet of Benjamin's angel of history. Neglecting to acknowledge or to connect them, we fail our accountability to an oppressed past, in which even the dead, as Benjamin warns us, "will not be safe."[41] As a documentary of affect, *History and Memory* flaunts an institutional tradition that defines documentary as a genre dividing affect from reason, or what Nichols describes as "a difference between an erotics and an ethics" separating the realm of fiction from the domain of the real.[42] Refusing these binaries, Tajiri underscores how an ethics of history is constituted through an affective longing—a feeling of kinship with and for the mother—that refuses the notion of a present that is not in transition, skirts the borders of pathology, and provides a ghostly language for loss—a new story, a new history helping us to remember differently. Here, as Derrida reminds us, the capacity to be with specters lies at the core of justice and ethical politics.[43]

If *History and Memory* is a documentary of affect, we might also describe Tajiri as a historian of affect, one who "stops telling the sequence of events like the beads of a rosary."[44] We have yet to attend to the past adequately, Tajiri insists, and "one measure of that neglect arises at the affective level."[45] Encouraging us to grasp the historical constellation that our colorblind era has formed with an earlier one, Tajiri's philosophy of history as image and affect indexes a feeling of kinship that returns Japanese internment—its ostensible political resolution and its histories of forgetting—to us in an entirely different manner. The affective dissonance between the what-was and the what-could-have-been of history inhabits and saturates the emergence of our now, turning us to cause and affect as an alternative site for historical understanding. It is this affective reciprocity between what-was and what-could-have-been that allows Benjamin to observe: "The past carries with it a temporal index by which it is referred to redemption. There is a secret agreement between past generations and the present one. Our coming was expected on earth. Like every generation that preceded us, we have been endowed with a *weak* Messianic power, a power to which the past has a claim. That claim cannot be settled cheaply."[46]

Identity Politics in a Colorblind Age

Affect is often thought to be eccentric to the domain of the political. It is usually managed and erased, as Cvetkovich notes, "in the public sphere through official discourses of recognition and commemoration that don't fully address everyday affects or through legal measures . . . that don't fully provide emotional justice."[47] *History and Memory* emphasizes how affect might help us not only to rethink the politics of historicism but also to reformulate questions of identity, family, and kinship in our colorblind age. Since the advent of poststructuralism, we have typically attributed to language (and to linguistic theories of performativity) powerful social functions relating to identity formation. We have grown accustomed, for instance, to describing our identities as linguistically inscribed, as discursive positions, as interpellative events.[48] Numerous critics of the politics of recognition have pointed out the failure of identity labels to map or to grasp fully our subjectivities. The practice of intersectionality has sought to address this critical impasse by providing an account of the ways in which identity is simultaneously constituted through multiple axes of difference. We continue to explore identity largely within linguistic traditions of poststructuralism, however, rather than diverse and convergent modes of affective recognition and particularity.

The deconstructive insights of poststructuralism emphasize identity as a discursive position. They provide a powerful theory of social construction and thus a critique of essentialism and the evidence of experience as the bedrock of the universal subject's critical authority.[49] However, in all these critical conversations, less attention has been paid to the ways in which affect might work to supplement linguistic theories of identity. *History and Memory*'s exploration of affect helps to address the current impasses of identity politics and colorblindness by offering a way of "worlding" forgotten creatures and things, bringing them into the time and space of the now in a manner radically divergent from that of a liberal humanist tradition.[50] Such a critical project not only requires a rethinking of the language of psychoanalysis after poststructuralism but also, as Tajiri's documentary proposes, a new account of identity formation across psychoanalytic and phenomenological registers (a consideration to which I will return shortly).

In rethinking the conventional divide between affect and history, *History and Memory* also calls for the implicit reconsideration of the divide between affect and language, for the reevaluation of language as the privileged frame through which both history and identity are largely mobilized. Such a rethinking of affect and language would insist on reevaluating the conceptual links, for example, between symbolic accounts of language in French poststructuralism and theories of affect in British object relations—between Lacan and Klein, to invoke two paradigmatic figures from previous chapters. Here, language and affect are traditionally cast as oppositional, with linguistically oriented and affectively oriented conceptions of the psyche at definitive odds with one another.

For Lacan, the unconscious is organized like a language, with the symbolic prototypically closed to affective transfers, to itself, and indeed to the world. In Lacan's famous "either-or" formulation, we forfeit being for meaning, presence for language, *jouissance* for symbolic legibility. To be sure, conventional readings of Freud would also seem to endorse such a distinction. In *The Interpretation of Dreams*, for example, language is said to bind affect, while affect is thought to exceed symbolic inscription beyond the occasion of its discursive deployment and decathexis.[51] From a different angle, Terada points out that we have "assumed that the very idea of strong emotion is inconsistent with poststructuralism,"[52] and although he suggests that emotion and subjectivity seem to be deeply connected, Jameson also speaks about a "waning of affect" that is the distinct mark of our postmodern times.[53]

What are the effects of upholding this traditional division between language and affect? In *New Maladies of the Soul*, Julia Kristeva suggests that what ails the contemporary subject is precisely the fact that language has become severed from affect. The cleaving of discourse from emotional life, she argues, curtails the subject's ability to make existential or historical sense of his or her own existence. Attempting to reconcile French poststructuralist approaches to language with a theory of affect, Kristeva argues that the postmodern subject has lost the capacity to articulate satisfying personal narratives and to conceive of itself as a psychic being with depth and substance.[54] Along similar lines, Mari Ruti calls for an account of identity that does not discard the deconstructive insights of poststructuralism or anti-essentialist theories of the subject, but uses these insights to modify a theory of object relations that allows us to reconsider relationality in the larger social sphere. As such, she argues for a new conception of the subject as both a discursive construct and an intricate psychic being with existential needs and concerns, with great psychic depth and capacity for feeling. It might be tempting to dismiss these existential needs and concerns, to argue that they expired with the deconstruction of the universal liberal humanist subject. But as Ruti asserts, the poststructuralist tendency to view the psyche as a site of alienation rather than potentiality only exacerbates the political and historical problems of the marginalized and subordinated.

Ruti wonders whether it is a coincidence that the proliferation of identity positions has resulted in the increased difficulty, if not impossibility, of claiming agency? She asks: "What do we make of the fact that the more subjectivity has ceased to be restricted to a small subsection of the population, the more its has come to connote subjection rather than autonomy."[55] If there is no universal subject but only, as Kandice Chuh asserts, "infinite differences that we discursively cohere into epistemological objects," how might affect be returned to language so as to advance rather than impede Chuh's political insight about identity formation and the social?[56] Even more, how might affect help in worlding those forgotten creatures and things leveled by historicism's endless march of progress? If the rhetoric of colorblindness refuses to recognize the ways in which race and racism continue to constitute and divide our national and social order, how might affect provide one way of moving beyond the binds of liberalism and its politics of representation? Indeed, how might affect help us to recalibrate the intellectual afterlife of post-identity politics?

To begin, affect need not be cast as oppositional to language but, as *History and Memory* suggests, they must be seen as supplemental to one another. Freud provides us with one way to approach this project and to conceive of affect as mediating rather than interrupting a relationship between language and identity, between language and history. Like Sartre's insistence that "emotion is a certain way of apprehending the world," Freud endows affect with a certain phenomenological quality. In his essay on "The Unconscious," Freud writes that it "is surely of the essence of an emotion that we should be aware of it, i.e. that it should become known to consciousness."[57] However, while emotions are consciously perceived as such, their meanings can often be misconstrued: "Owing to the repression of its proper representative has been forced to become connected with another idea, and is now regarded by consciousness as the manifestation of that idea. If we restore the true connection, we call the original affective impulse an 'unconscious' one. Yet its affect was never unconscious; all that had happened was that its *idea* had undergone repression."[58] By introducing the concept of unconscious affect, in which an affective impulse is perceived albeit misinterpreted, Freud suggests that what is repressed from consciousness is not the affect as such, but the interdicted idea to which this affect was initially (though provisionally) connected. Thus, he encourages us to understand affect as mediating a relationship between words and things. Affect transports us across different levels of signification, registers of pre-consciousness and unconscious thought, "not all of which can be admitted in the present."[59] In such a psychic economy of displacement, affect becomes the privileged vehicle through which unacknowledged correspondences between words and things, between linguistic signifiers and visual perceptions, are brought together or forced apart.

In *History and Memory*, affect is configured precisely as that psychic glue that allows unexpected correspondences between story and picture to emerge and stick. In other words, affective correspondences provide the means of (re)connecting through unexpected pairings disconnected words and things, unconscious links through which identity and history might come to be redefined in psychic and social life. Here, words do not bind affect so much as affect comes to reconstitute words and things through unacknowledged correspondences—dialectical images driven apart by historicism but driven together by emotion. In this regard, I would like to reprise my earlier discussion of transnational adoption, of girl love, the negative Oedipus complex, and the creation of psychic space for two good-enough mothers. In chapter three, I suggested that the deployment of the negative Oedipus complex's affective intensity reveals a forgotten but crucial new form of symbolization where libidinal openness, rather than fixity, holds pride of place, and where words rather than binding affect come under the influence of affect's unconscious impulses and motivations. In this manner, racial reparation describes a psychic process by which affect comes to re-symbolize racial melancholia and a debased and hated mother can emerge as good enough.

Like *First Person Plural*, *History and Memory* underscores how affect comes to be the privileged category through which, to borrow Freud's terminology, "thing-presentations" (images and perceptions) become associated with new "word-presentations" (linguistic and verbal signifiers), giving over to new histories of the subject. The enigma of Tajiri's mother—the picture without a story—returns as inexplicable pain, one eluding symbolic inscription. However, through a process of affective correspondences, this picture without a story brings forth a set of unacknowledged emotional pairings, creating anew a different historical sense. Tajiri's affective correspondences ultimately restore the mother—to return to our discussion from the previous two chapters— as a good-enough racialized object. In the same breath, it returns racial melancholia to the domain of the social and to the politics of historicism as a collective problem and collaborative endeavor. In the final analysis, affect serves to world the mother and the daughter as different historical subjects, unfolding them into an alternative time and space, one in which they might appear in a new guise to themselves and others. If a forgotten history initially assumes a displaced relationship between language and affect at the opening of Tajiri's documentary, affect ultimately comes to bear upon language, history, identity, family, and kinship not in a disjunctive or oppositional but in a transformative manner. It returns the mother and Tajiri to the world in a different mode of becoming.

Importantly, this worlding and return to the domain of the social does not reinscribe the everyday terms of liberal representation and identity. It does not, in other words, conflate political with psychic reparation, shore up the autonomy of the minority subject, or restore history to its referential pedestal. Tajiri's affective correspondences do not recuperate or recover the mother, moving backward in order to attempt the recapture an ever-receding origin or a set of lost representations. Instead, they move forward to generate a new and unexpected set of emotional analogies as well as historical links and images that allow Tajiri both to apprehend the mother from a different perspective and to inhabit the world in a less painful manner. Thus, she can forgive her mother her loss of memory. Tajiri's affective correspondences do not bring history to the past, but instead bring the past to history—a history of the present. Delineating the aesthetic and political processes through which affective correspondences come to be animated and sustained for a new racial politics in our colorblind age, *History and Memory* illustrates how the linguistic binds of identity might be loosened by affect to redefine affirmation (of freedom) and forgetting (of race).

If Heidegger saw the process of naming as bringing Being into the world and into the time and space of history, Tajiri's affective correspondences ultimately insist upon a reconsideration of affect's supplemental value to language not as "an instrument of domination over beings," but as "the house of the truth of Being."[60] Rethinking affect and language from such an idealist perspective might be worth exploring, for it is my hope that reconsidering the critical impasses between affect and language after poststructuralism might finally yield new understandings of family, kinship, and the racialization of intimacy in our colorblind age.

The Feeling of Kinship

Throughout this book, I have been asking why we have numerous poststructuralist accounts of language but few poststructuralist accounts of kinship. *History and Memory* helps us to advance such a project by insisting on the need to move beyond the binds of liberalism and its politics of representation to account for a new method of historical understanding, a new conception of psychic and political reparation that refuses the closure of the past. Tajiri's documentary concludes with a rather dramatic aesthetic shift, one moving us from the vertiginous frenzy of the visible to a more phenomenological framing of the affective horizons of Being. This aesthetic shift is marked by the director's closing voiceover, which has an indeterminate meaning. "I could forgive my mother her loss of memory," Tajiri tells us, "and could make this image for her." What, we need to ask, is the referent of this image?

On the one hand, "this image" could refer to the film as a whole, one in which the juxtaposition of image, sound, and text situates debates regarding history, identity, and kinship in an analytic tradition concerning liberal representation and visibility, the limits of which I have been exploring throughout this chapter. On the other hand, "this image" could also refer to the final visual sequence accompanying Tajiri's concluding voiceover, a sequence in distinct contrast to the rest of the film's busy aesthetic. This final image is of a desolate road near the Poston desert. As the camera slowly pans into the distance, the visual and acoustic regimes merge. We hear the accompanying squawks of a flock of birds as the picture of a distant horizon slowly fades from view. Unlike the highly edited sequences that populate the rest of Tajiri's film, this is not a "full" but an "empty" picture, one devoid of human subjects altogether.

Yet it would not be entirely accurate to describe this final image as an empty picture, for insofar as it marks the final coming together of the visual and acoustic registers, it also marks a different time and space of the film. It signals not Adams's vistas of "immensity and opportunity of America." To the contrary, it presents a scene of unfolding, a scene of discursive emptiness but affective fullness, one through which Tajiri can finally forgive her mother her loss of memory and create a new historical image *for* as well as *of* her. This affective tone and shift marking the end of Tajiri's documentary indicates a being in and for the world not dissimilar to that of Lai's emergence into the Taipei landscape at the conclusion of *Happy Together*, discussed in chapter two. They are "unexpected revelations of scenes of spring" that appear to Lai and in which Lai can finally appear.

In this respect, Tajiri's closing image might be likened to a phenomenological horizon, in both Edmund Husserl's and Heidegger's sense of the world as a horizon and of horizon as a nexus of being, an ephemeral ontological field in which we must strain our vision in order to imagine otherwise. Muñoz describes this kind of a phenomenological turn as a deliberate idealist endeavor seeking to understand the rhythms, particularities, and potentialities that constitute the world as cleaved from a natural attitude and naturalized epistemologies.[61] Set against the positivism of the analytic tradition, such an affective turn returns us to Chakrabarty's hermeneutic tradition, a human life-world not fully

Desert horizon. From
*History and Memory: For
Akiko and Takashige.*

knowable by standard modes of historical perspective or perception. Unlike poststructuralist accounts of language, in which the linguistic signifier is said to induce a fading of being by separating us from the world, such affective attentiveness keeps us open to the world, to its inexhaustible phenomenal shapes and forms.

In this regard, psychic reparation in *History and Memory* presents itself not as something to be surmounted or left behind. Unlike political theories of reparation, which seek to write history into a definitive past, psychic reparation does not delineate such a finite process, but rather a process of *working through*. Like the depressive position in Klein, it moves us from the sphere of paranoid splitting and racial melancholia to present us with the possibility of love and the creative impulse that loss, grief, and forgetting might be temporally conjoined with new ideas.[62] The world is a picture, Lacan explains in *The Four Fundamental Concepts of Psychoanalysis*, because it gives itself to be seen. But even more, as *History and Memory* insists, it gives itself to be felt, it gives itself to be loved.[63]

It is precisely on the terrain of the affective, Tajiri suggests, where the visual and the discursive might interact, not in an over-determined or bound manner, but in a way that might unfold the world to us in its manifest shapes and forms. This is a feeling of kinship in and with the world that exceeds the analytic prescriptions of traditional perception, legal recognition, and social belonging. Heidegger writes, "the essence of action is accomplishment [and that] to accomplish means to unfold something into the fullness of its essence."[64] Rethinking the linguistic

signifier from an affective position brings together more phenomenological notions of being and becoming with the politics of identity and
performativity that constitute the intellectual and political limits of
identity in our colorblind age.

When Tajiri's nephew speculates that he may not have a right to criti-
cize Parker's *Come See the Paradise* because, "being half white, maybe I
don't have the moral authority," we again inhabit a significant critical
impasse in identity politics, concerned with the ownership of representation and its proper appropriations and mis-appropriations. Essence in
phenomenology, keyed into affective horizons of Being, is not the essence, the evidence of experience, underwriting the conventional tenets
of identity politics. While essentialism in identity politics encloses the
world, essence in phenomenology unfolds it. In turning away from the
referential to the affective, Tajiri suggests one new approach to rethinking essence in the context of a transformative politics.[65] She invites the
viewer to inhabit her picture, but prevents the recovery of history in its
conventional guise. She uses her camera to create a new set of correspondences.

As *History and Memory*, *The Book of Salt*, *Happy Together*, *First Person
Plural*, and our case history on Mina eloquently underscore, such an
affective enterprise must necessarily belong to the world in neither a
bound nor pre-determined manner. Confined within the narrow stric-
tures of the normative Oedipus complex, affect functions to regulate
and reinscribe the traditional boundaries of family and kinship, dictat-
ing the constrained ways in which we are coerced to displace (away from
the mother) and to affiliate (with the father). We are repeatedly inserted
into the grammar of bodily action and speech as performative demand
and conscription.[66] Importantly, if affect at the beginning of Tajiri's film
is circumscribed by the trauma of nationalist politics configuring Japanese Americans as "target" and "enemy"—circumscribed by conventional rules of racial identity, family, and kinship—by the end of *History
and Memory* it is transformed and released into the world through an
alternative register.

Tajiri's phenomenological turn insists upon a consideration of the
ways in which affect might respond to new identities and social formations still searching for a form. As Tajiri shows us, this appropriation
and resignifying of affect may serve to mend not only those psychic
struggles marked by filial connection but also those political struggles

that exceed its privatized boundaries. If such affective responsibility is to have greater ethical traction, or larger social significance, we must come to recognize that no one person rightfully owns it. No one person either is its proper receiver. There is no one law of kinship, no one structure of kinship, no one language of kinship, and no one prospect of kinship. Rather, the feeling of kinship belongs to everyone.

Notes

Introduction

1. See Eve Kosofsky Sedgwick, "Queer Performativity: Henry James's *The Art of the Novel*," 12. Writing about shame in queer studies, Sedgwick observes:

> But I don't, either, want it to sound as though my project has mainly to do with recuperating for deconstruction (or other anti-essentialist projects) a queerness drained of specificity or political reference. To the contrary, I'd suggest that to view performativity in terms of habitual shame and its transformations opens a lot of new doors for thinking about identity politics. Part of the interest of shame is that it is an affect that delineates identity—but delineates it without defining it or giving it content. Shame, as opposed to guilt, is a bad feeling that does not attach to what one does, but to what one is. (Ibid.)

On the vexed relationship between gay and racial shame, see Judith Halberstam, "Shame and Gay White Masculinity."

2. Raymond Williams, *Marxism and Literature*, 132.

3. See David L. Eng, Judith Halberstam, and José Esteban Muñoz, Introduction to "What's Queer about Queer Studies Now?" For a discussion of subjectless critique, see Judith Butler, "Critically Queer"; and Michael Warner, Introduction to *Fear of a Queer Planet: Queer Politics and Social Theory*.

4. See "Times Will Begin Reporting Gay Couples' Ceremonies," *New York Times*, August 18, 2002, I:30.

5. See *Lawrence v. Texas,* 539 U.S. 558 (2003). See also *Goodridge et al. v. Department of Public Health,* 440 Mass. 309 (2003); *Marriage Cases, In re,* 43 Cal. 4th 757 (2008); *Kerrigan and Mock v. Connecticut Department of Public Health* (2008).

6. See Kath Weston, *Families We Choose: Lesbians, Gays, Kinship.*

7. As I mention in my preface, this is true even as it demands the inexorable growth of the prison industrial complex and ever-increasing militarization and unfreedom in global locales such as the Middle East, Afghanistan, and Guantánamo Bay, heightened racialized violence and racialized labor exploitation, and the vast redistribution of wealth to the already richest few as the just desserts of multicultural world citizens. See Ruth Wilson Gilmore, *Golden Gulag: Prisons, Surplus, Crisis, and Opposition in Globalizing California*; Amy Kaplan, "Where is Guantánamo?"; and Jodi Melamed, "The Spirit of Neoliberalism: From Racial Liberalism to Neoliberal Multiculturalism."

8. Of course, the public and the private are mutually constitutive and interconnected; one of the primary though unstated anxieties of opponents to desegregation in schools was the fear that it would encourage private intimacies and relationships among white and black students.

9. Rachel Moran, *Interracial Intimacy: The Regulation of Race and Romance*, 7.

10. See Twila L. Perry, "Transracial Adoption and Gentrification: An Essay on Race, Power, Family, and Community."

11. Cheryl I. Harris, "Whiteness as Property," 1714.

12. Ibid.

13. Lauren Berlant, *The Queen of America Goes to Washington City: Essays on Sex and Citizenship*, 1–24.

14. Moran, *Interracial Intimacy*, 13. She writes, "after three hundred years of antimiscegenation laws, it would be surprising if thirty years of official colorblindness have truly rendered race irrelevant in the choice of a marital or sexual partner" (6).

15. Randall Kennedy, *Interracial Intimacies: Sex, Marriage, Identity, and Adoption*, 33.

16. Eve Kosofsky Sedgwick, "How to Bring Your Kids Up Gay: The War on Effeminate Boys," 158.

17. See *Gratz and Hamacher v. Bollinger*, 123 U.S. 2411 (2003); *Grutter v. Bollinger*, 123 U.S. 2325 (2003); *Parents Involved in Community Schools v. Seattle School District No. 1*, 551 U.S. 701 (2007); Harris, "Whiteness as Property," 1715.

18. Legal scholar James G. Whitman argues that privacy in the U.S. has traditionally been inscribed within capitalist relations, as opposed to France, for example, where privacy was linked to dignity and considered a defense against the vicissitudes of the market and "wild capitalism." See Whitman, "The Two Western Cultures of Privacy: Dignity Versus Liberty."

19. See Cathy N. Davidson, Introduction to "No More Separate Spheres!"

20. See Karl Marx, "On the Jewish Question."

21. Amy Kaplan, *The Anarchy of Empire in the Making of U.S. Culture*, 1.

22. Ibid.

23. See Amartya Sen, *Development as Freedom*, and Melamed, who notes that racial liberalism laid the ideological foundations for our present colorblind moment by suturing an official anti-racism to U.S. nationalism, and by introducing the language of abstract equality, market individualism, and the proliferation of capitalism as the just political response to the Cold War specter of communism. See Melamed, "The Spirit of Neoliberalism."

24. Melamed, "The Spirit of Neoliberalism," 1.

25. Ibid.

26. Susan Bibler Coutin, Bill Maurer, and Barbara Yngvesson, "In the Mirror: The Legitimation Work of Globalization," 825.

27. Lisa Lowe, "The Intimacies of Four Continents," 193; 204.

28. Ibid., 206–7.

29. Fernand Braudel, *On History*, 25–54.

30. Jacques Derrida, *Spectres of Marx: The State of Debt, the Work of Mourning, and the New International*.

31. Lowe, "The Intimacies of Four Continents," 196.

32. See Eng, Halberstam, and Muñoz, Introduction to "What's Queer about Queer Studies Now?" See also recent publications by Jacqui Alexander, Licia Fiol-Matta, Gayatri Gopinath, Arnaldo Cruz-Malave, Martin Manalansan, José Esteban Muñoz, José Quiroga, Jasbir Puar, and Chandan Reddy.

33. Khachig Tölölyan, "The Nation-State and Its Others: In Lieu of a Preface," 4.

34. Ibid., 5.

35. Gayatri Gopinath, *Impossible Subjects: Queer Diasporas and South Asian Public Cultures*, 13.

36. Ibid., 11.

37. See Lisa Lowe and David Lloyd's Introduction to *The Politics of Culture in the Shadow of Capital*.

38. See Arjun Appadurai, *Modernity at Large: Cultural Dimensions in Globalization*.

39. Dipesh Chakrabarty, *Provincializing Europe: Postcolonial Thought and Historical Difference*, 18.

40. Williams, *Marxism and Literature*, 132; Walter Benjamin, "Theses on the Philosophy of History," 255.

41. Williams, *Marxism and Literature*, 132.

42. See Gayle Rubin, "The Traffic in Women: Notes on the 'Political Economy' of Sex"; Claude Lévi-Strauss, *The Elementary Structures of Kinship*. At the end of this book, Lévi-Strauss also refers to the exchange of women and words, as does Jacques Lacan in his "Roman Discourse" of 1953 ("The Function and Field of Speech and Language in Psychoanalysis"). Rubin singles out Lévi-Strauss and Lacan for developing a "sex/gender" system linking the exchange of women to a symbolic economy mediated on heterosexual kinship.

43. Judith Butler, *Antigone's Claim: Kinship between Life and Death*, 29–30.

44. See Dale Carpenter, "The Unknown Past of *Lawrence v. Texas*."

45. Joseph Roach, *Cities of the Dead: Circum-Atlantic Performance*, 2.

1. Aihwa Ong, *Neoliberalism as Exception: Mutations in Citizenship and Sovereignty*, 4.

2. See Gayatri Chakravorty Spivak, *A Critique of Postcolonial Reason: Toward a History of the Vanishing Present*.

3. *Lawrence v. Texas,* 539 U.S. 558 (2003) and *Bowers v. Hardwick,* 478 U.S. 186 (1986).

4. The Georgia statute formally applied to both homosexual and heterosexual sodomy, but the Court sidestepped the issue of equal protection, stating that the "only claim properly before the Court . . . is Hardwick's challenge to the Georgia statute as applied to consensual homosexual sodomy." While John and Mary Doe, a heterosexual couple, signed onto the original *Hardwick* suit filed in District Court, the Court expressed "no opinion on the constitutionality of the Georgia statute as applied to other acts of sodomy." See *Bowers v. Hardwick,* 188. As the Texas statute applied only to same-sex sodomy, *Lawrence* opened up the possibility of equal protection and heightened scrutiny arguments though, ultimately, the Court's reasoning in the majority opinion pivoted on rights to privacy arguments.

5. *Bowers v. Hardwick,* 190. See Teemu Ruskola, "Gay Rights versus Queer Theory."

6. See Ruskola, "Gay Rights versus Queer Theory."

7. *Lawrence v. Texas,* 567; 562, my emphasis.

8. On the ambivalence of the political construction of "cannot not want," see Gayatri Chakravorty Spivak, *Outside in the Teaching Machine*, 279.

9. See Chakrabarty, *Provincializing Europe*, 8.

10. See Eng, Halberstam, and Muñoz, Introduction to "What's Queer about Queer Studies Now?" For a discussion of subjectless critique, see Butler, "Critically Queer"; and Warner, Introduction to *Fear of a Queer Planet*.

11. See *Goodridge et al. v. Department of Public Health*, 440 Mass. 309 (2003); *Marriage Cases, In re*, 43 Cal. 4th 757 (2008); *Kerrigan and Mock v. Connecticut Department of Public Health* (2008). Of course, as I note in the preface, legalized marriage for gays and lesbians in California was taken away through the passage of Proposition 8 by the state's voters six months after the ruling.

12. John D'Emilio, "Capitalism and Gay Identity."

13. Ibid., 469.

14. For an analysis of this historical evolution, see Berlant, *The Queen of American Goes to Washington City*.

15. Janet R. Jakobsen, "Sex + Freedom = Regulation: Why?" 291.

16. Andrew Sullivan, *Virtually Normal: An Argument about Homosexuality*.

17. Hannah Arendt, *The Origins of Totalitarianism*, 296.

18. See Butler, "Critically Queer."

19. Ruskola, "Gay Rights versus Queer Theory," 237.

20. Giorgio Agamben, *Homo Sacer: Sovereign Power and Bare Life*, 121.

21. See Judith Butler, *The Psychic Life of Power: Theories in Subjection*, 6–10.

22. Saidiya V. Hartman, *Scenes of Subjection: Terror, Slavery, and Self-Making in Nineteenth-Century America*, 6.

23. See Linda Bosniak, "Citizenship Denationalized." Bosniak untangles the ways in which notions of citizenship implicate several distinct discourses, namely citizenship as legal status, as rights, as political activity, and as identity/solidarity.

24. Michel Foucault calls attention to the relationship between rights and subjugation rather than rights and legitimacy. See Foucault, "Two Lectures," 95–96.

25. See Melamed, "The Spirit of Neoliberalism."

26. An exceedingly popular television show in the U.S. today is Bravo's *Queer Eye for the Straight Guy*, winner of the 2004 Emmy Award for Outstanding Reality Program. Now in its 225th episode (at this writing), the motto of *Queer Eye for the Straight Guy*—"Five gay men, out to make over the world, one straight guy at a time"—summarizes the show's dubious conceit, one dedicated to the simple virtues of style, taste, class, and beauty. Each week, the self described "Fab 5" (Ted Allen, Kyan Douglas, Thom Felicia, Carson Kressley, and Jai Rodriguez) perform a total makeover, transforming a style-deficient, culture-deprived straight man from "drab" to "fab" in five crucial areas: fashion, grooming, food and wine, culture, and home design. Every makeover is intended to buttress a severely flagging heterosexual masculinity so that, by the end of each episode, the transformed guy is able to get the girl. Often the program concludes with a sappy marriage proposal. This is what queer politics has come to today: an aestheticized, commodified, and consumable lifestyle meant not to contest or to transform but indeed to support and to reinforce normative heterosexual masculinity and the joys of the free market.

27. See Alexandra Chassin, *Selling Out: The Gay and Lesbian Movement Goes to the Market*. Writing about the growth of global gay tourism, M. Jacqui Alexander observes that while "citizenship based in political rights can be forfeited, these rights do not disappear entirely. Instead, they get reconfigured and restored under the rubric of gay consumer at this moment in capitalism." As brown bodies from the global South move northward to take up employment, white bodies in the global North move southward in search of leisure and pleasure. See Alexander, *Pedagogies of Crossing: Meditations on Feminism, Sexual Politics, Memory, and the Sacred*, 71.

28. See Lisa Duggan, *The Twilight of Equality: Neoliberalism, Cultural Politics, and the Attack on Democracy*, esp. chapter four and pages 65–66. By trying to delineate the ways in which a turn towards liberal rights not only accepts the heightened regulation of gay and lesbian life but also underwrites the economic principles of neoliberalism, we might begin to untangle national forms of homophobia from the Bush Administration's wholesale economic assault on the poor through the rubric of "family values." Indeed, Duggan's new research on same-sex marriage suggests that a majority of people in the U.S. are in favor of limited same-sex partnership rights, though at the same time many oppose same-sex marriage precisely because traditional marriage is increasingly the only way to access Federal welfare entitlements.

29. Lisa Duggan, "The New Homonormativity: The Sexual Politics of Neoliberalism," 179.

30. Chandan Reddy, "Asian Diasporas, Neoliberalism, and Family: Reviewing the Case for Homosexual Asylum in the Context of Family Rights," 109.

31. Ibid., 109–10.

32. Ibid., 110.

33. See Leti Volpp, "Blaming Culture for Bad Behavior."

34. See Étienne Balibar and Immanuel Wallerstein, *Race, Nation, Class: Ambiguous Identities.*

35. José Esteban Muñoz, "Thinking Beyond Antirelationality and Antiutopianism in Queer Critique," 825. More generally, see "Forum: Conference Debates. The Antisocial Thesis in Queer Theory."

36. *Lawrence v. Texas* (2003), 562, 579, my emphasis.

37. For example, see William N. Eskridge, Jr., "Yale Law School and the Overruling of *Bowers v. Hardwick*"; Tobias Barrington Wolff, "Political Representation and Accountability Under Don't Ask, Don't Tell"; E.J. Graff, "The High Court Finally Gets It Right," *Boston Globe*, June 29, 2003: D11.

38. Dale Carpenter, "The Unknown Past of *Lawrence v. Texas.*"

39. *Lawrence v. Texas* (2003), 559.

40. *Lawrence v. Texas* (2003), 597.

41. Carpenter, "The Unknown Past of *Lawrence v. Texas*," 1509.

42. *Griswold v. Connecticut* (1965), *Eisenstadt v. Baird* (1972), *Roe v. Wade* (1973), *Carey v. Population Services International* (1977), and *Planned Parenthood of Southeastern Pennsylvania v. Casey* (1992).

43. The earliest conceptions of privacy in Anglo-American law concern trespass (privacy as space), assault (privacy as bodily integrity), and eavesdropping (privacy as knowledge about a person).

44. *Lawrence v. Texas* (2003), 577–78.

45. The *Loving* case began in 1958, when Mildred Jeter (an African American woman) and Richard Loving (a white man) were married in the Washington, DC. Shortly after, the couple moved to Virginia, where both had been raised, but where interracial marriage between whites and African Americans had been prohibited since 1924. The couple was arrested in their home and indicted by a grand jury in October 1958. In a series of appeals, the case finally reached the U.S. Supreme Court in 1967, which unanimously ruled that the Virginia law violated the equal protection and due process clauses of the 14th Amendment.

For an excellent intersectional analysis of *Loving,* see Siobhan B. Somerville,

"Queer Loving." Somerville analyzes a judicial history of same-sex marriage cases—including *Baker v. Nelson* (1971), *Baehr v. Lewin* (1993), *Lawrence v. Texas* (2003), and *Goodridge et al. v. Department of Public Health* (2003)—in relation to a judicial history of interracial sex and marriage cases—including *Perez v. Sharp* (1948), *McLaughlin v. Florida* (1964), and *Loving v. Virginia* (1967)—as well as a judicial history of Cold War immigration cases, such as *Boutilier v. Immigration Services* (1967).

46. *Boutilier v. Immigration Services* 387 U.S. 118 (1967).

47. *Boutilier v. Immigration Services* affirmed the constitutionality of this Federal law. Somerville traces the legal genealogy of *Boutilier* to the 1952 Immigration and Nationality Act (also known as the McCarren-Walter Act) and the Cold War politics of anti-Communism, marking for the first time the ways in which the language of homosexuality—"persons afflicted with psychopathic personality" and "sexual deviation"—had explicitly entered U.S. policy-making on naturalization. See also David K. Johnson, *The Lavender Scare: The Cold War Persecution of Gays and Lesbians in Federal Government*; and Robert J. Corber, *Homosexuality in Cold War America: Resistance and the Crisis of Masculinity*.

48. Somerville, "Queer Loving," 357. Somerville observes that this defensive constitution can be traced back to the 1952 Walter McCarren *Immigration and Naturalization Act*. Walter McCarren dropped the language of racial exclusion, shifting instead to a rhetoric of national inclusion through the national origins quota system while adding new language of exclusion concerning sexual outlaws, homosexuals, and adulterers.

49. From another angle, legal scholar Adrienne D. Davis points out that *Loving* should be contextualized in a long history of U.S. slavery, in which white slavemasters always had legal access to their black slave women. Seen in this light, a gendered analysis of *Loving* reveals that the legal right for white men to marry black women is quite different from the legal right of black men to marry white women. See Davis, "*Loving* Against the Law: The History and Jurisprudence of Interracial Sex."

50. *Lawrence v. Texas* (2003), 600.

51. Garner passed away at age 39 in 2006 from complications due to meningitis. See Douglas Martin, "Tyron Garner, 39, Plantiff in Pivotal Sodomy Case, Dies," *New York Times*, September 14, 2006. For a moving exploration of this subject of premature death, see Carla F.C. Holloway, *Passed On: African American Mourning Stories (A Memorial)*.

52. Somerville, "Queer Loving," 335.

53. Janet E. Halley, " 'Like Race' Arguments," 46.

54. Ibid., 67.

55. Miranda Joseph, "Family Affairs: The Discourse of Global/Localization," 80. See also, Janet R. Jakobsen, "Queers are Like Jews, Aren't They?"

56. Max Horkheimer and Theodor W. Adorno, *Dialectic of Enlightenment*, 9.

57. See Kandice Chuh, *Imagine Otherwise: On Asian Americanist Critique*.

58. See Kimberlé Williams Crenshaw, "Race, Reform and Retrenchment: Transformation and Legitimation in Antidiscrimination Law."

59. *Lawrence v. Texas* (2003), 578.

60. See Ruskola, "Gay Rights versus Queer Theory"; and Katherine Franke, "The Domesticated Liberty of *Lawrence v. Texas*."

61. *Lawrence v. Texas* (2003), 567.

62. Ibid.

63. Ruskola, "Gay Rights versus Queer Theory," 239, 239, 244, 241.

64. Lowe, "The Intimacies of Four Continents," 195–96.

65. See Ann Laura Stoler, "Tense and Tender Ties: The Politics of Comparison in North American History and (Post)Colonial Studies"; and *Carnal Knowledge and Imperial Power: Race and the Intimate In Colonial Rule*.

66. See G.W.F. Hegel, *The Philosophy of Right*.

67. Lowe, The Intimacies of Four Continents," 199.

68. Ibid., 201.

69. Indeed, Scalia writes in his dissenting opinion:

"At the end of its opinion—after having laid waste the foundations of our rational-basis jurisprudence—the Court says that the present case 'does not involve whether the government must give formal recognition to any relationship that homosexual persons seek to enter.' Do not believe it. More illuminating than this bald, unreasoned disclaimer is the progression of thought displayed by an earlier passage in the Court's opinion, which notes the constitutional protections afforded to 'personal decisions relating to *marriage*, procreation, contraception, family relationships, child rearing, and education,' and then declares that '[p]ersons in a homosexual relationship may seek autonomy for these purposes, just as heterosexual persons do.' Today's opinion dismantles the structure of constitutional law that has permitted a distinction to be made between heterosexual and homosexual unions, insofar as formal recognition in marriage is concerned. If moral disapprobation of homosexual conduct is 'no legitimate state interest' for purposes of proscribing that conduct; and if, as the Court coos (casting aside all pretense of neutrality), '[w]hen sexuality finds overt expression in intimate conduct with another person, the conduct can be but one element in a personal bond that is more enduring,' what justification could there possibly be for denying the benefits of marriage to homosexual couples exercising '[t]he liberty protected by the Constitution'? Surely not the encouragement of procreation, since the sterile and the elderly are allowed to marry. This case 'does not involve' the issue of homosexual marriage only if one entertains the belief that principle and logic have nothing to do with the decisions of this Court. Many will hope that, as the Court comfortingly assures us, this is so." (*Lawrence v. Texas* [2003], 604–5)

70. Jakobsen, "Sex + Freedom," 286, 293, 295.

71. Harris, "Whiteness as Property."

72. Ibid., 1721, 1714.

73. Ibid., 1725.

74. Wahneema Lubiano, "For Race."

75. Leti Volpp, "The Citizen and the Terrorist."

76. *Lawrence v. Texas* (2003), 573.

77. Quoted in Emily Eakin, "All Roads Lead to D.C.," *New York Times*, Week in Review, March 31, 2002: 4.

78. See Eric Santner, *My Own Private Germany: Daniel Paul Schreber's Secret History of Modernity*.

79. Daniel Paul Schreber, *Memoirs of My Nervous Illness*. It is interesting to note that the two major non-clinical analyses Freud publishes at this point in his career concern homosexuals and primitives: Schreber and the anthropological accounts of savage tribes in *Totem and Taboo*.

80. Sigmund Freud, " 'Civilized' Sexual Morality and Modern Nervous Illness," 192.

81. Sigmund Freud, "On Narcissism: An Introduction," 101–2.

82. Sigmund Freud, "Psychoanalytic Notes Upon an Autobiographical Account of a Case of Paranoia (Dementia Paranoides)," 49.

83. Ibid., 71.

84. Freud, "On Narcissism," 102.

85. Freud, "Psychoanalytic Notes," 79.

86. Ibid., 10.

87. Sigmund Freud, "April 22, 1910 Letter to Jung."

88. Freud, "On Narcissism," 96. I am indebted to the participants in my seminar on Freud at Rutgers in Spring 2005, and in particular to Jonathan Foltz, for developing this idea about the confusion of voices.

89. Freud, "Psychoanalytic Notes," 71.

90. Ibid., 20.

91. Ibid., 13.

92. Ibid.

93. Ibid., 19.

94. Ibid.

95. See Elias Canetti, *Crowds and Power*; and Gilles Deleuze and Félix Guattari, *Anti-Oedipus: Capitalism and Schizophrenia*.

96. Freud, "Psychoanalytic Notes," 16.

97. Schreber, *Memoirs of My Nervous Illness*, 165.

98. Kendall Thomas, "Corpus Juris (Hetero)Sexualis: Doctrine, Discourse, and Desire in *Bowers v. Hardwick*," 34.

99. Ibid.

100. Freud, "Psychoanalytic Notes," 43.

101. Ibid., 57.

102. Ibid., 58.

103. In this scenario, as Elizabeth Freeman suggests, same-sex marriage func-

tions as a private economic solution that cannot make good on large-scale structural problems including the collapse of health care, the criminalization of immigrants, and the wider dissolution of the social safety net. See Elizabeth Freeman, *The Wedding Complex: Forms of Belonging in Modern American Culture*; and "Still After."

104. Lisa Duggan writes: "In a bid for equality, some gay groups are producing rhetoric that insults and marginalizes unmarried people, while promoting marriage in much the same terms as the welfare reformers use to stigmatize single-parent households, divorce, and 'out of wedlock' births. If pursued in this way, the drive for gay marriage equality can undermine rather than support the broader movement for social justice and democratic diversity." See Duggan, "Holy Matrimony!"

105. Duggan and Richard Kim write: "Marital reproduction households are no longer in the majority, and most Americans spend half their adult lives outside marriage. The average age at which people marry has steadily risen as young people live together longer; the number of cohabiting couples rose 72 percent between 1990 and 2000. More people live alone, and many live in multigenerational, nonmarital households; 41 percent of these unmarried households include children. Increasing numbers of elderly, particularly women, live in companionate nonconjugal unions . . . Household diversity is a fact of American life rooted not just in the cultural revolutions of feminism and gay liberation but in long-term changes in aging, housing, childcare and labor." See Duggan and Kim, "Beyond Gay Marriage."

106. Ibid.

107. Ibid.

TWO *The Structure of Kinship*

1. William Faulkner, *Absalom, Absalom!*, 15.

2. Monique Truong, *The Book of Salt*. The novel grew from a short story, "Seeds," originally published in *Watermark: An Anthology of Vietnamese Writings*, and garnered several prizes, including 2003 Bard Fiction Prize, the Stonewall Book Award-Barbara Gittings Literature Award, the New York Public Library Young Lions Fiction Award, and the Association for Asian American Studies Book Award; Wong Kar-wai, director, *Happy Together*.

3. Alice B. Toklas, *The Alice B. Toklas Cookbook*, 186. Toklas writes: "When it was evident that connections in the quarter were no longer able to find a servant for us, it was necessary to go to the employment office. That was indeed a humiliating experience, from which I withdrew not certain whether it was more so for me or for the applicants. It was then that we commenced our insecure, unstable, unreliable but thoroughly enjoyable experiences with the Indo-Chinese" (186). Toklas tells us that Stein and she employed "a succession" (187) of Vietnamese cooks, but Toklas writes mainly about two men, Trac and Nguyen, the former without his surname and the latter without his given name.

4. Gayatri Chakravorty Spivak, "Subaltern Studies: Deconstructing Historiography," 207. Elda Tsou notes that *The Book of Salt* begins with two photographs of Bình, which appear to rectify a historical omission, to conjure forth the historically absent body, and to give voice to Bình as a missing subject. Yet the photographs are fictitious, one of many symptoms in Truong's novel that "stages over and over the equivocation of authorship and the fiction of testimony as access to authenticity" (147). See Elda Tsou, "Figures of Identity: Rereading Asian American Literature."

5. Martin Heidegger, "The Thing," esp. 177.

6. Truong, *Salt*, 86; 89.

7. Ibid., 98.

8. Ibid., 99.

9. Brent Edwards has written on the life of Nguyen Ai Quoc in France, "who may well stand as the most important and prodigious writer in radical circles in Paris during the first part of the 1920s" (33). Edwards connects Nguyen to a diasporic group of anticolonial and anticapitalist black activists, in particular, Léopold Senghor, indexing another historical incarnation of Asia and Africa in the metropole. See Edwards, "The Shadow of Shadows."

10. By historicism, I mean the attempt, found especially among German historians around the mid-nineteenth century, to view all social and cultural phenomena, all categories, truths, and values, as relative and historically determined, and in consequence to be understood only by examining their historical context, in complete detachment from present-day attitudes. For a trenchant critique of historicism, see Walter Benjamin, "Theses on the Philosophy of History," 255.

11. Ibid., 257.

12. Tani Barlow, *The Question of Chinese Woman in Feminism*, 3.

13. Michel Foucault, *Aesthetics, Method, and Epistemology: Essential Works of Foucault, 1954–1984, Volume 2*, 430.

14. See Maria Josefina Saldaña-Portillo, *The Revolutionary Imagination in the Americas and the Age of Development*.

15. Giorgio Agamben explains medieval conceptions of melancholia as a process of materializing the ghostly remains of an unrealized object or ideal. He highlights melancholia's insistent compulsion to transform an object of loss into an amorous embrace, thereby magically preserving it in the realm of the phantasmagoric. For Agamben, melancholia opens up an alternative time and space of the phantasm in which lost objects appear lost precisely so that they might become real. In this regard, Agamben's "ghostly matters" supplement what Avery Gordon describes as the haunting of the "sociological imagination" and its abiding fidelity to the empirical. These ghostly matters open onto the terrain of "complex personhood" (4), intricate ways of life and living that fall below the radar of conventional political representation and the protocols of market exchange. See Giorgio Agamben, "The Lost Object," in *Stanzas: Word and Phantasm in Western Culture*, 20. See also Avery Gordon, *Ghostly Matters: Haunting and the Sociological Imagination*.

16. Truong, *Salt*, 100.

17. Chakrabarty, *Provincializing Europe*, 111.

18. See Martin Heidegger, "Letter on Humanism." See also Ranjana Khanna, *Dark Continents: Psychoanalysis and Colonialism*.

19. Chakrabarty, *Provincializing Europe*, 7.

20. Ibid., 18.

21. Ibid.

22. See Williams, *Marxism and Literature*.

23. Vilashini Cooppan, "Hauntologies of Form: Race, Genre, and the Literary World System," 81.

24. Truong, *Salt*, 154.

25. Ibid., 135; my emphasis.

26. See Johannes Fabian, *Time and the Other: How Anthropology Makes Its Objects*, especially the first two chapters.

27. Chakrabarty, *Provincializing Europe*, 8.

28. See Derrida, *Spectres of Marx*.

29. Brian Massumi, *Parables for the Virtual: Movement, Affect, Sensation*, 70. Massumi further clarifies: "For the in-between, as such, is not a middling being but rather the being *of* the middle—the being of a relation. A positioned being, central, middling, or marginal, is a *term* of a relation. It may seem odd to insist that a relation has an ontological status separate from the terms of the relation. But, as the work of Gilles Deleuze repeatedly emphasizes, it is in fact an indispensable step toward conceptualizing change as anything more or other than a negation, deviation, rupture, or subversion."

30. Truong, *Salt*, 111.

31. Ibid.

32. Ibid., 189.

33. Ibid., 37.

34. See Jacques Lacan, "The Mirror Stage as Formative of the Function of the I as Revealed in Psychoanalytic Experience." See also Jacques Lacan, "Aggressivity and Psychoanalysis," 23.

35. Jane Gallop, *Reading Lacan*, 81; Jacques Lacan, "The Function and Field of Speech and Language in Psychoanalysis," 86.

36. Ranajit Guha, *Elementary Aspects of Peasant Insurgency in Colonial India*, 333.

37. See Paul Gilroy, *The Black Atlantic: Modernity and Double Consciousness*.

38. Truong, *Salt*, 190.

39. See Braudel, *On History*.

40. Carla Freccero, "Theorizing Queer Temporalities: A Roundtable Discussion," 184.

41. The Wolf, "*Happy Together*," *Inside Out Film*, www.insideout.co.uk (accessed April 18, 2000); David Dalgleish, "*Happy Together* Review," *Killer Movies*, www.killermovies.com (accessed October 8, 2009); Derek Elley, "*Happy Together*," *Daily Variety*, May 20, 1997.

42. Jay Carr, "Down and Out in Buenos Aires," *Boston Globe*, October 31, 1997.

43. Elley, "*Happy Together.*"

44. Eve Kosofsky Sedgwick, *Epistemology of the Closet*, 71.

45. *The Wedding Banquet*. Directed by Ang Lee.

46. Mark Chiang, "Coming Out in the Global System: Postmodern Patriarchies and Transnational Sexualities in *The Wedding Banquet*." See also my reading of Lee's film in *Racial Castration: Managing Masculinity in Asian America*, 204–28.

47. *The Wedding Banquet* is recognizable to a Western audience as a "gay" film. Queer diaspora in *The Wedding Banquet* depends on the strict alignment of the Taiwanese Gao Wai-tung (Winston Chao) with the management of transnational capital and the Mainlander Wei-Wei (May Chin) as the source of third-world labor. The narrative resolution to *The Wedding Banquet* relies upon Wei-Wei's acquiescence to keep and not to abort their unborn (male) child. In Lee's film, Wai-tung's purchase of an individuated Western gay lifestyle with his white lover Simon (Mitchell Lichtenstein), along with the placating of his heir-demanding Chinese parents (Lung Sihung and Gua Ah-la), depends upon the subordination of women and labor, such that women become the very sign of labor. *The Wedding Banquet* thus illustrates the regrettable cleaving of queerness from feminist political concerns.

48. Filmically and thematically this scene represents for Ho and Lai the original ineffable experience Kaja Silverman theorizes as the beginning point of all human desire and longing: "The experience of being within the 'here and now' is completely ineffable—it defies every kind of symbolization. Once presence evaporates, however, it assumes a status which it did not have before: it comes to signify a lost fullness. This is because we are able to constitute something as an object of desire only when we are able to make it a representative of something anterior, something no longer available to us . . . To desire is thus initially to incarnate, and later to reincarnate, the 'what-has-been.'" (Silverman, *World Spectators*, 39)

49. I borrow this term from Parreñas. See Rhacel Salazar Parreñas, *Servants of Globalization: Women, Migration, and Domestic Work*.

50. Gayatri Chakravorty Spivak, "Diasporas Old and New," 90.

51. See Alexander's analysis of the emergence and development of gay tourism around the globe in *Pedagogies of Crossing*.

52. In a *Salon* review, Charles Taylor notes, "It's one of the recurring jokes in Wong's movies that no matter where the characters travel, they end up in the same crummy bars and apartments and fast-food joints." See Charles Taylor, "Review of *Happy Together*," *Salon.com*, www.salon.com (accessed October 8, 2009).

53. Elizabeth Freeman, "Introduction: Queer Temporalities," 164.

54. See Marta E. Savigliano, *Tango and the Political Economy of Passion*. Tango,

Savigliano notes, exposes the dark side of development. Tango traces its roots back to the milonga, and black men and women probably initiated the first tango steps in the Río de le Plata in the mid-nineteenth century. She observes that the worldwide increasing popularity of the tango has been associated with the scandal of the public display of passion performed by a heterosexual couple. As the tango made its way from the countryside to the slums and brothels of Bueños Aires, and to the cabarets and ballrooms of Paris, London, New York, and Tokyo in the early decades of the twentieth century, the sins of tango's erotic suggestiveness became entangled with its debased status, associated with its racial and class origins.

Globally exoticized, the tango underwrites what Savigliano describes as a "political economy of Passion . . . [one] intertwined with the economies usually described on materialist and ideological grounds" (1). Tango's political economy of passion, Savigliano contends, is a traffic in "emotions and affects [that] paralleled the processes by which core countries of the capitalist world system have extracted material goods and labor from . . . the Third World (periphery)" (1–2).

But this imperial domestication and management of passion—of emotional capital—accumulated and consumed as exotic culture, cannot fully regulate its affective deviations. Savigliano writes, "Untamable interpretations . . . of bodies performing excessive movement, despite all efforts invested in domesticating them, are good signs for a decolonizing project" (13).

55. Massumi, *Parables for the Virtual*, 28.

56. See Lévi-Strauss, *The Elementary Structures of Kinship*.

57. Rubin, "The Traffic in Women," 173.

58. Ibid., 198.

59. Numerous psychoanalytic feminist critics note that Lacan often conflates and confuses these two losses, through the privileging of the paternal metaphor and through the implicit inscription of the name of the father with meaning and the maternal body with being, i.e. that the phallus is equivalent to a penis. See the special issue of *differences: A Journal of Feminist Cultural Studies* 4, no. 1 (Spring 1992) on the "Lacanian Phallus."

60. Butler, *Antigone's Claim*, 41.

61. Ibid., 29–30; 70.

62. See Chris Doyle, "To the End of the World." In his diary of the shooting of *Happy Together*, Chris Doyle writes, "He [Wong Kai-wai] feels that what Zhang Zhen gives Tony (and what Tony gives Leslie) is not 'love' but 'courage'—'a will to live.' It's our brightest film in all senses of the word and looks like having the happiest ending of any [Wong Kar-wai] film" (17).

63. Silverman, *World Spectators*, 38–39.

64. See Butler, *Antigone's Claim*, 66. She continues: "From the presumption that one cannot—or ought not to—choose one's closest family members as one's lovers and marital partners, it does not follow that the bonds of kinship that *are* possible assume any particular form."

65. There are three men and a woman working at the Chang food stand. While Wong Kar-wai suggests that two of these are Chang's parents, we are left with an image of a non-Oedipal communal family unit. Moreover, Lai's "adoption" into Chang's family unit demonstrates that Asian queer subjectivity does not necessarily occur, as some Western critics insist, outside the sphere of the traditional nuclear family but can coexist within it as a different kind of "individualism."

66. Silverman, *World Spectators*, 29.

THREE *The Language of Kinship*

1. Deann Borshay Liem, director, *First Person Plural*.

2. See Kirsten Lovelock, "Intercountry Adoption as a Migratory Practice." Lovelock divides post-war transnational adoption into two historical periods: the first wave was a humanitarian response to orphans in war-torn countries; the second wave, which began in the 1970s, was a response to infertility rates in the West.

3. While there is not a lot of scholarship on the topic, in recent years there have been a number of documentaries and memoirs on the transnational adoption from Asia. For a list of documentaries, see Sunny Jo, "Korean Adoption Films." For memoirs, see Tonya Bishoff and Jo Rankin, *Seeds from a Silent Tree*; Susan Soon-Keum Cox, *Voices from Another Place*; Elizabeth Kim, *Ten Thousand Sorrows*; Katy Robinson, Sook Wilkinson, and Nancy Fox, *After the Morning Calm: Reflections on Korean Adoptees*; and Jane Jeong Trenka, *The Language of Blood*. For recent scholarship, see Tobias Hübinette, *Comforting an Orphaned Nation*; Jane Jeong Trenka, Julia Chinyere Oparah, and Sun Yung Shin, *Outsiders Within: Writing on Transracial Adoption*; and Toby Alice Volkman, *Cultures of Transnational Adoption*.

4. Amy Kaplan, "'Left Alone with America': The Absence of Empire in the Study of American Culture," 16.

5. See Volkman, *Cultures of Transnational Adoption,* which was originally published as a special issue of the journal *Social Text*. Volkman's collection is largely about the topic of transnational parenting, from the point of view of adoptive parents. It is curated from the disciplinary angle of anthropology, using ethnographies and personal anecdotes. This chapter is, in part, a response to a necessary critical reframing of current approaches to the topic, broadening the political, economic, and cultural issues raised by the practice of transnational adoption as well as opening up new critical perspectives from the point of view of the adoptees and the (even more silent) birth mothers.

6. See Elizabeth Bartholet, "Commentary: Cultural Stereotypes Can and Do Die: It's Time to Move on With Transracial Adoption." Tobias Hübinette, a Korean adoptee raised in Sweden, has controversially compared the practice of transnational adoption to the Black Atlantic slave trade. See his "Orphan Trains to Babylifts: Colonial Trafficking, Empire Building, and Social Engineering."

7. *John Hancock Financial Services Advertisement*, available at http://www .commercialcloset.org/ (accessed June 28, 2008).

8. See "Hancock Ad Raises Alarm in Adoption Communities," *Wall Street Journal*, September 14, 2000. After protests from right-wing conservatives, the commercial was reedited without the final exchange about being great mothers. In addition, fearing reprisals from Chinese government authorities that lesbians were snatching up Chinese baby girls, an audio was added, stating that a flight from Phnom Penh, Cambodia had just arrived.

9. We need to dissociate the relationship between economic entitlement and political rights. That is, the current practice of transnational adoption suggests that family is available to those gays and lesbians with access to capital. The legal treatment of this group by courts, however, has by and large excluded them from the sphere of non-economic rights (adoption, marriage, inheritance, service in the military, consensual sex). As a legal matter, adoption is a privilege. Hence, the contemporary reconsolidation of family by gays and lesbians has become an economic privilege and entitlement for few rather than a political right for all.

10. Ann Anagnost, "Scenes of Misrecognition."

11. Ibid., 395.

12. Berlant, *The Queen of America Goes to Washington City*, 4–24. See also Perry, "Transracial Adoption and Gentrification."

13. Linda Gordon, *The Great Arizona Orphan Abduction*.

14. Ann Laura Stoler, "Making Empire Respectable," 648.

15. See Evan B. Donaldson Adoption Institute, "Adoption Facts," http:// www.adoptioninstitute.org, accessed June 28, 2008.

16. These figures are based on U.S. Department of State "Immigrant Visas Issued to Orphans Coming to the U.S. See http://travel.state.gov, accessed June 28, 2008.

17. See, for instance, Cynthia H. Enloe, *Bananas, Beaches and Bases: Making Feminist Sense of International Politics*.

18. This tax credit is for all adoptions, although the process for credit differs depending on the context, domestic or international. See "The Adoption Tax Credit." http://tax-credit.adoption.com. See also Robert S. Gordon, "The New Chinese Export: Orphaned Children, An Overview of Adopting Children from China." In the 1990s, Americans spent over U.S. $300 million to adopt 18,751 children from China. In 1999, adoption costs from China per child were approximately $20,000–27,000.

Hollee McGinnis, founder of the transnational adoption group "Also Known As," points out that while one of the original justifications for transnational adoption from Korea was a failing post-war national economy, today Korea is the ninth largest industrialized economy in the world. Yet, Korea is still the fourth largest sending nation to the U.S. According to McGinnis, this is because there is an elaborate infrastructure already established in Korea for transnational adoption. In short, it is a big business there.

Finally, from another angle, the economic profits from transnational adoption are central for understanding the political development and economic transformations marking the advent of Asian modernity. How, for instance, does transnational adoption relate to Korea's official narratives of its post-war economic miracle as one of Asia's "four tigers," its struggles for democratic rule, and its more recent and visible debates on the plight of comfort women during World War II?

19. For instance, see the 1989 United Nations Convention on the Rights of the Child, the 1993 Hague Convention on the Protection of Children and the Cooperation in Respect of Intercountry Adoption, and Brazil's Children's Code.

20. Twila L. Perry, "Transracial and International Adoptions: Mothers, Hierarchy, Race, and Feminist Legal Theory," 155.

21. Leti Volpp, "Disappearing Acts: On Gendered Violence, Pathological Cultures, and Civil Society," 1631.

22. Arlie Hochschild's comment that "when poor mothers get pregnant to sell babies—and we do not yet know the degree to which this practice might go on—[the] commodification paradigm fits squarely" is an instance of such ascription of female agency to the Third World woman by First World liberal white feminists. See roundtable on Hochschild and Barbara Ehrenreich's *Global Woman: Nannies, Maids, and Sex Workers in the New Economy* in *SGS: Studies in Gender and Sexuality: Psychoanalysis, Cultural Studies, Treatment, Research* 7, no. 1 (2006).

23. See Coutin, Maurer, and Yngvesson, "In the Mirror," 825.

24. See Janet Carsten, *After Kinship*.

25. I take this idea of the silent birth mother to be one of John Sayles's main themes in his film, *Casa de los babys*, about six American women who travel to an unnamed Latin American country to adopt babies. *Casa de los babys*, directed by John Sayles.

26. See Leti Volpp, "Divesting Citizenship: On Asian American History and the Loss of Citizenship Through Marriage."

27. See Lisa Lowe, *Immigrant Acts: On Asian American Cultural Politics*. See also Mae Ngai, *Impossible Subjects: Illegal Aliens and the Making of Modern America*.

28. Of course, the question of availability is not absolute but also a market-driven and discursive phenomenon. For a controversial analysis of the supply-and-demand aspect of baby adoption, see Elisabeth M. Landes and Richard A. Posner, "The Economics of the Baby Shortage." For a critique of Landes and Posner, see Patricia Williams, "Spare Parts, Family Values, Old Children, Cheap"; and Ana Teresa Ortiz and Laura Briggs, "The Culture of Poverty, Crack Babies, and Welfare Cheats: The Making of the 'Healthy White Baby Crisis.'" Ortiz and Briggs explore how the 1980s emerging discourse on "crack babies," damaged beyond repair, also fuels the desire to adopt "safe" babies from abroad.

29. For a discussion of the politics of interracial white parents/black child adoption, see R. Richard Banks, "The Color of Desire: Fulfilling Adoptive Parents' Racial Preferences through Discriminatory State Action."

30. Miranda Joseph, *Against the Romance of Community*, 42.

31. Siobhan B. Somerville, "Notes Toward a Queer History of Nationalization," 662.

32. See Viviana A. Zelizer, *Pricing the Priceless Child: The Changing Social Value of Children*.

33. See Marilyn Strathern, *The Gender of the Gift: Problems with Women and Problems with Society in Melanesia*.

34. In *First Person Plural*, Donald Borshay tells Deann: "You were so determined to learn. I guess to please us, whatever, I'm not sure. You actually made yourself ill and you became jaundiced. You got kind of yellow-looking. And the only thing we could think of was that you really tried too hard and were trying too hard."

35. Upon learning that she was switched for another child, Alveen tells Borshay Liem, "Well, I didn't care that they had switched a child on us. You couldn't be loved more. And just because suddenly you weren't Cha Jung Hee, you were Ok Jin Kang—Kang or whatever—didn't matter to me. You were Deann and you were mine."

36. Attitudes toward adoption (in general) and transnational adoption (in particular) have shifted considerably from forty years ago. However, given the ways in which racial difference is often appropriated and reinscribed by a politics of neoliberal multiculturalism, the current acknowledgement of the adoptee's racial, ethnic, or cultural difference may not have shifted the need for this management of affect in any significant manner.

37. See David L. Eng and Shinhee Han, "A Dialogue on Racial Melancholia."

38. Homi Bhabha, "Of Mimicry and Man: The Ambivalence of Colonial Discourse," 126; 130.

39. See Sigmund Freud, "Mourning and Melancholia." Later, in "The Ego and the Id," Freud comes to revise this distinction between mourning and melancholia, noting that the ego is, in fact, comprised of its abandoned and lost objects. See Sigmund Freud, "The Ego and the Id," 28–29.

40. See Williams, *Marxism and Literature*, 128–35.

41. See Lowe, *Immigrant Acts*, 63.

42. In another part of *First Person Plural*, Borshay Liem adds, "When I had learned enough English to talk to my parents, I decided that I should tell them who I really was. I remember going up to my mother and telling her 'I'm not who you think I am, I'm not Cha Jung Hee. And I think I have a mother and brother and sisters in Korea still.' And she turned to me and said, 'Oh honey you've just been dreaming. You don't have a mother. And you never had brothers and sisters. Look at these adoption documents. It says that you're Cha Jung Hee and your mother died giving birth to you.' And she said. 'You know what, this is just a natural part of you getting used to living in a new country. Don't worry about it. They're just bad dreams. They're going to go away soon.'"

43. Walter Benjamin, *The Arcades Project*, 456–75.

44. Here, I draw on this argument from Anagnost, "Scenes of Misrecognition," 395.

45. Sigmund Freud, "Femininity," 134.

46. Kaja Silverman, "Girl Love," 159.

47. Freud, "Femininity," 116.

48. Ibid., 121.

49. Melanie Klein, "A Contribution to the Psychogenesis of Manic-Depressive States," 125.

50. Patty Chu reads this painful scene as both women admitting their failings and taking on their status as post-Oedipal mothers: "Neither could provide the complete pre-Oedipal sense of emotional richness, safety, and continuity, and the mother as beautiful, nurturing, ever-present, and infallible, which Deann is trying to recover. But they are asking Deann not to hold them to that interior psychic standard of early infancy or early childhood." See Patty Chu, "The Orphan's Tales: Adoption, Mourning, and the Search for Roots."

51. It also complicates the notion of the gift, which often attaches itself to (transnational) adoption—a notion that the infant is a gift from the birth mother to the adoptive mother, a gift that can never be repaid. See Barbara Yngvesson, "Placing the 'Gift Child' in Transnational Adoption."

52. Here, let me gesture to Gail Dolgin and Vicente Franco's *Daughter from Danang*, another recent documentary exploring transnational adoption in the wake of the Vietnam War. The film is an elaborate and painful disquisition on adoptee Heidi Bub's successive rejection of two "bad" mothers—first her adoptive mother and subsequently her birth mother.

53. According to the United Nations High Commission on Refugees (UNHCR), "A person is a refugee whether or not a legal eligibility procedure has already recognized that status." Nevertheless, in order to gain the right of asylum in a particular nation-state, an asylum-seeker must be recognized by that nation-state's legal regime as a refugee.

The *U.S. Immigration and Nationality Act* defines "refugee" as "any person who is outside any country of such person's nationality or, in the case of a person having no nationality, is outside any country in which such person last habitually resided, and who is unable or unwilling to return to, and is unable or unwilling to avail himself or herself for the protection of, that country because of persecution or a well-founded fear of persecution on account of race, religion, nationality, membership in a particular social group, or political opinion."

54. See Sanda Lwin, *The Constitution of Asian America*, especially her discussion of the figure of the refugee in Wendy Law-Yone's *The Coffin Tree*.

55. Silverman, "Girl Love," 159.

56. Ibid., 156–57.

57. Ibid., 166.

58. Ibid., 161.

59. Anagnost, "Scenes of Misrecognition," 395.

1. Trenka, *The Language of Blood*, 207.

2. See, in addition, Eng and Han, "A Dialogue on Racial Melancholia."

3. See Klein, "A Contribution to the Psychogenesis of Manic-Depressive States."

4. See D.W. Winnicott, "Transitional Objects and Transitional Phenomena."

5. See Anagnost, "Scenes of Misrecognition."

6. Freud, "Mourning and Melancholia," 245.

7. Melanie Klein, "Love, Guilt, and Reparation," 68.

8. Melanie Klein, "The Psycho-analytic Play Technique: Its History and Significance," 48.

9. Melanie Klein, "Love, Guilt, and Reparation," 68.

10. Klein, "A Contribution," 125.

11. Ibid., 124.

12. Melanie Klein, "A Study of Envy and Gratitude," 217.

13. Klein, "A Contribution,"123.

14. See Eng and Han, "A Dialogue on Racial Melancholia," 696.

15. Judith Butler, "Moral Sadism and Doubting One's Own Love: Kleinian Reflections on Melancholia," 180.

16. Freud, "Mourning and Melancholia," 250.

17. Klein, "A Contribution," 131.

18. Melanie Klein, "Mourning and its Relation to Manic-Depressive States," 173.

19. Ibid.

20. Winnicott, "Transitional Objects," 3.

21. Ibid., 14–15.

22. Ibid., 10.

23. Ibid., 6.

24. Phillips, *Winnicott*, 114.

25. Winnicott, "Transitional Objects," 5.

26. Ibid., 13.

27. D.W. Winnicott, "Playing: A Theoretical Statement," 38. Passage italicized in the original.

28. See D.W. Winnicott, "The Use of an Object and Relating though Identifications."

29. See Michelle Friedman, "When the Analyst Becomes Pregnant Twice."

30. Winnicott, "The Use of an Object," 89; 87.

31. Ibid., 89.

32. The notion of positions and the concept of transitions that we encounter in object relations—in contrast to Freudian theories of stages that are accomplished, lived through, and overcome—force our attention to the everyday mechanisms of psychic coping that patients repeatedly employ to negotiate the social

realities and psychic pain of immigration, assimilation, and racialization. Like melancholia, positions and transitions do not have a temporal end. They are not stages to be mastered but are mechanisms fundamentally pertaining to psychic process of negotiation, adjustment, and coping.

33. Melanie Klein, "A Study of Envy," 217.

34. Ibid., 212.

35. Ibid., 213.

36. We are indebted to Robert Diaz for raising this concept of envy and racial spoilage with us.

FIVE *The Feeling of Kinship*

1. Rea Tajiri, director, *History and Memory: For Akiko and Takashige*.

2. Janet Sternburg, "Long Exposures: A Poetics of Film and History," 178. See also Robert M. Payne, "Visions of Silence." Payne describes *History and Memory* as blurring the distinction between the "avant-garde" and the "documentary."

3. See also Eng and Han, "A Dialogue on Racial Melancholia."

4. Sigmund Freud, "The Unconscious," 194.

5. Freud, "Mourning and Melacholia," 245.

6. Jean-Paul Sartre, *The Emotions: Outline of a Theory*, 52.

7. We might be tempted to describe this recurring visual tableau as a traumatic Freudian primal scene, defined by Jean Laplanche and Jean-Bertrand Pontalis as a retroactive childhood fantasy of origin and sexuality. However, this primal scene is one Tajiri never actually saw or heard (she was born after the Second World War) but *feels*. Even more, it is less concerned with the discovery of sexuality or sexual difference than with fundamental problems of history and historical understandings involving race, gender, and nation. See Laplanche and Pontalis, *The Language of Psycho-analysis*, 331–33.

8. See Sarah Ahmed, *The Cultural Politics of Emotion*; Ann Cvetkovich, *An Archive of Feelings: Trauma, Sexuality, and Lesbian Public Cultures*; Paul Gilroy, *Postcolonial Melancholia*; Massumi, *Parables for the Virtual: Movement, Affect, Sensation*; Sianne Ngai, *Ugly Feelings*; Jasbir K. Puar, *Terrorist Assemblages: Homonationalism in Queer Times*; Rei Terada, *Feeling in Theory: Emotion after the "Death of the Subject"*; Eve Kosofsky Sedgwick, *Touching Feeling: Affect, Pedagogy, Performativity*.

9. See Nicolas Abraham and Maria Torok, "The Illness of Mourning and the Fantasy of the Exquisite Corpse," and "Mourning *or* Melacholia: Introjections *versus* Incorporation," in *The Shell and the Kernel, Volume 1*, 107–38. See also Marianne Hirsch, *Family Frames: Photography, Narrative, and Postmemory*. Hirsch has written about the phenomenon of postmemory as it applies to children of Holocaust survivors. These children have an uncanny relation to their parents' experiences, in which images of the Holocaust continually reprised are so powerful that they come to constitute (virtual) memories in their own right.

10. Benjamin, "Theses on the Philosophy of History," 255.

11. Terada, *Feeling in Theory*, 1.

12. Lisa Yasui and Ann Tegnell, directors, *A Family Gathering*; Janice Tanaka, director, *Who's Going to Pay for These Donuts, Anyway?*, and *Memories from the Department of Amnesia*; Julie Otsuka, *When the Emperor Was Divine*; Lawson Fusao Inada, *Legends from Camp*.

13. Tanaka and Inada were both infants in camp.

14. House Resolution 422, The Civil Liberties Act of 1988. Enacted by the United States Congress, August 10, 1988.

> The Congress recognizes that, as described in the Commission on Wartime Relocation and Internment of Civilians, a grave injustice was done to both citizens and permanent residents of Japanese ancestry by the evacuation, relocation, and internment of civilians during World War II.
>
> As the Commission documents, these actions were carried out without adequate security reasons and without any acts of espionage or sabotage documented by the Commission, and were motivated largely by racial prejudice, wartime hysteria, and a failure of political leadership.
>
> The excluded individuals of Japanese ancestry suffered enormous damages, both material and intangible, and there were incalculable losses in education and job training, all of which resulted in significant human suffering for which appropriate compensation has not been made.
>
> For these fundamental violations of the basic civil liberties and constitutional rights of these individuals of Japanese ancestry, the Congress apologizes on behalf of the Nation.
>
> Based on the findings of the Commission on Wartime Relocation and Internment of Civilians (CWRIC), the purposes of the Civil Liberties Act of 1988 with respect to persons of Japanese ancestry included the following:
>
> 1) To acknowledge the fundamental injustice of the evacuation, relocation and internment of citizens and permanent resident aliens of Japanese ancestry during World War II;
>
> 2) To apologize on behalf of the people of the United States for the evacuation, internment, and relocations of such citizens and permanent residing aliens;
>
> 3) To provide for a public education fund to finance efforts to inform the public about the internment so as to prevent the recurrence of any similar event;
>
> 4) To make restitution to those individuals of Japanese ancestry who were interned;
>
> 5) To make more credible and sincere any declaration of concern by the United States over violations of human rights committed by other nations.

15. The temporal rhetoric of H.R. 422 deserves comment: "The excluded individuals of Japanese ancestry suffered enormous damages, both material and

intangible, and there were incalculable losses in education and job training, all of which resulted in significant human suffering *for which appropriate compensation has not been made*." On one hand, the passage implies that once "appropriate compensation" has been calculated and delivered, the injustices of Japanese internment—the "enormous damages," the "incalculable losses," the "significant human suffering"—can somehow be made good and thus written firmly into the nation's past. On the other hand, the grammar of the passage's final clause—*has not [yet] been made*—also defers such an anticipated moment of resolution and justice into an indeterminate future. In a colorblind age, that future has now apparently arrived.

16. Marita Sturken, "Absent Images of Memory: Remembering and Reenacting the Japanese American Internment," 704.

17. Victor Bascara, "Cultural Politics of Redress: Reassessing the Meaning of the Civil Liberties Act of 1988 after 9/11," 192.

18. Fredric Jameson, *The Political Unconscious: Narrative as a Socially Symbolic Act*, 90.

19. Cvetkovich, *An Archive of Feelings*, 10. Cvetkovich observes, whether "the language of trauma is used or not, the project of investigating racial histories needs to be part of an interdisciplinary trauma studies. Everyday forms of racism, many of which are institutional or casual and thus don't always appear visible except to those who are attuned to them, are among the effects of longer histories of racial trauma" (6).

20. Cathy Caruth, *Unclaimed Experience: Trauma, Narrative, and History*, 18. Caruth's trauma genealogy traces itself to Holocaust studies, in particular, Felman and Laub. See Shoshana Felman and Dori Laub, *Testimony: Crises of Witnessing in Literature, Psychoanalysis, and History*.

21. Victor Burgin, *In/Different Spaces: Place and Memory in Visual Space*, 130. Burgin continues: "The same logic that generates the opposition 'exile'/'nation' across national frontiers may oppose one racial group to another within national borders. History has familiarized us with the insidious movement in which 'nation' is confused with 'race.' Institutionalized racism may ensure that racial minorities live in a condition of internal exile within the nation of which they are citizens—an exile that, if it is not legal, cannot be named" (Ibid.).

22. Michel de Certeau, *The Practice of Everyday Life*.

23. Bill Nichols, *Representing Reality: Issues and Concepts in Documentary*, 1; 4–5. Nichols proposes four basic modes of documentary: expository, observational, interactive, and reflexive.

24. Benjamin, "Theses on the Philosophy of History," 257–58. He writes:

"A Klee painting named 'Angelus Novus' shows an angel looking as though he is about to move away from something he is fixedly contemplating. His eyes are staring, his mouth is open, his wings are spread. This is how one pictures the angel of history. His face is turned toward the past. Where we perceive a chain of events, he sees one single catastrophe which keeps piling wreckage upon wreckage and hurls it in front of his feet. The angel would like to stay, awaken the dead, and make whole what has been smashed. But a storm is blowing from Paradise; it has got caught in his wings with such violence that the angel can no longer close them. This storm irresistibly propels him into the future to which his back is turned, while the pile of debris before him grows skyward. This storm is what we call progress."

25. Chakrabarty, *Provincializing Europe*, 18.

26. Peter X. Feng, *Identities in Motion: Asian American Film and Video*, 78.

27. See Wendy Brown, *States of Injury: Power and Freedom in Late Modernity*.

28. See Eiichiro Azuma, *Between Two Empires: Race, History, and Transnationalism in Japanese America*. Azuma writes, "Although Yale Law Professor Eugene Rostow later characterized this episode [of Japanese American internment] as 'our worst wartime mistake,' it was not a mistake at all. The Japanese American incarceration signified a historical moment when the cultural, racial, and national otherness of the Asian was most lucidly articulated, most undisputed, and most resolutely dealt with by the American citizenry and state" (209).

29. Ngai, *Impossible Subjects*, 200. See also Kandice Chuh, "Nikkei Internment," in *Imagine Otherwise*, 58–84.

30. Ngai, *Impossible Subjects*, 179; 177.

31. Ansel Adams, *Born Free and Equal: Photographs of Japanese Americans at Manzanar Relocation Center, Inyo County, California*, 9. The book included a preface from Secretary of the Interior Harold Ickes, quoted in Ngai, *Impossible Subjects*, 180. Ngai writes: "Ever optimistic about the potential of mass social engineering, they envisioned the camps as 'planned communities' and 'Americanizing projects' that would speed the assimilation of Japanese Americans through democratic self-government, schooling, work, and other rehabilitative activities. Comparing their own experiments with the Nazis concentration camps, WRA officials believed their 'community building' project was an 'ironic testimony' to the value of American democracy. The greater irony, however, is that WRA's assimilationism led to the most disastrous and incendiary aspects of the internment experience—the loyalty questionnaire, segregation, and renunciation of citizenship" (177–79).

32. Feng also notes this paradox, stating "The video seeks to preserve space for the emotional truth of gaps in memory, for the emotional truth of memories of events that never happened, emotional truths that can be contradicted by the historical record. While offering a critique of cinematic institutions (such as Hollywood) that promotes a representational logic whereby the visible is legitimated, the video hesitates to offer up images of its own, for that would confirm that logic of visibility. Tajiri's video seeks to make a space for memory (and gaps in memory) within cinema, attempting to relocate that which is oral and private

in a space that is literate and public, while retaining an aura of indeterminacy not usually found in public discourse" (*Identities in Motion*, 91–92).

33. José Esteban Muñoz, "Queerness as Horizon: Utopian Hermeneutics in the Face of Gay Pragmatism," 455.

34. Chakrabarty, *Provincializing Europe*, 111.

35. Benjamin, "Theses on the Philosophy of History," 263.

36. Ibid., 262.

37. Ibid., 263.

38. Ibid., 262. See also Kaja Silverman, "Photography by Other Means."

39. Benjamin, "Theses on the Philosophy of History," 262.

40. In making these connections, I do not mean to level the differences between Japanese internment and our contemporary political moment as much as focus attention on a different historical narration of liberalism's good intentions, then and now. Ngai points out that Japanese internment occurred within a liberal story of assimilation and the rhetoric of good citizenship. With Guantánamo and indefinite detention, we witness the all-out assault on humanity, with discourses of "multicultural" and "monocultural," "human" and "nonhuman." But as Jodi Melamed points out, this shift occurs through the biopolitics of global capitalism, one that reconditions classic racial liberalism into a discourse of neoliberal multiculturalism. Neoliberal multiculturalism continues to "depreciate one form of humanity for the purpose of another's health, development, safety, profit or pleasure," not in the language of race but in the language of a U.S. multiculturalism that becomes "a marker of legitimate privilege and universality [as] monoculturalism becomes a category of stigma that justifies torture" and death. Extending racializing practices and discipline beyond the color-line, "multicultural" and "monocultural" become "new privileged and stigmatized racial formations semidetached from conventional racial categories." See Melamed, "The Spirit of Neoliberalism," 2; 16.

41. Benjamin, "Theses on the Philosophy of History," 255.

42. Nichols, *Representing Reality*, 76.

43. Derrida, *Spectres of Marx*, xviii.

44. Benjamin, "Theses on the Philosophy of History," 263.

45. Ann Cvetkovich, "Public Feelings," 465.

46. Benjamin, "Theses on the Philosophy of History," 254.

47. Cvetkovich, "Public Feelings," 465.

48. See Louis Althusser, "Ideology and Ideological State Apparatuses (Notes Toward an Investigation)."

49. Joan Scott, "The Evidence of Experience"; Gayatri Chakravorty Spivak, *Death of a Discipline*, 76. In terms similar to Scott, Spivak claims that ethnic studies will not let go of "the authority of experience as the bedrock of its theorizing" (Ibid.), although a similar claim can be leveled at the universal liberal subject.

50. Critics have not paid much attention to the ways in which emotions, like words, "do" things. Rather than being seen as indicative of a psychological dis-

position, we need to consider how emotions might be performative as well, how they work to interpellate subjects, how they impede or encourage individuals, for instance, to turn and face the voice of the law, to invoke Althusser's famous passage on hailing.

51. Indeed, some critics define emotion precisely as that which can be symbolically named and affect as that which escapes symbolic inscription. See Massumi, *Parables for the Virtual*, 27–28; 35.

52. Terada, *Feeling in Theory*, 1–2.

53. Fredric Jameson, *Postmodernism, or the Logic of Late Capital*, 10.

54. See Julia Kristeva, *New Maladies of the Soul*.

55. Mari Ruti, *Reinventing the Soul: Posthumanist Theory and Psychic Life*.

56. Chuh, *Imagine Otherwise*, 147.

57. Sartre, *The Emotions: Outline of a Theory*, 52. Freud, "The Unconscious," 177.

58. Freud, "The Unconscious," 177–78.

59. Sara Ahmed, "Affective Economies," 120.

60. Heidegger, "Letter on Humanism," 199.

61. Muñoz, "Queerness as Horizon," 452; 455.

62. See José Esteban Muñoz, "Feeling Brown, Feeling Down: Latina Affect, the Performativity of Race, and the Depressive Position," 687.

63. See Silverman, *World Spectators*, 133.

64. Heidegger, "Letter on Humanism," 193.

65. Judith Butler observes, "if identities were no longer fixed as the premises of a political syllogism, and politics no longer understood as a set of ready-made subjects, a new configuration of politics would surely emerge from the ruins of the old." See Butler, *Gender Trouble*, 149.

66. The horror of the incest taboo is one immediate way of considering how affective regulation secures particular social and psychic prohibitions of normative family and kinship. Like language, affect is performative. It "does" things. It serves to organize its subjects by interpellating them into Oedipal forms of family and kinship, aligning subjects with communities and subjecting them to particular historical narratives and understandings.

Bibliography

Films

Casa de los babys. Directed by John Sayles. New York: IFC Films, 2003.

Daughter from Danang. Directed by Gail Dolgin and Vicente Franco. Waltham, Mass.: Balcony Releasing, 2002.

A Family Gathering. Directed by Lisa Yasui and Ann Tegnell. San Francisco: National Asian American Telecommunications Association, 1988.

First Person Plural. Directed by Deanne Borshay Liem. San Francisco: National Asian American Telecommunications Association, 2000.

Happy Together. Directed by Wong Kar-wai. Hong Kong: Jet Tone Productions, 1997.

History and Memory: For Akiko and Takashige. Directed by Rea Tajiri. New York: Women Make Movies, 1991.

Memories from the Department of Amnesia. Directed by Janice Tanaka. San Francisco: National Asian American Telecommunications Association, 1991.

The Wedding Banquet. Directed by Ang Lee. Taipei: Central Motion Pictures Corporation, 1993.

Who's Going to Pay for These Donuts, Anyway? Directed by Janice Tanaka. San Francisco: National Asian American Telecommunications Association, 1992.

Legal Documents, Resolutions, and Cases

Griswold v. Connecticut, 381 U.S. 479 (1965).

Boutilier v. Immigration Services, 387 U.S. 118 (1967).

Loving v. Virginia, 388 U.S. 1 (1967).

Eisenstadt v. Baird, 405 U.S. 438 (1972).

Roe v. Wade, 410 U.S. 113 (1973).

Carey v. Population Services International, 431 U.S. 678 (1977).

Bowers v. Hardwick, 478 U.S. 186 (1986).

House Resolution 422, *111th Congress: To amend the Internal Revenue Code of 1986 to extend the research credit through 2010 and to . . .* [Civil Liberties Act] (1988).

United Nations Convention on the Rights of the Child. 1989.

Brazil's Childen's Code. 1990. (Estatuto de Criança e do Adolescente, lei n 8.069 de 13 de julho de 1990, Diário Oficial de Uniã de 16.07.1990).

Planned Parenthood of Southeastern Pennsylvania v. Casey, 505 U.S. 833 (1992).

Hague Convention on the Protection of Children and the Cooperation in Respect of Intercountry Adoption. 1993.

Goodridge et al. v. Department of Public Health, 440 Mass. 309 (2003).

Gratz and Hamacher v. Bollinger, 123 U.S. 2411 (2003).

Grutter v. Bollinger, 539 U.S. 306 (2003).

Lawrence v. Texas, 539 U.S. 558 (2003).

Parents Involved in Community Schools v. Seattle School District No. 1, 551 U.S. 701 (2007).

Marriage Cases, In re, 43 Cal. 4th 757 (2008).

Kerrigan and Mock v. Connecticut Department of Public Health, 289 Conn. 135, 957 A.2d 407 (2008).

Published Sources

Abraham, Nicolas and Maria Torok. *The Shell and the Kernel, Volume 1*. Translated by Nicholas T. Rand. Chicago: University of Chicago Press, 1994.

Adams, Ansel. *Born Free and Equal: Photographs of Japanese Americans at Manzanar Relocation Center, Inyo County, California*. New York: U.S. Camera, 1944.

Agamben, Giorgio. *Homo Sacer: Sovereign Power and Bare Life*. Translated by Daniel Heller-Roazen. Palo Alto, Calif.: Stanford University Press, 1998.

——. *Stanzas: Word and Phantasm in Western Culture*. Minneapolis: University of Minnesota Press, 1993. Originally published as *Stanze: La parola e il fantasma nella cultura occidentale*. Turin, Italy: Giulio Eianaudi, 1977.

Ahmed, Sara. "Affective Economies." *Social Text*, 22, no. 2 (2004): 117–39.

——. *The Cultural Politics of Emotion*. London: Routledge, 2004.

Alexander, M. Jacqui, *Pedagogies of Crossing: Meditations on Feminism, Sexual Politics, Memory, and the Sacred*. Durham, N.C.: Duke University Pres, 2005.

Althusser, Louis. "Ideology and Ideological State Apparatuses (Notes Toward an Investigation)." In *Lenin and Philosophy and Other Essays*, translated by Ben Brewster, 127–86. New York: Monthly Review Press, 1971.

Anagnost, Ann. "Scenes of Misrecognition: Maternal Citizenship in the Age of Transnational Adoption." *Positions: East Asia Cultures Critique* 8, no. 2 (2000): 389–421.

Appadurai, Arjun. *Modernity at Large: Cultural Dimensions in Globalization*. Minneapolis: University of Minnesota Press, 1997.

Arendt, Hannah. *The Origins of Totalitarianism*. New York: Harcourt, 1968.

Azuma, Eiichiro. *Between Two Empires: Race, History, and Transnationalism in Japanese America*. New York: Oxford University Press, 2005.

Balibar, Étienne and Immanuel Wallerstein. *Race, Nation, Class: Ambiguous Identities*. New York: Verso, 1991.

Banks, R. Richard. "The Color of Desire: Fulfilling Adoptive Parent's Racial Preferences through Discriminatory State Action." *Yale Law Journal* 107 (January 1998): 875–964.

Barlow, Tani E. *The Question of Chinese Woman in Feminism*. Durham, N.C.: Duke University Press, 2004.

Bartholet, Elizabeth. "Commentary: Cultural Stereotypes Can and Do Die: It's Time to Move on With Transracial Adoption." *Journal of American Psychiatry Law* 34 (2006): 315–20.

Bascara, Victor. "Cultural Politics of Redress: Reassessing the Meaning of the Civil Liberties Act of 1988 after 9/11." *Asian Law Journal* 10, no. 2 (2003): 185–214.

Benjamin, Walter. *The Arcades Project*. Translated by Howard Eilan and Kevin McLaughlin. Cambridge, Mass.: Harvard University Press, 1999.

——. "Theses on the Philosophy of History." In *Illuminations*, edited by Hannah Arendt, 253–64. New York: Schocken Books, 1969.

Berlant, Lauren. *The Queen of America Goes to Washington City: Essays on Sex and Citizenship*. Durham, N.C.: Duke University Press, 1997.

Bhabha, Homi. "Of Mimicry and Man: The Ambivalence of Colonial Discourse." *October* 28 (Spring 1984): 125–33.

Bishoff, Tonya and Jo Rankin. *Seeds from a Silent Tree*. San Diego: Pandal Press, 1997.

Bosniak, Linda. "Citizenship Denationalized." *Indiana Journal of Global Legal Studies* 7 (2000): 447–508.

Braudel, Fernand. *On History*. Chicago: University of Chicago Press, 1980.

Brown, Wendy. *States of Injury: Power and Freedom in Late Modernity*. Princeton, N.J.: Princeton University Press, 1995.

Burgin, Victor. *In/Different Spaces: Place and Memory in Visual Space*. Berkeley: University of California Press, 1996.

Butler, Judith. *Antigone's Claim: Kinship between Life and Death*. New York: Columbia University Press, 2000.

——. "Moral Sadism and Doubting One's Own Love: Kleinian Reflections on Melancholia." In *Reading Melanie Klein*, edited by John Phillips and Lyndsey Stonebridge, 179–89. London: Routledge, 1998.

——. *The Psychic Life of Power: Theories in Subjection*. Palo Alto, Calif.: Stanford University Press, 1997.

——. "Critically Queer." *GLQ: A Journal of Lesbian and Gay Studies* 1, no. 1 (1993): 17–32. Reprinted in *Bodies That Matter: On the Discursive Limits of "Sex,"* 223–42. New York: Routledge, 1993.

——. *Gender Trouble: Feminism and the Subversion of Identity*. New York: Routledge, 1989.

Canetti, Elias. *Crowds and Power*. Translated by Carol Stewart. New York: Farrar, Straus and Giroux, 1984.

Carpenter, Dale. "The Unknown Past of *Lawrence v. Texas*." *Michigan Law Review* 102 (2004): 1464–1527.

Carsten, Janet. *After Kinship*. Cambridge: Cambridge University Press, 2004.

Caruth, Cathy. *Unclaimed Experience: Trauma, Narrative, and History*. Baltimore, Md.: Johns Hopkins University Press, 1996.

Certeau, Michel de. *The Practice of Everyday Life*. Translated by Steven Rendall. Berkeley: University of California Press, 1984.

Chakrabarty, Dipesh. *Provincializing Europe: Postcolonial Thought and Historical Difference*. Princeton, N.J.: Princeton University Press, 2000.

Chassin, Alexandra. *Selling Out: The Gay and Lesbian Movement Goes to the Market*. New York: St. Martin's Press, 2000.

Chiang, Mark. "Coming Out in the Global System: Postmodern Patriarchies and Transnational Sexualities in *The Wedding Banquet*." In *Q & A: Queer in Asian America*, edited by David L. Eng and Alice Y. Hom, 374–96. Philadelphia: Temple University Press, 1998.

Chu, Patty. "The Orphan's Tales: Adoption, Mourning, and the Search for Roots." Presentation at the American Studies Association, Philadelphia, October 11, 2007.

Chuh, Kandice. *Imagine Otherwise: On Asian Americanist Critique*. Durham, N.C.: Duke University Press, 2003.

Cooppan, Vilashini. "Hauntologies of Form: Race, Genre, and the Literary World System." *Gamma: Journal of Theory and Criticism* 12 (2005): 71–86.

Corber, Robert J. *Homosexuality in Cold War America: Resistance and the Crisis of Masculinity*. Durham, N.C.: Duke University Press, 1997.

Coutin, Susan Bibler, Bill Maurer, and Barbara Yngvesson. "In the Mirror: The Legitimation Work of Globalization." *Law and Social Inquiry* 27 (Fall 2002): 801–43.

Cox, Susan Soon-Keum, ed. *Voices from Another Place*. St. Paul: Yeong and Yeong Book Company, 1999.

Crenshaw, Kimberlé Williams. "Race, Reform and Retrenchment: Transformation and Legitimation in Antidiscrimination Law." In *Critical Race Theory: The Key Writings that Formed the Movement*, edited by Kimberlé Williams Crenshaw, Neil Gotanda, Gary Peller, and Kendall Thomas, 103–22. New York: The New Press, 1995.

Cvetkovich, Ann. "Public Feelings." *South Atlantic Quarterly* 106, no. 3 (2007): 459–68.

———. *An Archive of Feelings: Trauma, Sexuality, and Lesbian Public Cultures*. Durham, N.C.: Duke University Press, 2003.

Davis, Adrienne D. "*Loving* Against the Law: The History and Jurisprudence of Interracial Sex." Unpublished manuscript, 142 pages, 2007.

Davidson, Cathy N. Introduction to "No More Separate Spheres!" *American Literature* 70, no. 3 (1998): 443–63.

Deleuze, Gilles and Félix Guattari. *Anti-Oedipus: Capitalism and Schizophrenia.* Translated by Robert Hurley, Mark Seem, and Helen R. Lane. Minneapolis: University of Minnesota Press, 1983.

D'Emilio, John. "Capitalism and Gay Identity." In *The Lesbian and Gay Studies Reader*, edited by Henry Abelove, Michèle Aina Barale, and David M. Halperin, 467–76. New York: Routledge, 1993.

Derrida, Jacques. *Spectres of Marx: The State of Debt, the Work of Mourning, and the New International.* Translated by Peggy Kamuf. New York: Routledge, 1994.

Doyle, Chris. "To the End of the World." *Sight and Sound* 73 (May 1997): 14–17.

Duggan, Lisa. "Holy Matrimony!" *The Nation*, March 15, 2004.

——. *The Twilight of Equality: Neoliberalism, Cultural Politics, and the Attack on Democracy.* Boston: Beacon Press, 2003.

——. "The New Homonormativity: The Sexual Politics of Neoliberalism." In *Materializing Democracy: Toward a Revitalized Cultural Politics*, edited by Russ Castronovo and Dana Nelson, 175–194. Durham, N.C.: Duke University Press, 2002.

Duggan, Lisa, and Richard Kim. "Beyond Gay Marriage." *The Nation*, July 18, 2005.

Edwards, Brent. "The Shadow of Shadows." *Positions: East Asia Cultures Critique* 11, no. 1 (2003): 11–49.

Eng, David L. *Racial Castration: Managing Masculinity in Asian America.* Durham, N.C.: Duke University Press, 2001.

Eng, David L., with Judith Halberstam and José Esteban Muñoz. Introduction to "What's Queer about Queer Studies Now?" *Social Text* 23, no. 3–4 (2005): 1–17.

Eng, David L. and Shinhee Han. "A Dialogue on Racial Melancholia." *Psychoanalytic Dialogues: A Journal of Relational Perspectives* 10, no. 4 (2000): 667–700.

Enloe, Cynthia H. *Bananas, Beaches and Bases: Making Feminist Sense of International Politics.* Berkeley: University of California Press, 2000.

Eskridge, William N. Jr. "Yale Law School and the Overruling of *Bowers v. Hardwick.*" *Yale Law Reporter* 51 (2004): 36.

Evan B. Donaldson Adoption Institute. "Adoption Facts." http://www.adoption institute.org/, accessed June 28, 2008.

Fabian, Johannes. *Time and the Other: How Anthropology Makes Its Objects.* New York: Columbia University Press, 1983.

Faulkner, William. *Absalom, Absalom!* New York: Vintage, 1990.

Felman, Shoshana and Dori Laub, eds. *Testimony: Crises of Witnessing in Literature, Psychoanalysis, and History.* New York: Routledge, 1992.

Feng, Peter X. *Identities in Motion: Asian American Film and Video.* Durham, N.C.: Duke University Press, 2002.

"Forum: Conference Debates. The Antisocial Thesis in Queer Theory." *PMLA: Publications of the Modern Language Association of America* 121, no. 3 (2006): 819–28.

Foucault, Michel. *Aesthetics, Method, and Epistemology: Essential Works of Foucault, 1954–1984, Volume 2*. Edited by James D. Faubion and Paul Rabinow. New York: The New Press, 1998.

———. "Two Lectures." In *Power/Knowledge: Selected Knowledge and Other Writings, 1972–1977*, edited by Colin Gordon, 78–108. New York: Pantheon, 1980.

Franke, Katherine. "The Domesticated Liberty of *Lawrence v. Texas.*" *Columbia Law Review* 104 (2004): 1399–1426.

Freccero, Carla. "Theorizing Queer Temporalities: A Roundtable Discussion." *GLQ: A Journal of Lesbian and Gay Studies* 13, no. 2–3 (2007): 177–95.

Freeman, Elizabeth. Introduction to "Queer Temporalities." *GLQ: A Journal of Lesbian and Gay Studies* 13, no. 2–3 (2007): 159–76.

———. "Still After." *South Atlantic Quarterly* 106, no. 3 (2007): 495–500.

———. *The Wedding Complex: Forms of Belonging in Modern American Culture*. Durham, N.C.: Duke University Press, 2002.

Friedman, Michelle. "When the Analyst Becomes Pregnant Twice." *Psychoanalytic Inquiry* 13 (1993): 226–39.

Freud, Sigmund. "Femininity" (1933). In *The Standard Edition of the Complete Psychological Works of Sigmund Freud, Volume XXII (1932–1936)*, translated and edited by James Strachey et al., 112–35. London: Hogarth, 1960.

———. "The Ego and the Id" (1923). In *The Standard Edition of the Complete Psychological Works of Sigmund Freud, Volume XIX (1923–1925)*, translated and edited by James Strachey et al., 12–66. London: Hogarth, 1961.

———. "Mourning and Melancholia" (1917). In *The Standard Edition of the Complete Psychological Works of Sigmund Freud, Volume XIV (1914–1916)*, translated and edited by James Strachey et al., 243–58. London: Hogarth, 1957.

———. "The Unconscious" (1915). In *The Standard Edition of the Complete Psychological Works of Sigmund Freud, Volume XIV (1914–1916)*, translated and edited by James Strachey et al., 166–215. London: Hogarth, 1957.

———. "On Narcissism: An Introduction" (1914). In *The Standard Edition of the Complete Psychological Works of Sigmund Freud, Volume XIV (1914–1916)*, translated and edited by James Strachey et al., 73–102. London: Hogarth, 1957.

———. "Psychoanalytic Notes On an Autobiographical Account of a Case of Paranoia (Dementia Paranoides)" (1911). In *The Standard Edition of the Complete Psychological Works of Sigmund Freud, Volume XII (1911–1913)*, translated and edited by James Strachey et al., 9–82. London: Hogarth, 1958.

———. "April 22, 1910 Letter to Jung." *The Freud/Jung Letters: The Correspondence Between Sigmund Freud and C. G. Jung*, edited by William McGuire, translated by Ralph Manheim and R. F. C. Hull, 311. Princeton, N.J.: Princeton University Press.

——. "'Civilized' Sexual Morality and Modern Nervous Illness" (1908). In *The Standard Edition of the Complete Psychological Works of Sigmund Freud, Volume IX (1906–1908)*, translated and edited by James Strachey et al., 181–204. London: Hogarth, 1959.

Gallop, Jane. *Reading Lacan*. Ithaca, N.Y.: Cornell University Press, 1985.

Gilmore, Ruth Wilson. *Golden Gulag: Prisons, Surplus, Crisis, and Opposition in Globalizing California*. Berkeley: University of California Press, 2006.

Gilroy, Paul. *Postcolonial Melancholia*. New York: Columbia University Press, 2006.

——. *The Black Atlantic: Modernity and Double Consciousness*. Cambridge, Mass.: Harvard University Press, 1993.

Gopinath, Gayatri. *Impossible Subjects: Queer Diasporas and South Asian Public Cultures*. Durham, N.C.: Duke University Press, 2005.

Gordon, Avery. *Ghostly Matters: Haunting and the Sociological Imagination*. Minneapolis: University of Minnesota Press, 1997.

Gordon, Linda. *The Great Arizona Orphan Abduction*. Cambridge, Mass.: Harvard University Press, 1999.

Gordon, Robert S. "The New Chinese Export: Orphaned Children, an Overview of Adopting Children from China." *Transnational Law* 10 (Spring 1997): 121–51.

Guha, Ranajit. *Elementary Aspects of Peasant Insurgency in Colonial India*. Durham, N.C.: Duke University Press, 1999.

Halberstam, Judith. "Shame and Gay White Masculinity." *Social Text* 23, no. 3–4 (2005): 218–23.

Halley, Janet E. "'Like Race' Arguments." In *What's Left of Theory? New Work on the Politics of Literary Theory*, edited by Judith Butler, John Guillory, and Kendall Thomas, 40–74. New York: Routledge, 2000.

Harris, Cheryl I. "Whiteness as Property." *Harvard Law Review* 106, no. 8 (1993): 1709–91.

Hartman, Saidiya V. *Scenes of Subjection: Terror, Slavery, and Self-Making in Nineteenth-Century America*. New York: Oxford University Press, 1997.

Hegel, G.W.F. *The Philosophy of Right*. Translated by Alan White. Newburyport, Mass.: Focus Publishing, 2002.

Heidegger, Martin. "Letter on Humanism." In *Basic Writings*, edited by David Farrell Krell, 189–242. New York: Harper Books, 1983.

——. "The Thing." In *Poetry, Language, Thought*, translated by Albert Hofstadler, 161–84. New York: Perennial Classics, 2001.

Hirsch, Marianne. *Family Frames: Photography, Narrative, and Postmemory*. Cambridge, Mass.: Harvard University Press, 1997.

Hochschild, Arlie, and Barbara Ehrenreich, eds. *Global Woman: Nannies, Maids, and Sex Workers in the New Economy*. New York: Metropolitan Books, 2003.

Holloway, Carla F. C. *Passed On: African American Mourning Stories (A Memorial)*. Durham, N.C.: Duke University Press, 2002.

Horkheimer, Max and Theodor W. Adorno. *Dialectic of Enlightenment*. Palo Alto, Calif.: Stanford University Press, 2002.

Hübinette, Tobias. *Comforting an Orphaned Nation*. Seoul, South Korea: Jimoon-dang, 2006.

———. "Orphan Trains to Babylifts: Colonial Trafficking, Empire Building, and Social Engineering." In *Outsiders Within: Writing on Transracial Adoption*, edited by Jane Jeong Trenka, Julia Chinyere Oparah, and Sun Yung Shin, 139–49. Cambridge, Mass.: South End Press, 2006.

Inada, Lawson Fusao. *Legends from Camp*. Minneapolis: Coffee House Press, 1993.

Jakobsen, Janet R. "Sex + Freedom = Regulation: Why?" *Social Text* 23, no. 3–4 (2005): 285–308.

———. "Queers are Like Jews, Aren't They?" In *Queers and the Jewish Question*, edited by Daniel Boyarin, Daniel Itzkovitz, and Ann Pellegrini, 64–89. New York: Columbia University Press, 2003.

Jameson, Fredric. *Postmodernism, or the Logic of Late Capital*. Durham, N.C.: Duke University Press, 1991.

———. *The Political Unconscious: Narrative as a Socially Symbolic Act*. Ithaca, N.Y.: Cornell University Press, 1981.

Jo, Sunny. "Korean Adoption Films." http://www.geocities.com/sunny_jo888/kadfilms.html (accessed 28 June 2008).

Johnson, David K. *The Lavender Scare: The Cold War Persecution of Gays and Lesbians in Federal Government*. Chicago: University of Chicago Press, 2004.

Joseph, Miranda. *Against the Romance of Community*. Minneapolis: University of Minnesota Press, 2002.

———. "Family Affairs: The Discourse of Global/Localization." In *Queer Globalization: Citizenship and the Afterlife of Colonialism*, edited by Arnaldo Cruz-Malavé and Martin Manalansan IV, 71–99. New York: New York University Press, 2002.

Kaplan, Amy. "Where is Guantánamo?" *American Quarterly* 57, no. 3 (2005): 831–58.

———. *The Anarchy of Empire in the Making of U.S. Culture*. Cambridge, Mass.: Harvard University Press, 2002.

———. "'Left Alone with America': The Absence of Empire in the Study of American Culture." In *Cultures of United States Imperialisms*, edited by Amy Kaplan and Donald E. Pease, 3–21. Durham, N.C.: Duke University Press, 1993.

Kennedy, Randall. *Interracial Intimacies: Sex, Marriage, Identity, and Adoption*. New York: Vintage, 2003.

Khanna, Ranjana. *Dark Continents: Psychoanalysis and Colonialism*. Durham, N.C.: Duke University Press, 2003.

Kim, Elizabeth. *Ten Thousand Sorrows*. New York: Doubleday, 2000.

Klein, Melanie. "A Study of Envy and Gratitude" (1956). In *The Selected Melanie Klein*, edited by Juliet Mitchell, 211–29. New York: The Free Press, 1986.

——. "The Psycho-analytic Play Technique: Its History and Significance" (1955). In *The Selected Melanie Klein*, edited by Juliet Mitchell, 35–54. New York: The Free Press, 1986.

——. "Mourning and its Relation to Manic-Depressive States" (1940). In *The Selected Melanie Klein*, edited by Juliet Mitchell, 146–74. New York: The Free Press, 1986.

——. "Love, Guilt, and Reparation" (1936). In *Love, Hate and Reparation*, by Melanie Klein and Joan Riviere. New York: Norton, 1964.

——. "A Contribution to the Psychogenesis of Manic-Depressive States" (1935). In *The Selected Melanie Klein*, edited by Juliet Mitchell, 116–45. New York: The Free Press, 1986.

Kristeva, Julia. *New Maladies of the Soul*. Translated by Ross Guberman. New York: Columbia University Press, 1995.

Lacan, Jacques. "The Function and Field of Speech and Language in Psycho-analysis" ("Roman Discourse") (1953). In *Écrits: A Selection*, translated by Alan Sheridan, 30–113. New York: W.W. Norton, 1977.

——. "The Mirror Stage as Formative of the Function of the I as Revealed in Psychoanalytic Experience" (1949). In *Écrits: A Selection*, translated by Alan Sheridan, 1–7. New York: W.W. Norton, 1977.

——. "Aggressivity and Psychoanalysis" (1948). In *Écrits: A Selection*, translated by Alan Sheridan, 8–29. New York: W.W. Norton, 1977.

Landes, Elisabeth M. and Richard A. Posner. "The Economics of the Baby Shortage." *The Journal of Legal Studies* 7, no. 2 (1978): 323–48.

Laplanche, Jean and Jean-Bertrand Pontalis. *The Language of Psycho-analysis*. Translated by Donald Nicholson-Smith. New York: W.W. Norton, 1973.

Lévi-Strauss, Claude. *The Elementary Structures of Kinship*. Translated by James Harle Bell and John Richard von Sturmer. Boston: Beacon Press, 1969.

Lovelock, Kirsten. "Intercountry Adoption as a Migratory Practice." *International Migration Review* 18 (1984): 907–49.

Lowe, Lisa. "The Intimacies of Four Continents." In *Haunted by Empire: Geographies of Intimacy in North American History*, edited by Ann Laura Stoler, 191–212. Durham, N.C.: Duke University Press, 2006.

——. *Immigrant Acts: On Asian American Cultural Politics*. Durham, N.C.: Duke University Press, 1996.

Lowe, Lisa, and David Lloyd. Introduction to *The Politics of Culture in the Shadow of Capital*, edited by Lisa Lowe and David Lloyd, 1–32. Durham, N.C.: Duke University Press, 1997.

Lubiano, Wahneema. "For Race." Keynote address presented at Bucknell University, "Color, Bone, and Hair: The Persistence of Race in the 21st Century." (Conference) September 25, 2002.

Lwin, Sanda. *The Constitution of Asian America*. Durham, N.C.: Duke University Press, forthcoming.

Marx, Karl. "On the Jewish Question" (1843). In *Early Writings*, translated by Rodney Livingstone and Gregor Benton, 211–41. New York: Penguin Books, 1975.

Massumi, Brian. *Parables for the Virtual: Movement, Affect, Sensation*. Durham, N.C.: Duke University Press, 2002.

Melamed, Jodi. "The Spirit of Neoliberalism: From Racial Liberalism to Neoliberal Multiculturalism." *Social Text* 24, no. 4 (2006): 1–24.

Moran, Rachel. *Interracial Intimacy: The Regulation of Race and Romance*. Chicago: University of Chicago Press, 2001.

Muñoz, José Esteban. "Queerness as Horizon: Utopian Hermeneutics in the Face of Gay Pragmatism." In *The Blackwell Companion to LGBT/Q Studies*, edited by George Haggerty and Molly McGarry, 450–61. London: Blackwell Publishing, 2007.

——. "Feeling Brown, Feeling Down: Latina Affect, the Performativity of Race, and the Depressive Position." *Signs: Journal of Women and Culture* 31, no. 3 (2006): 675–88.

——. "Thinking Beyond Antirelationality and Antiutopianism in Queer Critique." *PMLA: Publications of the Modern Language Association of America* 121, no. 3 (2006): 825–26.

Ngai, Mae. *Impossible Subjects: Illegal Aliens and the Making of Modern America*. Princeton, N.J.: Princeton University Press, 2004.

Ngai, Sianne. *Ugly Feelings*. Cambridge, Mass.: Harvard University Press, 2007.

Nichols, Bill. *Representing Reality: Issues and Concepts in Documentary*. Indianapolis: Indiana University Press, 1991.

Ong, Aihwa. *Neoliberalism as Exception: Mutations in Citizenship and Sovereignty*. Durham, N.C.: Duke University Press, 2006.

Ortiz, Ana Teresa and Laura Briggs. "The Culture of Poverty, Crack Babies, and Welfare Cheats: The Making of the 'Healthy White Baby Crisis.'" *Social Text* 21, no. 3 (2003): 39–57.

Otsuka, Julie. *When the Emperor Was Divine*. New York: Anchor Books, 2002.

Parreñas, Rhacel Salazar. *Servants of Globalization: Women, Migration, and Domestic Work*. Palo Alto, Calif.: Stanford University Press, 2001.

Payne, Robert M. "Visions of Silence." *Jump Cut* 41 (1997): 67–76.

Perry, Twila L. "Transracial Adoption and Gentrification: An Essay on Race, Power, Family, and Community." *Boston College Third World Law Journal* 26 (Winter 2006): 25–60.

——. "Transracial and International Adoptions: Mothers, Hierarchy, Race, and Feminist Legal Theory." *Yale Journal of Law and Feminism* 10 (1998): 101–64.

Phillips, Adam. *Winnicott*. Cambridge, Mass.: Harvard University Press, 1988.

Puar, Jasbir K. *Terrorist Assemblages: Homonationalism in Queer Times*. Durham, N.C.: Duke University Press, 2007.

Reddy, Chandan. "Asian Diasporas, Neoliberalism, and Family: Reviewing the Case for Homosexual Asylum in the Context of Family Rights." *Social Text* 23, no. 3–4 (2005): 109.

Roach, Joseph. *Cities of the Dead: Circum-Atlantic Performance*. New York: Columbia University Press, 1996.

Robinson, Katy. *A Single Square Picture*. New York: Berkeley Publishing Group, 2002.

Rubin, Gayle. "The Traffic in Women: Notes on the 'Political Economy' of Sex." In *Toward an Anthropology of Women*, edited by Rayna R. Reiter, 157–210. New York: Monthly Review Press, 1975.

Ruskola, Teemu. "Gay Rights versus Queer Theory." *Social Text* 23, no. 3–4 (2005): 235–49.

Ruti, Mari. *Reinventing the Soul: Posthumanist Theory and Psychic Life*. New York: The Other Press, 2006.

Saldaña-Portillo, Maria Josefina. *The Revolutionary Imagination in the Americas and the Age of Development*. Durham, N.C.: Duke University Press, 2003.

Santner, Eric. *My Own Private Germany: Daniel Paul Schreber's Secret History of Modernity*. Princeton, N.J.: Princeton University Press, 1996.

Sartre, Jean-Paul. *The Emotions: Outline of a Theory*. New York: Citadel, 1975.

Sassen, Saskia. "Global Cities and Survival Circuits." In *Global Woman: Nannies, Maids, and Sex Workers in the New Economy*, edited by Arlie Hochschild and Barbara Erenreich, 254–74. New York: Metropolitan Books, 2002.

Savigliano, Marta E. *Tango and the Political Economy of Passion*. Boulder, Colo.: Westview Press, 1995.

Schreber, Daniel Paul. *Memoirs of My Nervous Illness*. Translated by Ida Macalpine and Richard A. Hunter. New York: New York Review of Books, 2000.

Scott, Joan. "The Evidence of Experience." *Critical Inquiry* 17 (Summer 1991): 773–97.

Sedgwick, Eve Kosofsky. *Touching Feeling: Affect, Pedagogy, Performativity*. Durham, N.C.: Duke University Press, 2003.

——. "Queer Performativity: Henry James's *The Art of the Novel*." *GLQ: A Journal of Lesbian and Gay Studies* 1, no. 1 (1993): 1–16.

——. "How to Bring Your Kids Up Gay: The War on Effeminate Boys." In *Tendencies*, 154–64. Durham, N.C.: Duke University Press, 1993.

——. *Epistemology of the Closet*. Berkeley: University of California Press, 1991.

Sen, Amartya. *Development as Freedom*. New York: Anchor Books, 2000.

Silverman, Kaja. "Photography by Other Means." In *Flesh of My Flesh*, 168–223. Palo Alto: Stanford University Press, 2009.

——. "Girl Love." In *James Coleman*, 150–71. Munich: Lenbachhaus München, 2002.

——. *World Spectators*. Palo Alto, Calif.: Stanford University Press, 2000.

Somerville, Siobhan B. "Notes Toward a Queer History of Nationalization." *American Quarterly* 57, no. 3 (2005): 659–75.

——. "Queer Loving." *GLQ: A Journal of Lesbian and Gay Studies* 11, no. 3 (2005): 355–70.

Spivak, Gayatri Chakravorty. *Death of a Discipline*. New York: Columbia University Press, 2003.

——. *A Critique of Postcolonial Reason: Toward a History of the Vanishing Present*. Cambridge, Mass.: Harvard University Press, 1999.

——. "Diasporas Old and New." In *Class Issues: Pedagogy, Cultural Studies, and the Public Sphere*, edited by Amitava Kumar, 87–116. New York: New York University Press, 1997.

——. *Outside in the Teaching Machine*. New York: Routledge, 1993.

——. "Subaltern Studies: Deconstructing Historiography." In *Other Worlds: Essays in Cultural Politics*, 197–221. New York: Routledge, 1988.

Sternburg, Janet. "Long Exposures: A Poetics of Film and History." *Common Knowledge* 3, no. 1 (1994): 178–85.

Stoler, Ann Laura. *Carnal Knowledge and Imperial Power: Race and the Intimate in Colonial Rule*. Berkeley: University of California Press, 2002.

——. "Tense and Tender Ties: The Politics of Comparison in North American History and (Post)Colonial Studies." *Journal of American History* 88, no. 3 (2001): 829–65.

——. "Making Empire Respectable." *American Ethnologist* 16, no. 4 (1985): 643–60.

Strathern, Marilyn. *The Gender of the Gift: Problems with Women and Problems with Society in Melanesia*. Berkeley: University of California Press, 1988.

Sturken, Marita. "Absent Images of Memory: Remembering and Reenacting the Japanese American Internment." *Positions: East Asia Cultures Critique* 5, no. 3 (1997): 687–707.

Sullivan, Andrew. *Virtually Normal: An Argument about Homosexuality*. New York: Vintage, 1996.

Terada, Rei. *Feeling in Theory: Emotion after the "Death of the Subject."* Cambridge, Mass.: Harvard University Press, 2001.

Thomas, Kendall. "Corpus Juris (Hetero)Sexualis: Doctrine, Discourse, and Desire in *Bowers v. Hardwick*." *GLQ: A Journal of Lesbian and Gay Studies* 1, no. 1 (1993): 33–51.

Toklas, Alice B. *The Alice B. Toklas Cookbook*. New York: The Lyons Press, 1954.

Tölölyan, Khachig. "The Nation-State and Its Others: In Lieu of a Preface." *Diaspora: A Journal of Transnational Studies* 1, no. 1 (Spring 1991): 3–7.

Trenka, Jane Jeong. *The Language of Blood*. Minneapolis: Graywolf Press, 2005.

Trenka, Jane Jeong, Julia Chinyere Oparah, and Sun Yung Shin, eds. *Outsiders Within: Writing on Transracial Adoption*. Cambridge, Mass.: South End Press, 2006.

Truong, Monique. *The Book of Salt*. Boston: Houghton Mifflin, 2003.

——. T.D. "Seeds." In *Watermark: Vietnamese American Poetry and Prose*, edited by Barbara Tran, Monique T.D. Truong, and Luu Truong Khoi, 19–28. New York: Asian American Writers' Workshop, 1998.

Tsou, Elda. "Figures of Identity: Rereading Asian American Literature." PhD. dissertation, Columbia University, 2008.

U.S. Department of State. "Immigrant Visas Issued to Orphans Coming to the U.S." http://travel.state.gov/, accessed June 28, 2008.

Volkman, Toby Alice, ed. *Cultures of Transnational Adoption*. Durham, N.C.: Duke University Press, 2005.

Volpp, Leti. "Disappearing Acts: On Gendered Violence, Pathological Cultures, and Civil Society." *PMLA: Publications of the Modern Language Association of America* 121, no. 5 (2006): 1631–38.

——. "Divesting Citizenship: On Asian American History and the Loss of Citizenship Through Marriage." *UCLA Law Review* 53 (2005): 405–83.

——. "The Citizen and the Terrorist." *UCLA Law Review* 49 (2002): 1575–99.

——. "Blaming Culture for Bad Behavior." *Yale Journal of Law and Humanities* 12 (2000): 89–116.

Warner, Michael. Introduction to *Fear of a Queer Planet: Queer Politics and Social Theory*, edited by Michael Warner, vii–xxxi. Minneapolis: University of Minnesota Press, 1993.

Weston, Kath. *Families We Choose: Lesbians, Gays, Kinship*. New York: Columbia University Press, 1991.

Whitman, James Q. "The Two Western Cultures of Privacy: Dignity Versus Liberty." *Yale Law Journal* 113 (April 2004): 1158–1221.

Wilkinson, Sook and Nancy Fox, eds. *After the Morning Calm: Reflections on Korean Adoptees*. Detroit: Sunrise Ventures, 2002.

Williams, Patricia. "Spare Parts, Family Values, Old Children, Cheap." *New England Law Review* 28 (Summer 1994): 913–27.

Williams, Raymond. *Marxism and Literature*. Oxford: Oxford University Press, 1977.

Winnicott, D. W. "Playing: A Theoretical Statement." In *Playing and Reality*, 38–52. New York: Routledge, 1989.

——. "The Use of an Object and Relating through Identifications" (1969). In *Playing and Reality*, 86–94. New York: Routledge, 1989.

——. "Transitional Objects and Transitional Phenomena" (1953). In *Playing and Reality*, 1–25. New York: Routledge, 1989.

Wolff, Tobias Barrington. "Political Representation and Accountability Under Don't Ask, Don't Tell." *Iowa Law Review* 89 (2004): 1633–1716.

Yngvesson, Barbara. "Placing the 'Gift Child' in Transnational Adoption." *Law and Society Review* 36, no. 2 (2002): 227–56.

Zelizer, Viviana A. *Pricing the Priceless Child: The Changing Social Value of Children*. Princeton, N.J.: Princeton University Press, 1994.

Index

🕉 🕉 🕉

abortion rights, 37
Abraham, Nicolas, 168
abuse, 141
Adams, Ansel, 182, 195
adoption: as affective labor, 20, 98,
108–9, 136, 213n5; assimilation
and, 19–21, 107, 114–21; commodification of, 101–2, 215n22,
215n28; emergence of, 94; as form
of immigration, 102, 107, 131,
139, 150; globalization's politics
and, 135; identity and, 110, 127,
148–51; in popular culture, 99,
100; intersectionality of, 2, 8, 94–
95; isolation of racialized subjects
and, 121–22, 139, 151, 154; kinship feelings and, 121–23; language
and discourse of, 97, 111, 138; as
legal birth, 114; exploitative histories and, 103–5; management of
affect in, 114; military violence and,
20; neoliberal language of, 104–6;
as outsourcings of reproductive labor, 10, 106–9, 124; passing and,
71, 95, 117, 150; politics of, 78;
psychic predicaments of, 94, 96,
122–23, 151–52; psychoanalytic
case histories of, 20, 138–65; support for children of, 145–47; supporting narratives of, 102; as trace
of formerly public phenomena,

102–3; as transitional objects, 161.
See also family; intersectionality;
mothers
Adorno, Theodor, 41
Advocate, The, ix
affect: commodification of, 109, 113;
in film and literature, 70, 74, 79,
81, 84, 90–91, 114, 122–24, 135,
166–98; historicism and, 67–69,
176–80, 184–98; linguistic role of,
114–16, 121, 131, 170–72,
224n66; theory of, 20–22, 59–60,
126, 133–35; transnational adoptions and, 97–98, 109, 135, 140,
150, 154–62. *See also* labor; language
affirmative action, 7, 34–35, 38, 46
Afghanistan, x, 49, 106, 199n7
African Americans, ix, x, xi, 12, 145.
See also *Brown v. Board of Education*;
Lawrence v. Texas; race; racialization; slavery
Agamben, Giorgio, 28, 209n15
agency, 32, 77–81, 106, 123, 153, 184
AIDS epidemic, 3, 27
Alexander, M. Jacqui, 203n27
Alice B. Toklas Cookbook, The (Toklas),
19, 58–76, 208n3
Amache (internment camp), 171
American studies, 13
Anagnost, Ann, 101–2, 136

analogy: as comparative methodology, 38–41, 56–57

analytic philosophical tradition, 67, 180, 183, 195. *See also* historicism; neoliberalism

anthropology, 8, 16, 87

anxiety, 1

Arabs, 9

area studies, 13, 74, 94

Arendt, Hannah, 28

Arizona, 103–4

Asian Americans: as adoptees in white families, 96–137; cultural politics of, 121; immigration history of, 99, 116; literature of, 73, 93–137, 163–98; as migrant labor force, 10, 12, 59; prejudice against, 107, 142; racial identity of, 2, 138–65; racialization of, 115, 139; stereotypes of, 110; subjectivity of, 107. *See also* coolies; identity; immigrants; model minority myth; race

Asian American studies, 13, 97, 107

Asian studies, 94, 97

assimilation, 20, 107, 114–21

atomic bomb, 179

Auschwitz (concentration camp), 171

Bad Day at Black Rock (Sturges), 173

Bakhtin, Mikhail, 180

Balibar, Étienne, 33

Barlow, Tani, 63

Bascara, Victor, 171

belonging: homosexual, 77–78; racial, 14–15, 75, 122, 132; social, 2, 13, 29, 35, 60, 73, 97, 101, 140, 146. *See also* intersectionality

Benjamin, Walter, xiv, 15, 62, 75, 123, 166, 169, 172, 179, 186, 188–89, 221n24. *See also* historicism

Berlant, Lauren, 6, 103

Bhabha, Homi, 117

Bluest Eye, The (Morrison), 116

Book of Salt, The (Truong), 18–19, 59–77, 170, 172, 197, 208n2

Born Free and Equal (Adams), 182

Borshay, Alveen, 93, 123, 128–31

Borshay, Denise, 111, 113, 116

Borshay, Donald, 93, 113, 115, 128–29

Borshay, Duncan, 116–17

Borshay Liem, Deann, 20, 93–137, *112*, *115*, *118–20*, *124*, *133*, 138, 150

Boston Globe, 76

Boutilier, Clive Michael, 38

Boutilier v. Immigration Services, 37–38, 205n47

Bowers v. Hardwick, 16, 24, 34, 36–37, 42, 48, 202n4

Braudel, Fernand, 11, 73

Brown v. Board of Education, 4–5, 17, 35, 41, 47

Buchenwald (concentration camp), 171

Burgin, Victor, 174

Bush, George W., 30–31, 34, 106, 203n28

Bush, Laura, 106

Butler, Judith, 15, 28, 88, 157, 212n64, 224n65

California, 26, 106, 184; laws of, ix

Cambodia, 105

Cannes Film Festival, 76

capitalism: in Asian managerial class, 98; commodification of affect, 109, 113; exploitation and, x; family and kinship norms and, 8, 101, 214n9; forgetting of race and, 9; global, 23, 67, 76; identity and, 14, 79; immigration and, 32, 97; logics of, 15, 62, 64–65, 68, 99; as narrative structure, 16; political discourse and, 29, 135; private sphere and, 14. *See also* adoptions; family; globalization; neoliberalism

"Capitalism and Gay Identity" (D'Emilio), 25–26
Carey v. Population Services International, 37
Carlson, Michele, xiii–xiv
Carpenter, Dale, 17, 35–36
Carr, Jay, 76
Caruth, Cathy, 172
castration crisis, 126, 133
Castro, Fidel, 103
catachresis, 62–65
Certeau, Michel de, 179
Cha Jung Hee, 111, 113–14
Chakrabarty, Dipesh, 15, 25, 38, 66–67, 69, 179–80, 182–84, 195
Chang Chen, 90
Chao, Winston, 77
Cheung Kwok-wing, Leslie, 60
Chiang, Mark, 77–78
Chicago Tribune, 174
China, 105, 107, 145
Chinese: as othering identity, 102
choice: as neoliberal ideal, 5, 9, 45, 106, 110. *See also* language
Chu, Patty, 217n50
Chuh, Kandice, 191
citizenship: duties of, 30; excluded groups and, 38, 45, 47–48, 99, 174, 181–82; political rights of, 23, 28, 33–34, 68, 101, 107–8
"'Civilized' Sexual Morality and Modern Nervous Illness," (Freud), 51
Civil Liberties Act of 1988, 21–22, 170–71, 174
civil rights: gay and lesbian struggle for, x
civil rights movement, x, 5, 37, 74, 186
class. *See also* capitalism; displacement; immigrants; labor; migrations; mirroring; refugee
Clifton (Arizona Territory), 103

Clinton, Bill, 31
Clinton, Hillary, 31
closet, the, 1–2, 27, 77–78, 81
Cold War, 8, 94, 104, 110, 131
colonialism, x, 10–12, 73–74, 102–4
Colorado River Tribal Indian Reservation, The, 185–86
colorblindness: assumptions of, 23, 41; cultural discrimination and, 33; definition of, 4; language of, 3, 10, 17, 38, 47, 74–75, 110, 124, 184, 192; politics of, x, 18, 21, 23, 110, 136, 139, 165, 172, 189; psychic life of, 111; public/private distinction and, 7–8, 49; in transnational adoption phenomenology, 117
Come See the Paradise (Parker), 174–75, 176–77, 197
comfort women, 97, 105, 110
coming out, 27
commodification: of affect, 109, 113. *See also* affect
concentration camps, 171
Connecticut, 3, 26
"Contribution to the Psychogenesis of Manic-Depressive States" (Klein), 127, 154
coolies, 10, 23, 59–60, 75
Cooppan, Vilashini, 67
Coutin, Susan, 9, 106
critical race studies, xi, 2, 4, 8, 17, 33, 40, 46–47
cultural studies, 8
culture wars, 6
Curtiz, Michael, 173
Cvetkovich, Ann, 172, 189, 221n19

Dachau (concentration camp), 171
Daily Variety, 76
Davidson, Cathy, 8
Davis, Adrienne D., 205n49
death drive, 157–59, 164

Death Stalker III, Warriors from Hell (Corona), 175

D'Emilio, John, 25–27, 29, 33

depressive position, 21, 93, 115, 122, 140, 152–53, 166. *See also* Klein, Melanie

Derrida, Jacques, 11, 70, 189

"Dialogue on Racial Melancholia" (Eng and Han), 115, 117, 128

diasporas. *See* queer diasporas

diaspora studies, 8, 74

difference: analytic tradition's masking of, 180; continued impact of, 5; forgetting of, x, 2, 4, 40, 75, 124; mirroring and, 72. *See also* color-blindness; forgetting; historicism; (homo)sexuality; identity; race

discourse. *See* language

discrimination. *See* prejudice

displacement, 84, 86–89, 125, 171, 186, 197

domestic servants, 97

domesticity, 17, 25, 30–31, 34–35, 43–47, 55–56, 79. *See also* intimacy

Doyle, Chris, 82

Duggan, Lisa, 30–31, 57, 203n28, 207n105

Eisenstadt v. Baird, 37

Elley, Derek, 76

Emotions: Outline of a Theory, The (Sartre), 166

Eng, David L., 117, 121, 128

Enlightenment: criticisms of, 12; dialectical nature of, 62–71, 73; material preconditions for, 44; narrative structures of, 25, 47; privacy and, 12; racism and, 10–11, 22. *See also* freedom; historicism; neoliberalism; progress; queer liberalism

envy, 164–65

epistemology: definition of, 41; as thinking Being, 64

Epistemology of the Closet (Sedgwick), 77

ethnic studies, 64–65, 74, 94

Eubanks, Robert, 36, 42

European Court of Human Rights, 48

exclusion, 6, 46, 48

exile, 174

exploitation, x

Fabian, Johannes, 69

family: as affective unit, 27, 138–65; alternative structures of, 60; bourgeois ideals of, 43; capitalism and, 8, 27, 98–99, 101, 136; collective history and, 137; evolving forms of, 26; heteronormative structuring of, 103, 137, 152; homosexuality and, 3, 26; idealized versions of, 10, 17; immigration and, 32; language of, 20, 31–32, 42, 88, 97; the nation-state and, 14; normative politics of, 29, 33; Oedipal norms and, 18, 20, 31, 55, 135, 153, 161, 163; as political right, 111; politics of, 1, 141; poststructural theory and, 132; as private sphere, 4, 6, 30, 136; queer, 3, 17, 26, 29, 77–78, 99, 101–2; queer Asian diasporas and, 12; queer critiques of, 27; queer liberalism and, 25, 34; racialization of, 49, 121; segregation within, 120–22, 124, 154; structure of, xi, 6, 14, 25, 33, 91, 94; transnational adoption and, 108, 117, 136

Family Gathering, A (Yasui), 170

Faulkner, William, 59

feeling, structures of, 15, 58, 69

femininity. *See* women

feminism, 8, 40, 45–46, 88, 105, 109

Feng, Peter, 180, 222n32

First Person Plural (Borshay Liem), 20, 22, 93–137, *115*, *118–20*, *124*, *133*, 138, 167, 193, 197, 216n35, 216n42 flexible citizenship, 98

forgetting: of Asia and Africa, 73, 77; in creation of modernity, 64–70; of difference, x, 4, 19–20, 40–41, 60, 180–81; in historicism, 63–64; histories of, 167, 171, 182–85, 189, 193–95; of race and racism, 5, 9–18, 22, 36, 40, 45, 61, 75, 77, 81, 110, 150, 163, 188; as violent act, 11, 17, 25. *See also* historicism; modernity; race

Foucault, Michel, 63

Four Fundamental Concepts of Psychoanalysis, The (Lacan), 196

Franke, Katherine, 42

Freccero, Carla, 74

freedom, 13–14, 18, 23–25, 29, 35, 41, 47, 61, 79, 170, 180

Freeman, Elizabeth, 84

Freud, Sigmund: anthropological responses to, 87–88; on female development, 96, 115–17, 121, 125–37; Klein's responses to, 151, 157, 159, 163, 167, 190, 192–93; on Oedipal norms, 18, 20, 26, 50–57, 86

From Here to Eternity (Zinnemann), 183–84

Gallop, Jane, 72

Garner, Tyron, 35–37, 40–42

gay liberation, 27

gay marriage, ix, x, 3–4, 7, 26, 29–30, 38, 48, 53, 56, 99, 207n104

gays. *See* (homo)sexuality

gender(ing): of affective responsibility, 129; commodification and, 105, 110; forgetting of, 11; global histories of, 102; in human development, 153; of immigration, 107; of labor, 79, 97–98; normative influences on, 13; as property right, 87; violence and, 137. *See also* intersectionality

Germany, 104

Gila River (internment camp), 171

Gilroy, Paul, 72

girl love, 133–34, 193

"Girl Love" (Silverman), 133

"Global Cities and Survival Circuits" (Sassen), 93

globalization: capitalism and, xi, 23, 31, 66–67; forgetting and, 60; identity and, 79; narratives of, 14, 40, 90; politics of, 9, 11, 14–16, 29–31, 34, 135; transnational adoptions as window on, 95; U.S. identity and, 8, 45, 48

Godfather III (Coppola), 175

good-enough (mothers, analysts, daughters), 21, 135–36, 138–42, 145, 152–56, 160–165, 169, 193

Gopinath, Gayatri, 14

Gordon, Linda, 103

Grazt v. Bollinger, 7, 34

Great Arizona Orphan Abduction, The (Gordon), 103

grief, 115, 138, 167–68, 196

Griswold v. Connecticut, 37

Ground Zero, 188

Grutter v. Bollinger, 7, 34

Guantánamo Bay, x, 188, 200n7

Guatemala, 105

Guha, Ranajit, 72

guilt, 51, 153, 157

Halley, Janet, 40–41

Han, Shinhee, 20, 115, 117, 121, 128, 138–65

Happy Together (Wong), 18, 60, 76–92, 96, 195, 197

Hardwick, Michael, 24

Harris, Cheryl I., 5–7, 46

Hartman, Saidiya, 28

hate, 126–27, 142, 148–49, 154–56, 158–59, 161–62, 164

health care, x–xi

Heart Mountain (internment camp), 171

Hegel, G.W.F., 44

Heidegger, Martin, 61, 66–67, 166, 180, 194–96

hermeneutic philosophical tradition, 67, 69, 179–80, 183–85, 195. *See also* Heidegger, Martin

Hill Holiday, *100*

Hiroshima, 171, 179, 188

Hirsch, Marianne, 169, 219n9

historicism: affect as complement to, 185–86, 188; limitations of, 62–69, 74, 170, 172, 179, 189, 191; narrative structure of, 18, 38–40, 47, 182–83, 186, 188; political ramifications of, 60; presence and, 172; private and familial ramifications of, 113–16, 150; the racial project and, 74. *See also* Benjamin, Walter; neoliberalism

History and Memory (Tajiri), v, 22, 166–98, *169, 175, 176–78, 187*

Ho Chi Minh, 62–65, 75

homophobia, ix, 7, 33, 54, 145

(homo)sexuality: capitalism and, 29; citizenship and, 37–38; civil rights and, 3; domestication of, 17, 26, 30–31, 34–35, 43, 45; in *Happy Together*, 76–92; historicism and, 38, 77; identity and, xi, 14, 25–26, 28–29, 47; marriage and, x, 207n104; Oedipal complex and, 20, 56; privacy rights and, 24–49; racial aspects of, x, 4, 17, 33, 37, 38–40, 42, 45, 47; repression, psychosis, and, 50–55. *See also* gay marriage; *Lawrence v. Texas*; queer liberalism

Hong Kong, 19, 60, 80, 90–91

Horkheimer, Max, 41

House Resolution 422, 21–22, 170, 220nn14–15

human rights, 34, 48–49, 68, 105– 6, 131, 220n14. *See also* citizenship; civil rights; property; whiteness

Human Rights Campaign, 28

Husserl, Edmund, 195

identity: liberalism and, 65; Asian American, 107; capitalist narratives and, 14; conceptual boundaries of, 22; erasure of, 113; homosexual, 77–78; limitations of, 65; politics of, xi, 6, 8, 18, 49, 58, 172, 189, 197; post-, xi, 2, 8, 18, 95, 192; racial, 73, 75, 77, 140–65, 181. *See also* Asian Americans; (homo)sexuality; Japanese Americans; neoliberalism; race

immigrants: gender(ing) of, 107; homophobia and, 33; illegal, 101, 106–7; laboring class and, 10, 32; metaphorical tropes and, 131; politics of, 34, 73, 131; queer, 33; racialization of, 31, 47–49, 115; transnational adoptees as, 102, 107, 131, 139, 150. *See also* adoptions; citizenship; coolies; *Happy Together*; slavery; United States

Immigration and Nationality Act, 31

Inada, Lawson Fusao, 170

incest taboo, 16, 18–19, 84–91, 96, 125, 224n66

Inchon City, 143, 147

inclusion: liberal norm of, xi

India, 104

Indian schools, 103

internment: of Japanese Americans, 21–22, 166–98, 223n40; camps, 171

Interpretation of Dreams, The (Freud), 134, 190

intersectionality, 4, 25, 34, 37–42, 47, 49, 54, 74, 98, 103, 189–90

"Intimacies of Four Continents" (Lowe), 10–11, 74, 76

intimacy: definition of, 11; domestication of, 26; family structure as, 94; legal decisions concerning, 16, 24–49; legal definition of, 42–43; material preconditions of, 79; phenomenology of, 30–31; as private space, xi, 3, 12, 24, 26, 34, 44–45; as property, 44; racialization of, 1, 10–13, 20, 25, 36, 42–49, 77, 110, 117, 122, 136, 150, 194. *See also* domesticity; family; privacy; racialization

intimate public sphere, 6, 103, 124

Iraq War, 34, 49

issei (Japanese American first generation), 170

Jakobsen, Janet, 27, 45

Jameson, Fredric, 171–72, 190

Japanese Americans, 163–98

Jerome (internment camp), 171

"Jewish Question, On the" (Marx), 8

Jews, 145

John Hancock, 95, 98–99, *100*, 102, 137

Joseph, Miranda, 40–41, 108

Kang Ok Jin, 114

Kaplan, Amy, 8, 94–95

Kennedy, Anthony, 24, 35–37, 39–40, 42, 48

Kennedy, Randall, 7

Kim, Richard, 57

kinship: affect/language schism and, 131, 134; blood-line, 124, 150; bourgeois ideals of, 43; capitalism and, 8, 136; choice and, 3; definition of, 2; gays and lesbians, 3; gay identity and, 26; idealized versions of, 10, 17; language of, 20, 22, 31, 88, 96–99; legal aspects of, 4; marriage in relations of, 85–86; the

nation-state and, 14; normative politics of, 3, 29, 33; Oedipal complex and, 18, 20, 86, 135, 163; as political right, 111; politics of, 1, 88, 141; poststructuralist theory and, 132, 136; as private sphere, 30, 32, 169; queer, 3, 17, 29, 77–78, 99, 101–2; queer Asian diasporas and, 12; race and racism in, 7, 49, 153; structural linguistics and, 15, 33; structure of, xi, 6, 14, 25–26, 60, 81, 85, 91, 94. *See also* adoptions; affect; family; intimacy; queer liberalism

Klein, Melanie, 21, 127–28, 130, 139–40, 152–59, 163–64, 190, 195

Komoko, 173, 179, 182, 185, *187*

Korea: as origin, 123, 127–32, 147; orphanages of, 93; otherness of, 111, 114–17; racial identity and, 140–65

Korean language, 147, 149

Korean War, 104, 113

Krauthammer, Charles, 49

Kristeva, Julia, 191

Kunsan (Korea), 93, 129

labor (class), 32; affective, 98, 108–9; colonialism and, 44; consumptive, 108; reproductive, 10, 78–79, 106–9, 124

Lacan, Jacques, 72–73, 87–88, 134, 190, 196, 201n42

language: of affect, 114, 172, 188; the affective and, 190–93; in the analytic tradition, 180; of choice and free will, 106, 110; gendered, 65; limitations of, 168; as pre-Oedipal loss, 87, 130–31, 134; of rights and liberties, 28–29, 31, 68; transnational adoptions and, 129. *See also* affect; historicism; Lacan, Jacques; linguistics

Language of Blood, The (Trenka), 138–39

Latinos, 145

Lawrence, John, 17, 35–37, 41–42

Lawrence v. Texas, 3, 7–8, 16–18, 24–49, 79

Lee, Ang, 77–78

Lee, Anthony, 58

Legends from Camp (Inada), 170

lesbian baby boom, 3

lesbians. *See* (homo)sexuality; Stein, Gertrude; Toklas, Alice

"Letter on Humanism" (Heidegger), 166

Leung Chiu-wai, Tony, 60

Lévi-Strauss, Claude, 15, 85–87, 201n42

liberal humanism: alternatives to, 59, 190–91; imperial reach of, x, 48; intimacy and, 43; material conditions of, 15, 18, 77; philosophical foundations of, 22–23, 69–70; racialization and, 71, 73. *See also* neoliberalism

Lichtenstein, Mitchell, 77

Liem, Paul, 132

linguistics, 15, 88, 189–90

loss, 122, 149, 167, 169, 172, 183–85, 188, 194–96

love: images of, xiv, 59–60, 72, 76, 78; politics of, 27, 35–36, 42; theories of, 51, 91, 103, 125–29, 133–35, 144, 153–59, 162–64, 193, 196. *See also* family; girl love; intimacy; kinship; Klein, Melanie

Loving v. Virginia, x, 4–7, 17, 37–39, 41, 204n45, 205n49

Lowe, Lisa, 10–11, 44

Lubiano, Wahneema, 47

mail-order brides, 97, 105, 107, 110

manifest domesticity, 8

Manzanar (internment camp), 171, 182, 188

marriage rights. *See* family; gay marriage; intimacy; privacy; queer liberalism

Marx, Karl, 8, 14, 40, 66–67

Marxism, 8

Massachusetts, 3, 26

Massumi, Brian, 70, 84, 210n29

Maurer, Bill, 9, 106

McGinnis, Hollee, 214n18

McGreevy, James, 28

Melamed, Jodi, 9, 48, 200n23, 223n40

melancholia, 115–16, 122–23, 130–33, 158, 163, 167, 179, 186–88, 209n15

Memoirs of My Nervous Illness (Schreber), 23, 26, 50, 53–55

Memories from the Department of Amnesia (Tanaka), 170

memory: in the construction of histories, 163, 168, 194. *See also* forgetting; Freud, Sigmund; historicism; Mina

migrations: Asian, 1, 76; family reunification and, 32–33; labor as reason for, 10, 75–76; waiting and, 59. *See also* adoptions; globalization; immigrants; slavery

Mill, John Stuart, 69

Mina (case study subject), 139–65, 197

Minidoka (internment camp), 171

mirroring, 71–73

miscegenation, 17, 35, 37–39, 47, 54, 103

Mississippi Burning (Parker), 175

model minority myth, 110, 145

modernism, 19, 60, 67, 73–75

modernity, x, 15, 18–19, 22; exploitation and, 74: forgetting as precondition of, 70

Moore, Gary, 113

Moran, Rachel, 5, 7, 200n14

Morenci (Arizona Territory), 103
Morrison, Toni, 116
mothers: adoptive, 93, 111, 123–24,
    129, 151, 155, 162; birth, 93, 109,
    124, 128–29, 132, 143, 147–48,
    154, 162; good-enough, 21, 135–
    36, 138–42, 145, 152, 154–56,
    160–63, 165, 169, 193; Oedipal
    constructions of, 125–28, 138,
    140–41, 153; as origin trope, 13,
    20–21, 132, 135, 139, 152–55,
    179, 188; psychic space require-
    ments of, 94, 124, 130, 135–36,
    138–39, 154, 156, 162, 164–65,
    169, 193; racialization of, 139; as
    transitional objects, 158–60
"Mourning and Melancholia" (Freud),
    115, 117, 151, 167
mourning, 115–16, 122
multiculturalism, xi, 4, 6, 78, 97, 110,
    117, 137
Muñoz, José, 34, 183, 195
Muslims, 9, 48

Nagasaki, 171, 179, 188
naming, 62–65
National Association of Black Social
    Workers, 96
nationalism, 13–14, 95. See also inter-
    nment; United States; World War II
Native Americans, 103
neoliberalism: global capitalism and,
    25, 30, 48; (homo)sexuality and, 31;
    identity and, 65; language of, 5, 45;
    philosophical assumptions of, 4,
    23–24; tenets of, x, 5, 8, 14, 22,
    117, 194. See also Enlightenment;
    liberal humanism; queer liberalism
Netherlands, 104
New Jersey, 28
New Maladies of the Soul (Kristeva),
    191
New York City ballet company, 141

New York Foundling Hospital, 103–4
New York Times, 3
Ngai, Mae, 181, 222n31, 223n40
Nguyen Ai Quoc, 62, 209n9
Nguyen That Thanh, 62–63
Nichols, Bill, 179, 188
nisei (Japanese American second gen-
    eration), 170
no-no boys, 181

Obama, Barack, ix, x, 3–4, 31
object relations, 146, 158, 160–61.
    See also Winnicott, D. W.
O'Connor, Sandra Day, 37
Oedipus complex: adoptions and, 20;
    details of, 87–88; language and,
    18–20; negative, 20, 96, 125–26,
    130, 134–35, 158, 193; norms and
    normative aspects of, 26, 60, 81,
    90, 132, 136, 139, 153, 197; para-
    digmatic dominance of, 16, 19, 84–
    86, 88. See also Freud, Sigmund;
    Lacan, Jacques; language; mothers
Ong, Aihwa, 23
"On Narcissism" (Freud), 51, 53
Origins of Totalitarianism, The
    (Arendt), 28
orphans, 103–5, 109, 113
otherness, 24, 94, 102, 104, 116–17,
    136, 155
Otsuka, Julie, 170
ownership society, 23

Page Law, 107
Pakistan, 49
parachute kids, 98
paranoia, 51–53, 155, 163, 196
parenting: as emblem of full social
    membership, 101–2. See also adop-
    tions; family; mothers; privacy
Parents Involved in Community Schools
    v. Seattle School District, 7
Parker, Alan, 174–75, 197

passing, 2, 71, 95, 110, 117, 150

penis envy, 126

Perry, Twila L., 5, 105

phenomenology. *See* Heidegger, Martin; hermeneutic philosophical tradition

Phillips, Adam, 159

Philosophy of Right, The (Hegel), 44

Piazzola, Astor, 82

Picturing Chinatown (Lee), 58

Planned Parenthood of Southeastern Pennsylvania v. Casey, 37

play, 160, 162

Plessy v. Ferguson, 4–5

Poland, 104

postcolonial feminism, 105

postcolonial literature, 73–74

postmodernism, 74, 191

Poston (internment camp), 167, 171, 174, 178, 184–86, 195

poststructuralism: the affective and, 189–90; analytical methodology of, xi, 170; kinship relations and, 84, 135; language and, 16, 189–91, 194–96. *See also* Lacan, Jacques; structuralism

prejudice, 6, 141, 145. *See also* difference; gay marriage; homophobia; racism

prison-industrial complex, 34, 199n7

privacy: as Enlightenment product, xi, 12, 14, 17, 42–43; as guaranteed right, 24, 26, 35–37, 42, 200n18; legal decisions concerning, 4–6, 16, 36–49; litigating racism and, 8; racialization of, 49; relative inalienability of, 45–46. *See also* intimacy; queer liberalism

private sphere, 6–9, 27, 30, 43–44

progress, 13, 23, 25, 29, 41, 47, 79, 170, 180

property: citizenship as form of, 23, 28, 101; racialization of, 26, 46–

47; the self and, 44; whiteness as, 5–6, 25, 36, 46, 101, 104, 116, 146, 165

Proposition 8, ix, x, xi, 4

Proposition 187, 106

psychoanalysis: alternatives to, 90–91; as analytical method, xi, 81, 149, 163; displacement, 84, 86–89, 125, 171, 186, 197; incest taboo, 16, 18–19, 84–91, 96, 125, 224n66; melancholia, 115–16, 122–23, 130–33, 158, 163, 167, 179, 186–88, 209n15; mourning, 115–16, 122; narratives of, 125; poststructuralist accounts of, 135. *See also* ; Freud, Sigmund; Klein, Melanie; Oedipal complex; Winnicott, D. W.; *specific works and case histories*

psychoanalysts. *See specific analysts and therapists*

"Psychoanalytic Notes Upon an Autobiographical Account of a Case of Paranoia" (Freud), 18, 26, 50, 52, 54

psychotherapists. *See specific analysts and therapists*

public sphere, 2, 6, 8, 12, 27, 95, 102

Quaid, Dennis, 174–75

queer diasporas: as analytical lens, 2, 12–15, 58–59, 68, 94, 132, 186; conventional narrative and, 60; definition of, xi, 13; *Happy Together* and, 81, 90; Oedipal complex and, 16; psychic and material preconditions of, 76; psychology of, 18

Queer Eye for the Straight Guy (TV show), 30, 203n26

queer liberalism: avatars of, 90; captialist logic and, 30; colorblind logic and, 17; consumerism and, 26, 29–30; definition of, xi, 2–3, 24; *Happy*

Together and, 79; heteronormative family and, 25, 27–28, 31, 35, 42, 55, 74; intimacy's racialization and, 36, 43; language of, 28–29, 34, 38; material preconditions for, 77; methodological responses to, 13; the Oedipal and, 81; origins of, 3, 12, 24, 26, 78; psychic structure of, 18, 26; race and, 4, 25, 36, 45, 47; rights and citizenship and, 49–50, 56–57; scholarship on, 1; Schreber's *Memoirs* and, 51–56; waiting and, 77

queer literature, 73

queer studies, 2, 4, 8, 34, 40, 49, 74, 80, 94, 183

race: adoptions and, 96; colonialism and, 74; in the concept of belonging, 14, 97; continued importance of, 3, 7; definition of, 5; forgetting of, xi, 5, 9–13, 15, 17–18, 20, 22, 40–41, 45, 58, 61, 77, 81, 95, 103, 110, 117, 188; homosexuality and, x, 14, 25, 33, 37–40, 42, 45, 47; identity and, 75, 140–42, 149–51, 154–57, 161–62, 165, 179; language of, 49, 161; mirroring and, 72; in modernism, 67; mothers and, 128; phenomenology of, 9–10; politics of, 2, 75, 169; private sphere and, 6, 153. *See also* adoptions; forgetting; identity; intersectionality; queer liberalism

racialization of intimacy: as critical focus, 11; critical responses to, 13; definition of, 10; *Lawrence v. Texas* and, 17; mothers and, 130; neoliberalism's underwriting of, 49; transnational adoption and, 20, 95, 101, 110, 117, 121–24, 127, 136, 150. *See also* family; intimacy; privacy

racial melancholia, 20–21, 96, 115–16, 122–23, 138–40, 149–54, 165–67, 193–96

racism: Enlightenment and, 10–11, 22; eradication of, x; global histories of, 102; history of, 11; institutional, 121; narratological underwriting of, 13, 136; prejudice, 6, 141, 145; public discourse and, 3, 17; rationalizations of, 33. *See also* intersectionality

Reagan, Ronald, 6, 22, 31, 103, 170

Reddy, Chandan, 31–33

refugee status, 131, 174, 217n53

reparation: political, 22, 171, 188, 194; psychic, 22, 171, 186–88, 194, 196; racial, 21, 127, 138, 140, 152–55, 157–63, 169–70

repression, 116

Republican Party, ix

reverse settlers, 98

Roach, Joseph, 18

Roe v. Wade, 37

Rohwer (internment camp), 171

"Roses" (Carlson), *ii*, xiv

Rubin, Gayle, 15, 86–87

Ruskola, Teemu, 28, 42–43

Russia, 105

Ruti, Mari, 191

same-sex marriage. *See* gay marriage

San Francisco, 3

sansei (Japanese American third generation), 170

Sartre, Jean-Paul, 166, 192

Sassen, Saskia, 93

satellite people, 98

Savigliano, Marta, 211n54

Saxony Supreme Court of Appeals, 26, 50

Scalia, Antonin, 36, 39–40, 206n69

Schreber, Daniel Paul, 18, 23, 26, 47, 50, 52–58

Schreber, Moritz, 50

Sedgwick, Eve Kosofsky, 7, 54–55, 77, 199n1

Seoul (Korea), 143, 147

"separate but equal": in *Plessy v. Ferguson*, 4–5

September 11th, 30, 47, 136, 188

sexuality: domestication of, 43; legitimacy of, 31; normative influences on, 13, 153; power and, 141. *See also* (homo)sexuality; intersectionality; privacy; queer liberalism; sex workers

sex workers, 97, 105–6, 110

Silverman, Kaja, 91, 133–34, 211n48

slavery, 10, 23, 28, 43, 75, 103

social contract theory, 61

sodomy, 30, 36, 42–43, 202n4

Somerville, Siobhan, 38, 109, 205nn47–48

South Korea. *See* Korea

Spivak, Gayatri Chakravorty, 24–25, 60

Stein, Gertrude, 19, 59–76

stereotypes, 65, 76, 110

Sternburg, Janet, 167

Stevens, John Paul, 37

Stoler, Ann Laura, 44, 104

Stonewall, 26

structuralism, 15–16, 85, 89; *See also* poststructuralism

"Structures of Feeling" (Williams), 1–2, 15, 67

Sturges, John, 173

Sturken, Marita, 171

Sullivan, Andrew, 28

Tajiri, Rea, v, 22, 166–98

Tanaka, Janet, 170

Terada, Rei, 170, 190–91

terrorism, 30, 34, 47

Texas, 36, 42

Thatcher, Margaret, 6, 103

"Theses on the Philosophy of History" (Benjamin), 166

Thomas, Kendall, 54–55

Toklas, Alice, 19, 58–76, 208n3

Tölölyan, Khachig, 13

Tomita, Tamalyn, 174

Topaz (internment camp), 171

Torok, Maria, 168

Tracy, Spencer, 173, 185

"Traffic in Women, The" (Rubin), 87

transference, 146, 158, 160–61

"Transitional Objects and Transitional Phenomena" (Winnicott), 158

transitional objects, 158, 161–63, 218n32

trauma, 114, 124, 128, 167–68, 197. *See also* grief; loss

Trenka, Jane Jeong, 138–39

trespass: racial, 17, 36

Truong, Monique, 18–19, 59–76, 170

Tsou, Elda, 208–9n4

Tule Lake (internment camp), 171

"Unconscious, The" (Freud), 134, 167, 192

United States: as adopter of orphans, 104–5; army of, 173; Asian American identity status in, 116; conservative politics of, 30; domesticity in, 108; exceptionalism of, xi, 13, 48, 109; historicist narratives of, 180–81; immigration policies of, 31, 99, 106–7, 131, 217n53; imperialism of, 9, 34, 49, 103–5; liberal project of, x, 17, 102; militarism of, 8, 62, 102, 106; national culture of, 24, 171, 180, 182

United States Supreme Court, 7, 24–49, 104. *See also specific decisions and justices*

Vietnam, 62–64, 105, 131

Volpp, Leti, 47, 106

waiting: as historicist phenomenon, 25, 59, 63, 66–67, 69–70, 76, 81, 182

war brides, 105, 107, 110

War on Terror, 28, 47, 171

War Relocation Authority (WRA), 173, 175, 181

"We Are Seven" (Wordsworth), v

Wedding Banquet, The (Lee), 77–79, 211n47

Weston, Kath, 3

When the Emperor was Divine (Otsuka), 170

White, Byron, 24

whiteness: Asian Americans as partaking of, 110; as normative, xi, 36, 127, 140, 149, 151, 155–57, 164; as property, 5–6, 25, 36, 46, 101, 104, 116, 146, 165

"Whiteness as Property" (Harris), 46

Whitman, James, 200n18

Who's Going to Pay for These Donuts, Anyway? (Tanaka), 170

Williams, Raymond, 1–2, 15, 67

Winnicott, D. W., 21, 140, 158–60, 163

women: Freud's essays on, 96, 127, 133; Oedipal and capitalist roles of, 85–88; symbolic martyrdom of, 106. *See also* feminism; Freud, Sigmund; Klein, Melanie; mothers; Oedipus complex; Winnicott, D. W.; *specific authors and case history subjects*

Wong, Kar-wai, 18–19, 59, 61, 76–92

Wordsworth, William, v

worlding, 61, 66, 70–71, 78. *See also* Heidegger, Martin

World War II, 104, 166, 170–71, 173, 179

Yankee Doodle Dandy (Curtiz), 173

Yasui, Lisa, 170

Yellow Peril, 107

Yngvesson, Barbara, 9, 106

Zelizer, Viviana, 109

Zinnemann, Fred, 183–84

DAVID L. ENG is Professor in the Department
of English, the Program in Comparative Literature
and Literary Theory, and the Program in Asian
American Studies at the University of Pennsylva-
nia. He is the author of *Racial Castration: Managing
Masculinity in Asian America*, and co-editor of *Loss:
The Politics of Mourning*, and *Q&A: Queer in Asian
America*.

Library of Congress Cataloging-in-Publication Data
Eng, David L., 1967–
The feeling of kinship : queer liberalism and the
racialization of intimacy / David L. Eng.
p. cm.
Includes bibliographical references and index.
ISBN 978-0-8223-4715-6 (cloth : alk. paper)
ISBN 978-0-8223-4732-3 (pbk. : alk. paper)
1. Asian American gays—Family relationships.
2. Asian Americans—Family relationships.
3. Gay liberation movement—United States.
4. Kinship—United States. I. Title.
HQ76.3.U5E54 2010
306.85086′640973—dc22   2009048187

DATE DUE

GNSS1960Q	